# Dear Lilly

*From Father to Daughter: The Truth about Life, Love, and the World We Live In*

By Peter Greyson

iUniverse, Inc.
New York   Bloomington

# Dear Lilly

iUniverse books may be ordered through booksellers or by contacting:

iUniverse
1663 Liberty Drive
Bloomington, IN 47403
www.iuniverse.com
1-800-Authors (1-800-288-4677)

ISBN: 978-0-595-49306-7 (pbk)
ISBN: 978-0-595-61050-1 (ebk)

Printed in the United States of America

iUniverse rev. date: 6/2/2009

# CONTENTS

# PREFACE

Dear Lilly,

I can't believe it's been three years since you came into my world. It seems impossible to imagine what my days would be like without the infectious giggle, radiant smile, or precious "huggie buggies" of my beloved little pumpkin. As I watch you grow, millions of thoughts race through my mind, bombarding me with endless hopes and worries. I ponder things such as: What will you be like when you mature? How will you look? Who will you become? And, what will you believe in? With each breath you take, I grow more frightened and insecure, mostly about my own shortcomings as a father. Just what kind of a daddy will I be? Will I always be there for you, and teach you all you need to know to survive in this sometimes harsh world? Will I set good examples and prepare you adequately enough to make the right decisions when it is crucial that you do so?

Then one evening amidst a rainstorm of self-doubt, I had a moment of clarity; the kind where everything makes perfect sense and you are spontaneously gushing with amazing realizations. I realized a way that I could give you ongoing guidance throughout your life, without having to resort to those dreadfully uncomfortable father-daughter discussions. I could write you a handbook that tried to explain the vast complexities of our world, and just maybe, my words might help you navigate through the many trials and tribulations of your adolescence.

I wish I could tell you that life is always like a fairy tale with a wonderful ending, that good prevails over evil, and love is everlasting, but that would be far from the truth. Life can be enchanting sweetheart, yet it can also be horrifying. It all depends on how strong and prepared you are.

Every day I read about the heinous tragedies of our planet: the murders, the rapes, the abductions, abusive relationships, addictions, fatal accidents, and deadly diseases. I shudder at the thought that some day you may be confronted with something of this gruesome nature. How can I possibly teach you to stay clear of these dangers? It is a task too great for any one person. Besides, by the time you are ready to learn, I'll probably be the least important guy in your life. Hell, I'll probably be too chicken shit to say any of this to your face anyway; so it's best for both of us if I just write it down.

In my thirty-three years, I have seen more than my share of personal triumphs, defeats, and heartbreak. I feel it is my obligation to explain to you who I am and everything I have learned throughout my journey. How else could you ever truly know the man who has given you life? I cannot even fathom how some of these revelations may trouble you, but I can promise you this: everything I have put down on these pages is directly from my soul, and the absolute truth.

I haven't always been the carefree goofball that you know and love. It's taken me decades to come to grips with my past. I've been an abused child, a runaway, a drug addict, an alcoholic, a thief, a liar, a womanizing frat boy, a self-destructive musician, a college drop-out, a selective mute, a depressed teen, and, at times, even a suicidal adult. Although it pains me greatly to say, there was a time when I simply could not bear to see another day. It was then that an angel came to save me, to pick me up, and show me how to persevere. That angel's name was Lilly Skye. Yes, it was you, and from that moment on things have been very different. The hole in my heart has been healed, and I have been given the most glorious gift- a reason to live.

This book is a survival guide to help you through this crazy thing we call life, and still be able to maintain your sanity. One night I sat down, pen in hand, to scribble a few helpful tidbits for your future, and from there I never looked back. Nine months later I had multiple notebooks full of my stories, advice, and discoveries. Sometimes I would awaken at three in the morning and blurt ideas into a handheld tape recorder; other times I'd pull to the side of the road in traffic to jot down my thoughts on a Subway napkin. The words poured out of me faster than my hand could write or my brain could comprehend.

When I was finally finished, I knew in my heart that what I had was something extraordinary. These notebooks, soaked with my sweat and tears, contained much more than cute stories and amusing anecdotes; they contained all of life's truths as I knew them—with absolutely no bullshit! The truth about boys, sex, love, drugs, alcohol, partying, school, friends, family, popularity, music, teenage angst, depression, money, the media, religion, death, and so much more. I know that when you are finally old enough to read this, it will have a profound and positive affect on your life.

The only question I have now is, just when will you be ready? I guess you'll tell me when, not with words but with your actions. When the time comes that you're not my little cuddle bug anymore, when older boys start sniffing around our property, and your nights begin to consist of secretive phone calls and instant messages behind closed doors- I'll know it's time. I'm already dreading those days, but I know that it's just a part of growing up, and someday you will emerge from your bedroom, a beautiful and confident woman. I just want you to know that I'll be counting the seconds until I have my Lilly back in my arms again. I don't care if it takes twenty years. I'll be patiently waiting and just dying to know what you thought of my book. So if the truth is what you seek- then read on my dear.

# Chapter 1: Boys

Rather than having you skip ahead to this chapter, I figured I'd just make it easy for you and put it first. Once upon a time, I was the most important guy in your life. You gazed at me with loving admiration, and showered me with affection each and every day. Sometimes I felt like a superhero. I was "Superdad," boo-boo kisser, tent-maker, storyteller, and hide-and-seeker extraordinaire. We had such an incredible bond, like two best friends on a never-ending sleepover. For now, I guess those days are on temporary hiatus. In the meantime, it's my job to educate and protect you from one of the most insidious beings you will ever encounter throughout your adolescence. These creatures I speak of are unbelievably sinister, and the power they can possess over you is astonishing. They lurk in the shadows, waiting for the perfect opportunity to pounce on unsuspecting prey. They are called teenage boys!

Ahhh, the teenage boy—teeming with testosterone, willing to go to any means necessary to acquire a naïve female, one in which to conduct countless experiments on. I do speak from experience here. It wasn't too long ago that I was one of these predators on the prowl myself. I know it's hard for you to believe, but Daddy was quite the ladies man in his day. Luckily, I was blessed with a baby face, dark wavy hair, dimples in both sets of cheeks, and the innocent smile of an altar boy. For over fifteen years, I played the game and played it well; the game of conquering as many females as humanly possible.

In the neighborhood where I grew up, all of the kids my age just happened to be females. There was Kimmy Anderson across the street, the Stewart sisters next door, and Anne Marie Fassano three houses down. Add to that my older sister Joy and her crew of boy-crazy friends, and you could say that my house was like a daily estrogen convention. Rather than resisting, I just accepted my female cohorts and assumed my role as one of the girls, with no complaints. House, school, dolls, cheering, and dress up were the games of my youth. We even had slumber parties on occasion. It was during this time that I would learn one of the most valuable skills of my life: how to get along with and manipulate females.

As time passed, our bodies started changing in profound ways and so did the chemistry between the girls and myself. A few more boys moved into the neighborhood, and before long, our innocent childhood games became more aggressive and physical in nature. It happened to the girls first. "It" being puberty; a time when everything you know gets completely turned upside down and your life becomes an absolute mess. By now, I'm sure you've already entered the beginning stages of this traumatizing process. It must have been very scary for you. I hope this book can help keep things in proper perspective.

Anyway, after the girls in the neighborhood started to physically mature, the boys weren't too far behind. Our daily games of Tag soon morphed into an activity called Grab Ass, and the game Truth or Dare became an outlet for revealing secret crushes and harmless groping. To be this age was so exhilarating, like riding a roller coaster without the safety harness; hormones rushing, heart-pumping, and belly-churning. We were living in the moment and not looking back.

Then, like some ancient ritual passed down from generation to generation, the ultimate puberty game was magically unearthed. A game so simple, yet so mind blowing—Spin the Bottle! It was a sultry night in July of 1985, if memory serves correct. A frenzied circle of pimple-faced preteens watched a whirling Pepsi bottle in silent amazement, knowing that wherever it stopped would result in the most awkward of lip-locks. I sat there in disbelief as the bottle I had just spun stopped directly on Amanda Stewart, my huge crush since the third grade. Like a quivering buffoon, I inched my way toward her, eyes closed, and practically impaled her with my jagged braces and unruly lizard tongue. After it was over, I felt a change come over me, as if I had opened the door to a secret room filled with riches. Let's just say that my action figures and remote controlled cars were by the curb the very next morning.

As the summer weeks passed and this nightly ritual became more comfortable, the rules started adapting to our new found prowess. Soon, the lucky couples were pressured into going in a closet or another darkened space for the infamous "Seven Minutes in Heaven." During this time, you were expected to get some sort of bare-skin action, and mocked incessantly if you didn't. After my first trip to heaven, I emerged hair messed, cheeks flushed, clothes disheveled, and in shock as to having grazed my first boob. Having seen the other side of the mountain, so to speak, I was determined to venture on and experience whatever came next.

By now, you've probably discovered the answer to the age-old childhood mystery of "What is sex?" In this era of technological superiority, I'm sure it was rather easy. In my case, it was like trying to decode the ancient biblical scrolls uncovered in the deserts of the Holy Land. Until thirteen, I actually thought that sex was French kissing and believed that the exchanged saliva was the cause of pregnancy. Thanks to encyclopedias, neighborhood kids, cable television, and the occasional dirty magazine, I finally got the facts straight. It scared the hell out of me, but I was focused on becoming a man at any cost.

You must understand one thing: boys are just like the animals you see on the Discovery Channel; there is no difference. They are biologically programmed to conquer as many females as they possibly can. This urge cannot be suppressed. Every mature male on this planet is in constant battle with his insatiable sexual fantasies; some are just able to hide it better than others. When I turned sixteen, I felt it was time to step it up a notch. I had to devise a strategy to make my virginity a thing of the past. I would utilize my innocent smile to befriend every girl I met, and become someone they could talk to about their problems. I'd make them laugh with my goofy charm, and then when their defenses were down, I'd make my move. It was foolproof.

The only downfall was that most of the girls developed crushes and wanted to get serious with me; something I had no interest in at the time. While girls are forever in search of the perfect relationship, younger guys are merely looking for easy action. Some do unwillingly give into the serious relationship, but this is solely for the prospect of continuous action. I realize that this makes the male gender sound like despicable swine, but we simply cannot help it. Our dilemma is called the penis, a part of our anatomy that controls our every thought and action. We are powerless to its command and it very often leads to our demise.

While in the process of writing, I kept coming across statements that I felt were the undeniable truths of life. I will be calling them "Life Rules" and they are my words to live by. Even if you skim through this book and only read them, I will be satisfied. For the first rule may be the single most important thing I can ever teach you …

### Life Rule #1: Boys lie!

Picture the sweetest, most harmless guy you know. At this very moment he is most likely racking his brain trying to develop a plan to get you naked. Now, he may be a very upstanding young man with genuine admiration for you, but all of this gets tossed out the window once "the fever" sets in. You see, the penis is the root of our complete and utter deceit. It makes us become someone we are not, and continually remorseful of our actions. Almost every guy I knew in high school was a manipulator of females, and in my college years I lived in a fraternity house, jam-packed with the most depraved guys on Earth. Therefore, I consider this an area in which I am extremely knowledgeable.

I would love to get on my soapbox right now and preach to you about waiting until adulthood to become physical with guys. However, it would be terribly naïve of me to do so. I've been teaching middle school-age students for ten years now, and I know exactly what kids are up to these days. I can't even begin to explain the conversations I've overheard, or the notes I have intercepted in my classroom. The information contained would send any parent to an early grave. In one of the schools I taught, a sixth grade girl had to leave school after becoming pregnant by a ninth grade boy. Times sure have changed since I was your age, and by the time you read this, kids will be even more experienced.

When these tremendous decisions do present themselves, it is imperative that you ask yourself the following questions: Is this guy really worth it? Do I want to become another trophy in his display case? How will I feel if he never talks to me again afterward? And, do I want to be the topic of his perverted conversations with his friends? Because, believe me when I say this …

### *Life Rule #2: We tell our friends everything.*

While girls will tell each other everything about the inner workings of their relationship, guys will be much more graphic with the intimate details. Sex for a guy is like going hunting; when we get something, we want to display it for the world to see. There was a girl I went to high school with who was secretly videotaped while being with a guy on my wrestling team. He then proceeded to show it to every one of us. Her life and reputation were completely destroyed. People snickered behind her back, girls despised her, and from then on, guys only wanted one thing from her. In my eyes, she did nothing wrong except trust a teenage boy. He should have been labeled the trash instead of her.

Another dude I knew used to tell us to gather outside his bedroom window when he was getting intimate with his girlfriend; and like the shameless animals that we were, we complied. That's what seventeen-year-old boys do; they're disgusting pigs. It's not until we someday have daughters of our own, that we realize the errors of our ways.

## Your First Time

I can't tell you how many girls I've heard say that losing their virginity was the single worst experience of their life. It hurt; it was scary, rushed, forceful, in a nasty location, and worst of all, the guy never spoke to them again. Every girl fantasizes that their first time will be by candlelight, with rose petals on the bed, and soft music playing in the background. But instead, it's with some asshole guy who barely knows your name in the spare room of a hell-raising keg party. Or in my friend Emily's case, one of those disgusting portable toilets at a music festival. I almost vomited after hearing that story.

With one second of poor judgment, this can happen quite easily, and it will be this memory that will lay the foundation for the rest of your adult life. You only get one chance to have a first time, so make sure it's with someone who's proven he cares for you, and never makes you feel pressured. Any guy who would pressure a girl into having sex, I can assure you, cares nothing about her and is only out for his own satisfaction. I wish I could have been one of the few nice guys out there, but I was an ignorant fool. My parents never told me squat about sex, or how to treat a lady. Everything I learned was from dirty movies and my idiot friends. I broke many a heart and I'm not the slightest bit proud of it.

If you'd like to avoid having your heart broken time after time, then it is essential that you learn to differentiate between love and lust. These are two emotions that can feel exactly the same at first, but while one can last forever, the other can last mere minutes.

## Love vs. Lust

Love- There are two kinds of love in this world; the kind you feel for your family and friends, and then there's the other one. This is the one that can leave you feeling overjoyed at one moment and devastated the next. No one knows for sure what love is or what causes it. If you look at it scientifically, it's basically our bodies telling us that it's time to find a suitable partner in which to mate, and the one you've currently chosen meets all the proper criteria. However, it is so much more than that; especially when you're sixteen and everything is so new and exciting. Love is a magical feeling that goes far beyond the urges for sexual activity. It is a deep yearning for intimacy, for someone to truly know us, care for us, worry about us, and not be fully complete without us. To love and to be loved is all anyone genuinely wants in this world.

Some people will balk at love, calling it a wasted emotion that we are better off without. This is either because they have yet to find love, or they have been hurt so deeply that they are forever bitter. In my opinion, this is one of the main reasons why so many people are addicted to drugs and alcohol. They are desperately trying to silence their innate desire to be loved. This yearning is also the reason kids runaway from home, teenagers secretly elope, and people cheat on their spouses; because in the words of the prolific songwriter Greg Brown, "If you don't get it at home, you're gonna go looking."

Love is an undeniable necessity like water and oxygen. There have been countless songs, poems, stories, movies, and books written about how amazing it can be. It sounds so simple; you fall in love with your high school sweetheart, get married after graduation, have your two children, and live happily ever after. Well, I got news for you kid; this rarely happens anymore.

Let me know if any of this sounds familiar. You just started dating the perfect guy and he's exactly like you dreamed he would be since you were nine years old. He's sweet, charming, kind, funny, gorgeous, and he treats you like a princess. You feel like you're floating above the ground when you are with him. You think about him every second, dream about him, and spend every moment that he's not around feeling empty inside. Being with him is like taking a vacation in heaven; food tastes better, sunsets are more enjoyable, the air smells cleaner, and each day begins with a smile. What a wonderful world it would be if it could always be that easy. However, falling in love is such a phenomenal high in the beginning that it is impossible for it to continue its momentum. I know it's hard to imagine, but that fire will eventually fade over time.

There was a time in my life when I was so shallow, that the moment the initial spark of a relationship diminished, I took it as a sign to head for the hills. When that magic was gone, I'd break up with whomever I was with and immediately look for it again, thinking that it was actually feasible to feel that way forever. I gave up on a lot of amazing relationships because of my futile search for the eternal flame.

I hate to say it, but this will happen to you many times. Boys come and go like the breeze when you're a teenager. The absolute love of your life on Monday may become a guy you can't even stomach by Friday. And if it happens to be your first true love that was lost, you may never fully recover. Mommy still talks about the pain of her first love to this day. She was sixteen, and when it ended she cried for months; she couldn't eat or sleep, and ached all over her body. It can be that painful. My first love cheated on me with one of my good friends. I caught them tongue wrestling in a bedroom at a party, and I literally thought my life was over. I cried for weeks after that and vowed to never let a girl hurt me again.

This is a kind of pain that does not subside easily; not even your favorite song, ice cream, best friend, or your daddy can make it better. "First-love hurt" just has to run its course and be expelled through your tear ducts as each day passes. Hopefully, you will take my advice and wait before you become too emotionally invested in some guy who doesn't deserve you. This is when you will discover what true love is. Just promise me that you will always use common sense when choosing guys. If you come home one night with Joe Football and start getting serious with him too fast, I might have to shoot myself. So for my sake, please use utmost caution. I know it's difficult to ignore that dreamy smile and adorable little tush of his, but try to look beneath the skin, at his soul.

Your Aunt Joy made this mistake. She married a great looking meathead right out of college and was divorced within two years. She was completely annihilated. We all warned her that he was a total jerk-off, yet she did not care to listen. She was blinded by love, or should I say lust.

## Lust

Can anyone really deny the concept of "love at first sight"? Everyone has experienced this phenomenon at some point in their life. In college I used to fall in love every weekend. But in reality, it's impossible to truly love someone before you know who they are on the inside. Therefore, all of those explosive feelings that you undergo in the beginning of a relationship are actually something called lust, love's evil twin.

Lust is our animal instincts kicking into overdrive, when you become so attracted to someone that you actually ache for their scent. You can kiss them for hours, turn into Jell-O with one look into their eyes, and their touch becomes your sole reason for existence. Sadly enough, this is when most people get bit in the ass. You wind up falling so head over heals in lust that you become blinded and begin to make huge mistakes, ones that can have a major impact on your future.

This is when people start making rash decisions, like engaging in spontaneous sex or getting married before the relationship has even begun. Every cell in your body may be telling you it's the right decision, and you believe in your heart that it's meant to be, but think again my dear. That's what is so frightening about lust; it brainwashes you and skews your ability to think rationally. This is one of the main reasons why many teenage girls end up in abusive relationships, marry losers, get pregnant, or even all three.

And when the day comes that the lust has receded, most guys start singing a completely different tune. Once lust has vanished from our lives, we cannot help but go in search of it again. It's what makes us the Neanderthals that we are, leaving girls in the dust, bitter, broken-hearted, and permanently scarred.

### *Life Rule #3: Sex isn't love.*

While sex for a teenage girl is all about being in love, intimacy, and the ultimate right of passage into womanhood. For a teenage boy, it's merely about completing the act. I feel I would be doing you a tremendous disservice by not explaining something that younger guys revolve their whole world around: the male orgasm.

I'm probably the first father in history to ever mention this to his daughter, but it's the God's honest truth. From the onset of puberty until they reach their late twenties, this is their one and only objective. If they are not doing it to themselves, then they are looking for someone else to take part in the project. It doesn't even have to be someone they care the slightest bit about; any female will do. And as soon as they have gotten what they want, their eyes are usually on the door, wondering what their friends are up to. If you can comprehend this one absurd male characteristic, then you will truly understand the enigma that is teenage boys.

I mentioned "the fever" earlier; this is when all of the blood rushes out of a guy's brain and into an extremity with a brain of its own. It's a complete metamorphosis of the male personality that is a conundrum even to us. This is when guys will lie, sweet talk, and make empty promises galore to get girls to cooperate with their desires. Most young girls will only agree to sex because they want a guy to like them, but it actually has the adverse affect.

If getting you to sleep with him wasn't a challenge, he'll lose all respect for you, and you'll never be more than a late-night booty call. Now you'll be forever labeled a slut because you didn't say "No!"

***Life Rule #4: Treat your virginity like a solitary wish given to you by your fairy godmother; something you cherish and will only use on the most meaningful occasion.***

When you are finally able to find that special someone who loves you to death, and you feel you are ready for a physical commitment, make sure you are positive because you can never go back. Although making love can be an amazing experience, it can also have particularly negative and hazardous affects on your life. You can become the victim of an unwanted pregnancy, or even contract a dangerous disease from your partner. I'm sure you've already heard about sexually transmitted diseases (STDs) in school, but I just want to make sure that you understand their severity and potentially deadly implications.

I wish somebody would have sat me down when I was your age and set me straight on all of this stuff. Unfortunately, and it kills me to have to tell you this, but I've experienced one of these. While it wasn't life threatening, it has been an extremely humiliating ordeal and something I'll have to live with for the rest of my life.

1. **Herpes:** Out of all the disclosures in this book, this is the one that hurts the most. Believe me, the last thing I want to do is make you grossed out by me, but I feel that hearing this will teach you a valuable lesson. Before I contracted this virus, I had barely even heard of herpes, or anything else for that matter, that could be spread from the simple act of kissing. As one of the millions of Americans who share my problem, we have come to call them "cold sores." I can barely even say the other word without cringing.

The mere mention of it makes me nauseous and extremely pissed off. It actually sounds a lot worse than it is. Basically, they are little blisters that break out a few times a year and then dry up and go away. When they first appeared on my mouth, I was so clueless; I had no idea what they even were. After my doctor quickly filled me in, I felt like he just told me that I had six months to live. Although he tried to comfort me by saying that almost 75 percent of the adult population in America has this, I was inconsolable.

In April of 1995, my fraternity brothers and I went to spring break in Cancun, Mexico. No sooner had the plane touched down on the tarmac; than did the drunken debauchery begin. Spring break is like nothing you could ever imagine. Picture thousands of sex-crazed college kids in a tropical atmosphere, getting completely wasted, and hooking up with random strangers for seven straight days. During our stay, I don't think we ate an ounce of solid food, just beer, shots, and frozen drinks. Everywhere we went, it was wall-to-wall people drunk off their asses, dancing, singing, kissing, and throwing up. The whole trip is a fog for me, but between all the bars, clubs, and parties, I think I hooked up with at least eight different girls. I was twenty-two, in my prime, and southern belles from places like Mississippi, Oklahoma, and Texas melted with a single utterance of my New York accent. One moment you're dancing with your friends, and the next a perfect stranger would just walk right up and try to swallow your face. It was like a giant orgy with clothes on.

After returning to the states, I needed some serious detox. I had the worst case of "Montezuma's Revenge," my liver hurt from all the drinking, and I noticed a small cluster of sores on the left corner of my mouth. I had finally gotten burnt; all those years of indiscretion had finally caught up to me. I was mortified and felt like I could never date or leave the house again. The absolute worst thing about this virus is that, unlike other STDs that can be treated and eradicated from your system, herpes stays with you for life. It lies dormant in your spinal chord, reappearing at times of stress or sickness. In the ten years that I've had it, the first year was by far the worst. I got it four times and each outbreak was worse than the last. Since then my body has learned to fight it more efficiently, to the point where I only get it about once a year. It still sucks big time, but I've actually managed to find a bright side to this nightmare.

For one, it was a huge wake up call for me. I finally learned that the dangers of a promiscuous life aren't things that just happen to other people. After the initial shock wore off, I was grateful in a way that this was all I had gotten. I could have easily contracted AIDS or another deadly disease from the poor choices I made. This made living with a twelve-day annoyance with minimal health risks a tad easier to deal with, and it officially ended my days as a male slut. I'm living proof that a select few of them can change for the better.

Secondly, I consider myself extremely fortunate to have contracted herpes that appear only on my mouth. Many people have to live with the pain and humiliation of genital herpes. While it is extremely contagious and easily spread from mouth to genitals and vice versa, if you are careful this can be avoided. Luckily, after all these years, I've managed to keep it from Mommy. When I feel the initial tingle, I just abstain from kissing for two weeks until it goes away. I spent the months before my wedding desperately praying to God that if he could please prevent an outbreak on this most stressful of days, I would never spend another moment hating this virus. Can you imagine? Hundreds of people watching my every move, all the kissing, the video footage, endless pictures, and worst of all, your mom's broken heart. I was sick for weeks, but on that fateful morning I was as clean and smooth as a baby's ass. I was never happier in my life.

Since then I've tried to fulfill my promise and not give this virus another moment's thought. When it comes, I just suck it up and deal with it. Every time I look into a mirror, I breathe a sigh of relief that I chose to get married and end my life of meaningless sexual relations.

When you're a teenager, kissing is the most amazing rush in the world. I learned first hand that even something as innocent as this can have life-changing affects. I promised you full disclosure in this book, and that's what I have to do. Although it's very embarrassing for me to share stories like this, I'll take all the humiliation in the world if it means saving you from having to go through it.

2. **Chlamydia and Gonorrhea:** I chose to group these two diseases together because, after researching, I saw many similarities between them. Although they are caused by different strains of bacteria, both infections are contracted through unprotected sexual activity. They are two of the most common STDs in America with close to three million reported cases each year.* Symptoms may include: burning during urination, lower abdominal pain, discharge, and genital swelling. While they can be treated if caught early, serious infection can occur if they are not taken care of immediately. The real kicker is that people can have these diseases and not even know it, therefore silently spreading it throughout the dating pool. Right before you decide to become sexually active, I would advise you to search the internet for chlamydia and gonorrhea photos. Although they may shock you into a life of celibacy, you will most definitely re-evaluate your current situation.

3. **Syphilis:** Also spread through unprotected sex, this disease causes open sores called "chancres," appearing on

private areas, along with serious health concerns. Syphilis can come and go in stages of remission, leading it's victims to believe it has gone away. In fact, people can have this disease for years and not know it until it's too late. In the later stages, syphilis begins attacking the organs and can cause dementia, heart complications, blindness, or death. Women can also transfer the infection to their unborn baby or become permanently unable to conceive.

4. **Genital warts:** I didn't even know you could get warts down there until the day my college suitemate called me into the bathroom practically in tears. We both stood there in silence staring at these grotesque pustules on the head of his penis. That image will be engrained in my mind for as long as I live. After an immediate trip to the infirmary, he came back to tell me that he had contracted genital warts and had to have them chemically frozen off in the doctor's office. Like herpes, they were highly contagious and it was a virus that would be reoccurring for his life. This is when my suitemate began to spiral out of control.

Nick was from a small town in upstate New York of only a few hundred people. Before coming to college, he was an all-American boy, working on his dad's farm, playing varsity football, and planning on marrying his high school girlfriend after college. Hanna was a doll; she visited every weekend, mostly to try and keep Nick away from the dangerous party scene that our school was so famous for. It was actually quite pathetic how in love they were, and how whipped Nicky was. Would you believe that the one weekend Hanna couldn't make it to see him, Nick would go out on the town, get shit-faced drunk, and hook up with a perfect stranger? About two weeks later, we would both be standing in the bathroom staring at his weiner with perplexed looks on our faces. The tragic part of this story is that in those two weeks he had gone to visit his devoted girlfriend, and had unknowingly passed the virus on to her.

Much more dangerous for a woman, genital warts can manifest on the cervix and cause life threatening cancer, or be transferred to a baby during child birth. After several months of despair, Nick and Hanna were no more. Both of their lives were destroyed because of his one drunken blunder. In the ensuing months, Nick would go on a self-destructive drug and alcohol binge of epic proportion. After a DWI, three bar fights, and two disorderly conduct arrests, he eventually failed out of college and was never heard from again. Nick is a perfect example of how one alcohol induced lapse in judgment can ruin the rest of your life. I think of him often and feel sad, but mostly I feel sad for Hanna, the innocent victim.

5. **AIDS:** The mother of all STDs, a true killer, and the number one reason for the end of the sexual revolution of the 1960s. Before this disease came along, people pretty much had sex with whomever they wanted, with zero guilt. This all changed in the early 1980s. AIDS (acquired immune deficiency syndrome) is a disease brought on by its predecessor HIV (human immunodeficiency virus). Whenever one of my students inquires about this disease, I offer the following explanation.

Your body possesses an intricate defensive scheme called the immune system. It's made up of many different components whose job is to keep the body healthy and disease free. The main components in this fight are things called white blood cells, or as I call them, "soldier cells." Imagine that your body was a country, if it didn't have defenses like the army, navy, air force, or marines, then it would be constantly attacked by other countries in hopes of conquering it. However, your white blood cells come to the rescue and fight off any type of harmful foreign body that may enter you. Sometimes it may take a while, but usually the soldiers win in the end, defeating the virus and bringing you back to optimal health. What makes AIDS so dangerous, is that it attacks your soldier cells and eventually eradicates them, leaving your body like an unprotected island in a sea of hostility. As your white blood cell count gets lower and lower, you become more susceptible to harmful diseases, until you eventually lack the ability to fight off even the common cold.

There are many drugs to fight this sexual epidemic, but unfortunately this only prolongs the inevitable—that there is no cure. I read that close to five million people around the world contract AIDS every year, and in 2004, over three million died from it.^ In the beginning, it was believed that it was exclusively a disease of gay men; this is now known to be a myth. AIDS does not discriminate; people of all races, ages, and sexual orientations can get it, even unborn babies. There are no second chances with this disease; one night of unprotected sex can end your life. You may think you know everything about your current boyfriend's sexual past, but how well do you know the history of everyone of his past partners? A person can also catch AIDS from one of them, having never even met them.

Contrary to popular belief, the virus cannot be spread through casual human contact such as hugging, kissing, touching, sneezing, or sharing a drink. Yet, current studies have shown that it can be transferred through oral sex. And don't think for a minute that someone with this disease looks sickly and easy to spot. AIDS can take years to develop symptoms, so people can be walking around healthy and sexually active, unknowingly infecting countless others.

6. **Hepatitis C:** This is another deadly disease that is transferred through blood-to-blood contact. This virus

attacks the liver and can cause cirrhosis, liver cancer, and even death. An estimated three hundred million people worldwide have this disease, with 3.9 million living in the United States. Although hepatitis C is primarily contracted from intra-venous drug usage and tainted tattoo needles, unprotected sex is also a common reason for its widespread infection rates.

7. **Crabs**: This shouldn't even be listed among STDs, for it is not a disease and more of an annoyance than a health threat. Nonetheless, they can be sexually transmitted, so I figured I'd throw them into this depressing section for a little comic relief. Like the lice that people get in their hair, these little buggers make their home in your pubic hair, and it can be quite the bitch getting rid of them. After only a week in college, I was noticing an itch in my private area that would not go away. The bathroom in our suite had these ultra-bright fluorescent lights on the ceiling, so I jumped up on the sink and dropped my skivvies. I couldn't believe what I saw: hundreds of tiny little bugs were jumping around and having a party in my short and curlies.

I knew exactly what they were, but I hadn't hooked up with anyone in school yet, so how the hell could I have gotten them? Then I remembered the piss stained and mold ridden mattress that I had underneath my nice new sheets. Being so psyched to unpack, meet my roommates, and start my life as a college student, I just threw a sheet over the revolting mattress I was assigned and forgot about it.

Not only do these suckers live on you, but they lay eggs on you, in your bed, and clothing, causing complete infestation. I freaked, shaved my whole body to the skin, used a special medicated shampoo, washed everything I owned in boiling water, and demanded a new mattress from the dorm director. The crabs were soon gone, but it definitely was a harrowing experience, one that I would hate to ever live through again. I start to itch just thinking about those little bastards. Although I'm pretty sure I got them from my bed, most people get them from each other during sex, and this is one thing that a condom won't protect you from.

## Pregnancy

As soon as a girl gets her first period she can become pregnant, pretty disturbing when you think that some girls are getting it by nine or ten years old these days. Nature played a cruel trick on humans with this one. Our bodies are physically ready for something that our minds are decades away from being able to comprehend: parenthood. If you were to analyze what our purpose is for being on this planet, you'd see that it is simply to make more people. We must perpetuate the species and assure our survival at all costs. This is the primal message encoded in our DNA: reproduce, reproduce, reproduce.

This is why sex is all we can think about once puberty sets in. Our bodies desperately want us to make babies; it's undeniable. While becoming a parent was the single greatest moment of my life at thirty-one, teenage pregnancy can be quite the horrific experience. I've known girls who got pregnant in high school and it ruined their lives. Their childhood ended the moment that home pregnancy test came up positive. The days of parties, proms, the mall, crushes, first dates, and talking on the phone were now gone forever. Their whole life became about the baby: sleepless nights, changing diapers, 3:00 AM feedings, and endless hours of screaming. And in almost every case, the boy responsible for this fiasco vanished into thin air.

Do you really think that a seventeen-year-old boy with shit for brains and a perpetual boner is prepared to embrace that kind of responsibility? Even the "Mr. Wonderful" types with great grades, family values, and an awesome future ahead of them are simply unable to handle that kind of lifelong commitment. The good ones may promise to stick by you, sometimes even until the baby comes. However, most likely after a few months of the new lifestyle, it will be too much to bear. He will eventually leave you with this baby, a constant reminder of him.

While some girls choose to become sixteen-year-old mothers, others opt to have an abortion, ending the baby's life before it even had a chance. No matter what your feelings on abortion may be, living with that kind of guilt is something that may be impossible to get over. Abortion is one of those topics that are just so difficult to comprehend. I've spent hours talking with people who were either strictly pro-life or pro-choice, and they both make each side of the fence sound morally justified. As I see it, it's impossible to adhere to one belief system for every situation. Who's to say that a girl impregnated by her sadistic stepfather should be forced to have the baby? While on the other hand, who's to say that there isn't a loving home for that baby somewhere in the world?

What I do know is this: one of my good friends from high school had an abortion at fifteen and is still living with the emotional pain it caused almost twenty years later. So much so, that in college she attempted suicide by slitting her wrists with a razor blade. We still talk on occasion; she's a happily married mom now and ironically the director of "The Pregnancy Support Center," a non-profit organization that counsels girls on the alternatives to abortion. I don't think a day goes by that she doesn't feel deep regret for the decision she made.

I realize that much of the above is quite terrifying to read about, but sex is a dangerous topic that should not be taken lightly. However, there are certain precautions you can take to keep yourself out of harm's way. There are things that can prevent most STDs and unwanted pregnancies; if used correctly, you can avoid many of the pitfalls that sexual maturity can bring.

## Sexual Precautions and Birth Control

1. **Abstinence:** This means a total conscious decision to avoid sex until a later stage in life. I would be ecstatic if this was the road you chose; there are many girls out there who still practice this for one reason or another. I've known some who lost their virginity in their twenties; they held out for true love and considered this the greatest decision they ever made. Always remember that love is proven through actions and not words. Guys learn very young that saying the magical words "I love you," whether they mean it or not, will usually lead to quicker sex. I'm not holding my breath that you'll practice this method. Just promise me that you'll give it some serious thought.

2. **Condoms:** I know you probably think they're gross, but this little piece of latex can be the difference between a little harmless experimenting and a wasted life of regret. While they are not 100 percent effective against fighting STDs and pregnancy, they are pretty damn close. You just have to be very careful with them because they do have some flaws, the biggest being that they break quite easily and can expire like a carton of milk. When a condom breaks during usage, it's pretty much the same thing as having unprotected sex with all of the aforementioned risks. This has happened to me a few times, including once when I was seventeen. The weeks following were a living hell as I waited for my girlfriend to get her monthly friend. Luckily, I avoided the worst, but I really sweat it out there for a while, crying at night as to what would become of me as a teenage dad.

   Another tremendous flaw with condoms doesn't even involve the product at all, but the user. Most guys hate condoms and will only use one if they have to. They'll use lies, urban legends, or even the infamous, "I'll be extra careful" promise. Don't ever fall for any of this garbage; allowing a guy this privilege will only bring you misery. You should absolutely use a condom every time, no questions asked. If he refuses, how much do you think he truly cares about you? He doesn't; you're merely the flavor of the month to him, or should I say the night.

If you feel that you are getting close to this stage in your life, then go to the drug store, get yourself a three pack of Trojans, and carry them wherever you go. I'll even buy them for you if you're too embarrassed. When I was growing up, none of my friends carried condoms in their wallets, we only used them when the girls forced us to. The idea that guys are actually into these things is a myth. Use your head, and remember this famous quote from an unknown author, "No glove, no love!"

3. **The Pill:** This is the greatest invention in the history of the world, as far as young guys are concerned. However, the pill cannot protect you from any sexually transmitted diseases, and you still have a slim chance of conceiving a baby, so it should never be used as your sole method of birth control. While it claims 99 percent effectiveness, I feel that that statement is quite the double-edged sword. Mainly because once young girls begin taking the pill, they feel that they are indestructible and are able to sleep around indiscriminately. The reason guys love the pill so much is because it takes all of the responsibility off their shoulders, and allows them do whatever they want. Proper birth control should always be using the pill and a condom together, keeping you safe from any diseases and unwanted pregnancies. The moment you let your boyfriend talk you into abandoning the condom, you are giving up a lot more than it seems. Now if he cheats on you, he's endangering your health greatly.

When the time comes, come to us and we will make an appointment for you to see a doctor and get a prescription. Don't listen to all the negatives stigmas attached to the pill, like that it makes you fat, moody, and acne ridden. Three of my girlfriends (including Mommy) were on it for many years and, while there were definite side effects, they thought the pros significantly outweighed the cons. Which would you rather have, moodiness and zits a few times a month or becoming a seventeen-year-old unwed mother?

4. **Diaphragm, Sponge, and Spermicidal Jelly:** I mention these three together because they all have the same thing in common: they suck! These methods of birth control are all for females who aren't extra cautious when it comes to sex, and don't give proper thought to the risks of STDs. The first one blocks the sperm, the second absorbs it, and the third kills it. But what about all of the diseases that snuck by? None of these three birth control methods are very effective and shouldn't even be considered by a teenager with so much to lose. I only mention them because you will probably bump into girls from time to time who swear by them. Pay them no mind, for they are also the girls who truly believe that their teenage boyfriend is their future husband and is completely faithful to them.

There may be a few other ones that I have forgotten to mention, but they are most likely worthless. I don't care what new groundbreaking methods come about in the near future, using the condom and the pill together is the only way to guarantee yourself a healthy sex life with little to no regrets. Now, I can't stop you from living your life and making your own decisions; I just hope that you take all that I have said to heart. This will be invaluable information for you during this difficult time. However, no matter what happens, I will always be there to help and will never judge you.

## Finding Mr. Right

You've probably been dreaming about him for years now, Prince Charming—the guy who will come to rescue you from the depths of adolescence and bring you all the joy in the world. You never know, you could meet him tomorrow or thirty years from now. But odds are you will go through many failed relationships before you finally find him. During your search, you will most likely fall in love many times and have your heart ripped out just as much, but in all you will learn a great deal from both types of experiences. As a father and former manipulator of females, I can't help but be extremely concerned about this topic. While there are indeed good guys out there with true intentions, they are very few and far between.

Your cousin Brett comes to mind, I met him over fifteen years ago when he was eight years old. In that time, I don't think I've ever known a more responsible, mature, and kind-hearted guy. He never got into the drinking/drug scene and, as far as I know, his long term girlfriend Kerri has always been treated with utmost respect. Brett is one of the few young guys out there who truly understands how to treat a girl. I know in my heart that you will someday find your special someone, and I can't wait to welcome him into our family with open arms.

Just be careful when you are interpreting signals from perspective guys. Misreading a situation like this can lead to certain humiliation. Like the time I mistook a friendly lab partner for my long lost soul-mate. I put a note in her locker professing my undying devotion, which was later found by her 200 pound boyfriend and resulted in a minor ass beating.

## Ten signs he's into you:

1. **Whenever you are around, he either completely clams up or starts being loud and obnoxious.** Either extreme can show interest, depending on his overall demeanor.
2. **He teases you constantly.** We're talking harmless teasing here, any malicious name calling means you probably have a psycho on your hands who should be avoided rather than a future boyfriend.
3. **He stares at you constantly.** This has always been my choice of advances for some bizarre reason. Although it has probably made many a girl consider me a deranged stalker, it has worked well at showing girls I was interested.
4. **Any attempt at face-to-face small talk.** "Where are you from? How many siblings do you have?" etc. Guys hate small talk, so if he does this, there's no doubt he digs you.
5. **He constantly shows up where you are.** The mall, parties, sporting events, wherever; it's no coincidence you two keep bumping into each other.
6. **He makes friends with your friends.** This is a tricky one because he could be either trying to get at you or them. But it means he is definitely interested in someone in your circle.
7. **He has his friends question you.** A biggie with the shy ones; usually a sure sign there's interest brewing.
8. **Any form of written communication.** Whether it's a note, email, instant message, or anything else he took the time to write, it's another sure sign. Teenage boys hate writing to girls. They know that within the hour you'll be giggling over their every word with your friends.
9. **Any attempt at phone contact.** Whether it's for a missed homework assignment or just to say hi, any phone call is a huge sign he likes you.

10. **Any display of an adept memory concerning you.** If he remembers something you said, did, or told him in passing, he digs you.

## Ten signs he's Not into you:

1. **"I just want to be friends."** Guys never want to be just friends with a girl, they always have ulterior motives. If he says this, there is definitely zero interest and no changing his mind.

2. **"I don't want a girlfriend right now."** With the tempting possibilities of daily intimacy, guys always want a girlfriend right now. It just happens to not be you.

3. **"I've been busy."** Guys would blow off sleep, work, a sporting event, concert, party, school, or pretty much anything else at the slightest chance of being with a girl they like. They are never too busy.

4. **Doesn't even know you exist.** Another tricky one because he could just be deathly shy. I've come across many of the bitchiest girls from my high school who later turned out to be sweethearts, and admitted that they were just incredibly insecure when they were younger.

5. **He pays more attention to your friend than you.** Back off; he's totally into her. And don't hate her either, the time will come when the tables are turned and her crush is into you.

6. **After you hook up with him, he never looks at you again.** What can I say, guys suck!

7. **Lack of written communication.** As I said above, guys hate writing to girls, but they will if they are into you. If they care not to respond to your written advances, it's time to move on.

8. **He showed initial interest and then backed off.**
The moment you show too much interest for someone, they lose all interest in you. Most likely your mutual admiration was the culprit. Acting aloof with guys is usually the best policy.

9. **He forgets everything you tell him.** If guys are into a girl, they'll write things on their hands if they have to. Most likely he's lazy, thick-headed, and not a keeper.
10. **He's rude to your family.** Even the biggest meatheads know that this is a tremendous mistake. If he's anything but courteous to your kin, don't waste your time.

## Finding Mr. Wrong

Until you do find your knight in shining armor, I feel it is my duty to properly warn you about something I know a great deal about: the Pretty Boy Snake. They are so easy to spot; great-looking, dreamy eyes, outgoing personality, utmost confidence, athletic build, and a million-dollar smile to boot. These are the ones to be extremely leery of; for once they set their sights on you, there is little chance of not falling head over heals in love with them. You may even envision the two of you getting serious and possibly married somewhere down the road. Yet, after a few memorable months of dating, he's gone from your life as quickly as he entered it. All the promises he made, all the times he said he loved you were all for naught. You trusted him, loved him with all your heart, gave yourself to him unconditionally, and now he's moved on, maybe even to your best girl friend.

That's the way the snake works, they divide and conquer, leaving no survivors; it happens to everyone. You must be quite vigilant and constantly on the lookout for this type of guy. If suddenly out of the blue, the local hottie that every girl adores starts showing an interest in you, consider this a red flag. Don't think for a second that he's a changed man and ready to commit to you for the first time in his life, because most likely you'll get burnt.

One of Mommy's good friends from childhood learned this harsh lesson first hand. A few years ago, Beth was introduced to a local blues musician and became instantly enamored by his charm. After years of dating one bastard after another, she had finally found her one true love. Rory had it going on; looks, personality, and serious musical talent as well. They moved in together right away and were engaged to be married within months. Although they hardly knew each other, we all adored him and were completely supportive of their whirlwind romance. If I was into guys, I would have even fallen under his spell.

As the wedding approached, Rory began to exhibit traces of a shady past filled with money issues and many unanswered questions. Love would prevail however, and Beth soon accepted his faults and hoped for the future. They exchanged vows in Barbados, bought a house in a swanky neighborhood, and became expecting parents of a bundle of joy. Yet within months of the birth of his daughter, Rory had once again moved onto greener pastures; leaving his bride with a broken heart, hefty mortgage payment, and a fatherless child.

During the messy divorce proceedings, Beth would discover that Rory not only had a string of ex-girlfriends to whom he owed money and promised the world, but he also had a young son living in Virginia. She was now just one of the many girls left in his wake, desperately trying to pick up the pieces of her shattered life. Beth thought she could change him, believed his lies, and gave him everything possible; if only she knew.

Most of the snakes in the world aren't boyfriend material anyway, never mind husband material. In reality, they'll probably end up three times divorced, skirt-chasing bar-flies as adults. Still, even some of the worst male specimens on Earth can be quite the charmers in the beginning. There's something called the "first date persona." This is where a guy is on his best behavior for the first few months of a new relationship. They open doors, pull out chairs, abstain from harsh language, call you every minute, and spew out compliments ad nauseam. For a guy determined to get you into bed, this can even last eight months to a year. I've personally kept it up for longer.

However, it all comes to an abrupt halt once sex has taken place; now they know they've got you. No girl in her right mind would dump a guy right after first sex; her reputation would be trashed. Now she's vested and in for the long haul. The transformation from the first date persona to the real him can be quite disturbing. So, for your own good, don't ever be easy. Guys fill each other in on the easy girls; who they are and just what it takes to score with them. It's part of our code.

### Life Rule #5: An easy girl will eventually become a lonely girl.

After they get you to finally say yes, if they even choose to stick around, you will lose all the power in the relationship. In the mind of the snake, you have now given up your right to say no in the future. Now he'll use all the mind games in the book to turn you into his little sex toy: guilt trips, threats of a break up, anger, or even the legendary "blue balls" excuse. This classic has been around for a long time and has convinced many a girl to do things against her will. You see, when a guy has participated in a lot of foreplay but no actual sex has occurred, he will develop a gut wrenching pain in his scrotal area referred to in the medical field as "prostatic congestion." I don't know why this happens, but it is extremely painful. According to the pretty boy, this is a very serious condition that can even be life threatening if not taken care of immediately. In reality, it's no big deal and goes away in about an hour; so don't fall for this old gag.

When searching for the keepers it's best to just start out as friends. Get to know him, learn about his past relationships, likes, dislikes, attitudes, moods, and slowly learn more and more. If negative attributes start appearing, move on immediately. The worst thing you can do is think that you have the power to change a snake into Mr. Wonderful. He's not changing for you or anybody else for that matter.

## When to Dump His Ass

Remember, dating is just a game to them. In high school my friends and I would actually argue and brag about whose girlfriend was more whipped and pathetic. When you feel that you are being even the slightest bit disrespected by a guy, there is only one solution: dump his ass. Nothing can empower a girl more than a preemptive break up. This captivating move can turn even the most experienced pretty boy into a slobbering disgrace of a human being. No one likes to be dumped, especially when they are used to doing the dumping. As soon as he starts talking down to you, ignoring you, ordering you around, forgetting important dates, raising his voice, eyeing other girls, or lying to you about where he's been, it's pretty much over anyway. Many times behaviors like these mean he's either thinking of dumping you, he's cheating on you, or both.

Cheating—not my honey! I hate to break this to you, but teenage boys cheat like crazy. Come to think of it, married men cheat like crazy, but with boys who have less to lose, it's much more rampant. I'd bet that 90 percent of guys would cheat on their girlfriends if chances of getting caught were slim. We just can't help it; even the slightest glance from a pretty girl makes us gush with excitement. Just imagine the reaction we get when a female shows genuine interest in us.

Every teenage guy I knew was occasionally unfaithful in their relationships, including myself. When certain situations arose it was just too difficult to deny. However, if you are aware of the telltale signs of infidelity, and remain cognizant of your boyfriend's behavior; you can most certainly avoid being unknowingly betrayed.

## The Five Signs of an Unfaithful Boyfriend

1. **The sudden appearance of a new wardrobe.** Usually when a guy purchases a slew of new clothes it means there's someone new he's trying to impress (unless he's a fashion model or something). And if it's the underwear supply that was replenished, be on high alert!

2. **Stops including you in his plans.** Guys love alone time with their friends. But if you get wind that girls are involved in their nightly excursions, this may call for an unexpected pop-in where they hang out.

3. **Directly to voicemail.** If this happens every time you call him, there's definitely a reason his phone is always turned off.

4. **Acting aloof and forgetful.** If your once omnipresent boyfriend suddenly appears emotionally distant and forgetful of your every plan, chances are there's someone else occupying his mind.

5. **Constantly checking email, social websites, text messages, or voicemail.** Three or four times a day is a tad extreme, but a few times an hour is a dead give away. Any guy who does this is without a doubt in a relationship he cares nothing about.

No girl wants to believe that her guy could be secretly intimate with someone else. Well, it's not intimacy that we crave, but the excitement of being desired by a new person that is irresistible. Trust me, you'll find a faithful one someday if you're patient. They are out there. Until then, just kick him to the curb. This will either be a huge slap in his face and he'll come back to you on his hands and knees begging for forgiveness, never to cross you again; or, his pride will be crushed and he'll runaway with his tail between his legs. Either way you've won, maintained your self-worth, and got the word out among the other snakes that you are no easy chick.

## *Life Rule #6: Guys will treat you how you allow them to treat you.*

## Relationships and Dating

The most important trait you should be looking for in a guy is strong family values. I'm not saying you should go out and date repulsive dweebs or anything, but looks should definitely not be number one on your list. At the age you are reading this, it probably will be. Yet, as you mature this will slowly change with each heart break. You'll be one step closer to finding that guy who maybe doesn't set your soul on fire, but instead thaws your frozen heart and makes you feel appreciated. Marriage may be the last thing on your mind right now. However, when you're both thirty, do you want a guy who still wants to get wasted with his friends every night, and can barely even stomach a weekend home with his family?

Give this some thought; the perfect guy doesn't always have to be the stud of the group, or the one with the killer bod that all the girls have their eye on. Maybe it's the shy one of the bunch that hardly anyone notices at all, the one who sits right next to you in math class. You never know, underneath that baseball cap could be the cutest and most sensitive guy ever, simply dying for you to notice him. That just might be where you'll find him. This young man will be more interested in you than he is in himself, and he'll appreciate more in life than beer, football, and getting laid. And most importantly, he won't be in such a rush to get you out of your clothes. Spicy physical attractions will always fade. When it does, don't you want to be with a guy who will listen to you, nurture you, and include you in every aspect of his life? That's exactly what healthy long-lasting relationships are made of.

When you do ultimately come across your handsome prince and all you can think about is making him happy, review the following list of what I believe guys really want in their relationships. All the complex advice in *Cosmopolitan* and *Vogue* will only confuse you further. Guys are quite simple to figure out actually. Follow these clear-cut rules and you can forever be the number one girlfriend.

## What Guys Want from their Girlfriends (Besides Sex):

1. **Have your own life.** While in the beginning we want you to drop your whole life for us, this gets old pretty fast. Once you've dismissed all your friends, interests, and become totally dependent on him for everything, this is the exact moment when guys start to feel smothered and start thinking about maybe moving on to a less needy girl. When that inevitable time comes and your relationship has gone awry, you will now have to go crawling back to the girls you abandoned months ago.

### *Life Rule #7: Never drop your friends for a guy.*

Other than looks, one of the biggest reasons that guys fall for a girl is because they are interesting and seem to have a lot going on. A perfect example of this is one of the girls I dated in high school. Jenna was a die-hard music fan, ridiculously smart in school, and had a ton of friends. As time passed, one of the things that kept me so attracted to her was that she never gave up her life for me. In fact, I was often the one who felt neglected and wanted to be included more in her activities. Don't ever become that girl who sits home alone every night waiting for her man to call, this is a major turnoff. Also, be careful not to turn into the, "Chameleon girlfriend." You know the kind I mean; they have no true identity for themselves and become exact clones of their current boyfriend. This week she's a hippy, next week she's into the Goth scene, followed by a brief stint as a baggy pants-wearing rapper chick. This is a sure way to show people that you have no personal interests, and also makes you look quite flakey.

2.  **Let us hang with the boys.** This is probably the biggest mistake a girlfriend can make. Never underestimate the power of his friends, for they can manipulate him almost as easily as you can. I know the thought of him hanging out at all hours; driving around with drugs, alcohol, and slutty girls makes you insane. But the moment you start to bad mouth or even forbid him to see his friends, your relationship is very close to being over. Guys need other guys in their life almost as much as they need girls. Our boys are part of our identity, without them we'd become a no-name loser with zero chance of getting a girl like you again in the future. I probably would have still been a virgin into my twenties, if not for the happening crowd of my late teens. So for us to give up our friends is very much like asking us to give up our manhood, coolness, and even our gonads. I have had many obnoxious friends that I'm sure Mommy hated deep down, but she never made the mistake of being vocal about these feelings. Nevertheless, as much as you loathe their perverted faces you must pretend you can tolerate them, or else start shopping for a new boyfriend.

3.  **Jealousy is a fine line.** While a little bit of jealousy from both sides of a relationship may keep it strong, too much can turn even the most adoring lovebirds into that screaming couple you see in the mall and swear could never be you. Jealousy can bring out the animal in even the most timid of people. I've done horrible things in my life under its power. I've also had girls freak out on me, claws drawn and teeth bared. You should definitely mention to him when you are feeling jealous every now and then to show that you are into him, just try not to make a daily habit out of it. It can also work for your benefit. Let him know when guys compliment you or someone likes you, and don't keep your guy friends a secret. This will no doubt

drive him crazy and make your happiness his number one priority. Be very careful you don't go overboard with this though, or you might have a roid-raging lunatic on your hands, primed for battle.

4. **Don't nag him.** HUGE! No girl likes to think that they are a nag. They believe that they are merely being a loving, caring, and cautious girlfriend. After you have been with a guy for a while and you begin to let your guard down; this is when it happens. You start vocalizing every thought that enters your mind to him, questions about your future together, the present, his past, etc. We hate this with a passion. While guys don't want a mute girlfriend, they don't want a girl who never shuts up even more. You have to be confident enough in yourself to be quiet every now and then. Let there be silences between you, saying every thought makes you look insecure in who you are. And as soon as you become known as the "bitchy nag" by his family and friends, they will most certainly start pressuring him to dump you. They will even go so far as setting him up with new girls; anything to get you out of his life.

5. **Never mention marriage to a guy of any age.** This is a tricky one because many guys will be very responsive to the idea of marriage in their future, even in the beginning of a relationship. However, this is another one of our secret ploys to get you into bed quicker. After sex has taken place, I'd be shocked to hear of any young guy ever acknowledging the topic again. Guys don't want to hear about your fantasies of the dream wedding, or when you want to be married and have your first child. This scares the shit out of us to be quite frank. Even if you've been with a guy ten years, always let him bring up the topic and then just casually dance around the idea; don't get all crazy about it. Getting a guy to commit to something like

marriage is like trying to get a baby deer to eat out of your hand; any sudden movements and he's gone.

6. **Body upkeep and hygiene.** *Seinfeld*, a 1990s sitcom, was one of the most popular TV shows in the history of entertainment. One of the running gags on this show was that the guys were constantly breaking up with girls because of silly superficial reasons, like the one girl who had "man hands," for example. I think the reason this was so hysterical is because there is some definite truth to that. Men are 100 percent visual creatures; we live with our eyes and can be totally neurotic about even the slightest imperfections. This is not our fault however; ever since we can remember, television and advertising has shown us the perfect woman. The very one we imagine marrying someday. I'm sad to say, but I fall into this shallow puddle myself. I'd be lying if I said any different. I once broke up with a girl after my friends nicknamed her Scaley, instead of Haley, for her dry skin.

I'm not saying for one moment that you should strive for perfection in your physical attributes. I'm merely suggesting that you should take pride in your appearance, for it says a lot about who you are. Staying attractive in the dating game can be achieved through actions as simple as plucking a few stray hairs, moisturizing, standing up straight, not slathering on too much make-up, having good oral hygiene, maintaining a proper diet, and exercising regularly. Nobody has to have the body of a supermodel, but the two things that every guy secretly desires are tone and proportion. If this is a problem, fixing it doesn't require surgery, starving, throwing up, or anything drastic like that; just being health-conscious and striving to maintain an active lifestyle.

As we get older it's inevitable that our bodies will start to sag a little, guys get the gut and girls get the butt. It takes a willful effort to avoid this; brisk walking, use of light free weights, and skipping the after-school McDonald's run can be the solution. Your mother and I have had a pact since we both turned thirty. I promised I would never get a jelly belly, if she promised never to pack too much junk into her trunk. This keeps us both motivated to stay healthy and very much attracted to each other. True beauty is definitely something that is within a person. However, I've learned that people who do not care about their appearance usually have a lot of other issues as well.

7. **Food.** Guys love to eat almost as much as they love to have sex. Nothing shows a guy you care more than surprising him with yummy treats every once in a while. We're not talking gourmet cuisine here; it can be franks and beans from the can, as long as it's made with love it will get the point across. Just the act of you buying the ingredients, planning the meal, and spending time preparing it is more than enough to impress any guy. Bring him lunch at work, save leftovers for him when you go out to eat, or come out with his favorite snack when you run into the store. It's little things like this that mean a lot. And one more thing, when you are eating out together offer to pay every now and then. Most teenage boys are broke and even if he doesn't accept the money, the gesture says a lot about your commitment to him.

8. **Don't get "lovey dovey" too fast.** From the first date, always be careful of showing interest too quickly. Even if you believe you've found your soul mate, you should hide it as best you can. While you want to show him that you are interested, showing that you are completely under his spell could have the opposite effects that you desire. Some girls go into warp-speed moments after that first magical kiss. They profess their undying love, make hourly phone

calls, write three page letters, and drop every plan for him. Doing these things will most likely make the guy see you as leachy and annoying, a big turn off. Follow his lead, but never overdo the mushiness, pet names, and baby talk; it may scare him away for good.

I didn't figure this out until I was in my late twenties. When a girl liked me I was as cool as an autumn breeze. Yet when I liked her, I became a blathering pile of mush and compliments. When you fall hard for someone, you want to climb the tallest mountain and scream to the world that you love them. The three major loves in my life (Mommy included) were all girls that I played the game with and always kept them wondering. That's why it is so important that you don't get intimate with a guy too quickly; that is the ultimate recipe for disaster. Let the lovey dovey crap slowly build over time. Mommy and I say "I love you" to each other at least fifty times a day, but this is after twelve years together. If you notice yourself calling him things like, "muffin ass," "pumpkin pie," or "honey bunny" within the first six to eight months of the relationship, it's too soon; back off a little.

9. **Befriend the females in his life.** Unlike the rest; this one is more for your own personal gain than his. Regardless, he will appreciate you reaching out to the women in his life. These are the people who will be watching you very closely, so always be aware of every utterance you make in their presence. Even if his mom and sisters are total bitches, try showering them with kindness; be polite, warm, and honest, and they will let their guard down soon enough. Although, be extremely careful of the nosey mom. After getting close to you, she may try to use you as an unknowing spy into her son's secret life. If this happens, Mr. Wonderful will start viewing you as an untrustworthy blabbermouth and soon cut you out of the loop. When you feel mom

beginning to pry, simply smile, play dumb, and do your best to change the subject. Part of your job as his girlfriend is to always make him look like a perfect little angel to his family. These women can be your biggest supporters or your biggest adversaries, so use them wisely.

10. **Be able to watch sports with the guys.** Even the guys who have little interest in sports, still enjoy hanging with their friends at sporting events. At every Super bowl party I ever attended, there was always one guy who brought along his super-cool girlfriend. This was not just your average hottie, who would sit there looking pretty, impatiently looking at her watch, and fetching beers for her man. This was something quite different; a girl that almost every guy would kill to have, one who can enjoy sports and really hang with the guys. A girl that not only understands the intricacies of competition, but can also watch events with the same testosterone-induced enthusiasm as men.

I can't even count the number of amazing nail-biting games I watched on the edge of my seat, screaming at the television, as my girlfriend at the time sat next to me painting her nails and thumbing through a magazine. I can still see Allison Moran, my buddy Mark's girlfriend/ wife now, sitting there in her official Giants jersey with her favorite player's name embroidered on the back, screaming at the referees, warning about blitzes, and discussing how a loss could affect possible playoff implications. We all marveled at her love for sports and wondered how great it must be to be able to share that with a female. It just so happened that Ally grew up with four older brothers and a dad who was a football coach at a junior college, so she had been breathing sports since she was in diapers.

Now she was an extreme case; in order to become one of these girls all one needs to do is learn the basics of the major sports and merely pretend to be into them.

Nothing is worse than the girlfriend who asks, "What quarter is the baseball game in?" or yells, "We need a homerun here!" during a football game. With just a little background knowledge on each of the big four (football, baseball, hockey, and basketball), anyone can appear to be a true sports fan. It will take some homework, but in the long run, you'll be one of the cool girlfriends, the one that others admire and wish they had.

First and foremost, you have to learn a little bit about the teams of the sporting event in which you are about to view; learn where they are from, and one or two of their star players. This can easily be done through the use of the internet, skimming the sports section of the local newspaper, or watching a few minutes of *Sports Center* on ESPN. You don't need to go crazy here, just learn the basics. No one is going to quiz you on the spot, but it's very impressive when a girl calls a player by his nickname, or can spew a trivial stat every now and then. Just remember that whatever the event, it's all about attitude, choosing a team to cheer for, and being ruthless to the core. If you choose to go this route, you'll be set if you learn the meanings of the following terms:

**football**: end-zone, touch down, field goal, offense, defense, punt, first down, quarterback, running back, sack, blitz, turnovers (fumble and interception), AFC, and NFC

**baseball**: National and American leagues, all nine field positions, single, double, triple, homerun, stealing, walk, double play, strike out, perfect game, no hitter, the cycle, error, relief pitching, bullpen, balk, dugout, and designated hitter

**basketball**: all five positions, dunk, lay-up, three pointers, rebounds, NBA, NCAA, March Madness, the Final Four, fouls (personal, technical, and flagrant), and traveling

**hockey**: the net, offense (wings), defense, goalie, power play, hat trick, assists, the crease, slap shot, break away, short-handed goal, Stanley Cup, and penalty shots

You never know; you just might get hooked into the hype and become somewhat of a fan. Even your mother, who literally has negative interest in sports, has gotten sucked into a few playoff games in her day. So it's your call; I just thought I'd give you the lowdown on sports.

Now that I've more or less scared you into a life of lesbianism with all of my wild stories and opinions of young men, I must recap. Boys lie, and blah, blah, blah; I'm sure you're sick of hearing it. It's not that I want you to be afraid to date or anything, but I would much rather you hear all of this from me instead of learning it the hard way. Nothing in this world is more rewarding than a loving relationship. I am only trying to guide you towards finding one sooner rather than later. In the meantime, go out on dates, have fun, be yourself, and discover life and love, but never forget …

*Life Rule #8: No guy will ever love you as much as your daddy does!*

* Centers for Disease Control and Prevention. May 1999. CDC Fact Sheet: *Some facts about Chlamydia.*

^ A.I.D.S. Epidemic Update, December 2005. UNAIDS/05.19E.

~ Arthur Schoenstadt, MD. July 2006. www.hepatitis-c.emedtv.com.

# CHAPTER 2:
# TEENAGE ANGST

When I was a teenager, nothing was worse than getting out of bed and venturing to the bathroom mirror for a morning gaze; only to find a minefield of zits scattered about my face, with some so big they had their own pulse. Add to that lovely image a mouthful of metal, un-proportioned body parts, and a matted mane of unkempt hair, and it was just the perfect start to yet another angst ridden teenage day. As if over night, my thoughts switched from video games and cartoons to hating my life, constant feelings of insecurity, and dying to fit in with the cool crowd.

These feelings I am describing are called teenage angst. This is a five-to-seven-year stretch of your life roughly starting with the onset of puberty, when your childish world becomes shattered and you can barely tolerate being inside your own skin. I'm not going to sugarcoat this one for you honey, it can be hell! But I can assure you that this is only temporary, and soon enough, your life and mind will return to their normal state.

I've given this topic many years of thought, and I just might be able to get you through it in one piece. There are three main reasons for teenage angst, and they all have to do with different aspects of science: biology, psychology, and sociology.

**Reason #1: Biological.** Puberty has triggered the release of sexual chemicals in your bloodstream called hormones. These chemicals have begun to wreak havoc on your mind and body, leaving you powerless to thoughts and urges for the opposite sex. Boys will become an obsession, if they haven't already, and the only things that will matter to you will be: who they are, where they hang out, and whether or not they find you attractive. You will soon be trying on hundreds of outfits a day, constantly looking into full length mirrors from every angle, and wondering what guys see when they walk behind you in the hallway. Self-deprecating thoughts will consume your every waking moment, like: Do people like me? Are my clothes in style? Should I change my hair? Am I too fat, skinny, flat-chested, short, tall, lanky? You will never be pretty enough in your own mind, especially when the guy of your dreams begins dating Buffy Buffington, the sixteen-year-old supermodel in training. It's things like this that can drive a teenage girl insane and fuel the angst to unbearable levels. But fear not my child, there is a solution.

As your body develops from girl to woman, it will have an overwhelming affect on your emotional well-being. Don't expect a complete spiritual transformation overnight; you will need plenty of time to adjust to the new you. It's like breaking in a new pair of shoes: at first they are stiff and awkward, but after a while they just feel so right. Until then, you will need a plan to help you stay focused on the positives of maturation.

One surefire way to make it through this difficult period unscathed is to approach it with a strong sense of humor. I would have never survived puberty if not for the endless hours of penis size and masturbation jokes within my social circle. This will be a time that you need your friends greatly, for they are going through the same exact drama inside their own heads. Use this opportunity as a bonding experience; take comfort in each other and learn to take life less seriously. And always remember, nothing cures the puberty blues better than an old fashioned wet-your-pants giggle party.

**Reason #2: Psychological.** It is now time for you to try and break free from your parents' shackles and explore all that this exciting world has to offer. The more we try to hold you back at this point with our rules and restrictions, the more you will feel the urge to rebel. It is time to press on and find your own way, discover who you are, and what you believe in. For all of these years, you have existed merely as Pete and Gina's daughter, believing what we believed and taking all that we told you as fact. But now you are coming of age and that just doesn't cut it anymore. Experience is the only true teacher in this world, and experiences of every kind are what you shall seek.

In my younger days, my dad would lecture me incessantly until I wanted to die. Did I listen? Hell no! Should I have? Hell yes! He was no idiot. I could have saved myself infinite heartache if I had listened to him even 10 percent of the time. I thought I knew everything, chose to ignore his advice, and got the shaft many times. I hope that you can be more open minded than I was and try to learn from your parents' advice. Why should you have to fall on your face as often as we did?

**Reason #3: Sociological.** This was one issue that I struggled with severely in high school: the pressure to be liked and fit in with the "cool crowd." Everyday, I would walk the halls on full alert for kids that I perceived as popular to shoot a wave or a nod to. As if their acknowledgement of me was some kind of reassurance of my coolness. God forbid anyone snubbed me, and I would lie awake that whole night wondering why. I wanted more than anything to be accepted into the clique society that my high school was broken down into. They probably don't use the word "clique" anymore, but I'm sure it still exists.

Cliques were social groups, where the members shared the same fashion styles, interests, and took shelter in each other's company. You know how an adult's occupation soon becomes their identity (Jim the cop and Gloria the teacher)? Well, cliques work the same way for teenagers (Ron the burnout and Sarah the jock). When I was your age, there were many cliques. Some of which were: the juice heads, band geeks, preps, skaters, drama dorks, jock straps, burnouts, computer nerds, Goths, hippies, and the Dungeons and Dragons dweebs. Much like you have now only morphed backward through time.

These select groups of people seemed so different to me at the time. Yet in hindsight, they were all exactly the same, insecure kids desperately trying to fit in and be accepted. If you can find the courage to look a little deeper than a person's appearance, you might discover really interesting individuals and make some great friends. Your mom was much better at this than I was. Did you know that she was voted homecoming queen of her high school? This may seem like no big deal, but it was a tremendous honor in our day. The lucky couple that was chosen as king and queen were crowned at the homecoming dance, driven around in a parade, and treated like royalty for the two weeks prior. They were usually the most conceited guy and girl in school, but not your mother. She somehow managed to be popular and still be friendly with various types of people. Whether it was a juice head, Goth chick, or a "sexually active band geek," she always managed to see through the facade and appreciate people for who they were. I guess it was because even though she was gorgeous and confident on the outside, she still always felt shy and awkward on the inside, so she could relate.

Daddy on the other hand was the complete opposite. I was so insecure and terrified of being discovered as a geek myself, that I completely avoided everyone I perceived as a social misfit. In the latter part of sophomore year, I joined the wrestling team and latched onto the jock-straps as my associates. Although I was way out of my element, I managed to slip under the radar by dressing the part and keeping my mouth shut most of the time. I was hell-bent on becoming popular, even if it meant stepping on people I cared about.

One of my best friends throughout junior high was a kid named Ray Anson. He came from an impoverished family, was a little overweight, and extremely awkward. You know that kid who always strikes out in kickball? Well, that was Ray, but he was always there for me in bad times and was the true definition of a friend. When high school rolled around, we made a promise to stick together no matter what. It was only two months into our freshman year before I began blatantly ignoring him in the hallways, blowing off weekend plans, and mocking him behind his back. I even stooped as low as "flagging" him once in a crowded hallway.

As I said, Ray was a pretty heavy kid, so he would often wear sweatpants to school. Well, the guys thought it would be a real scream if someone pulled those sweats down one day. Like the soulless monkey that I was, I snuck up behind him and yanked his waste band clear to his ankles. However, strictly by accident, I had some underwear in my grip as well. The crowd erupted into hysterics as Ray dropped his books, spun around in horror, and looked at me with tears in his eyes. I knew at that moment that I had just crossed a line in morality and that my heart was beginning to harden, but I chose to bury the emotions and joined in the laughter.

After that day, Ray and I never spoke a word or even made eye contact for the remainder of high school. Thinking about Ray and the way I treated him still makes me remorseful, even after all this time. Please don't ever let yourself behave this way. I hope Mommy and I have instilled feelings of compassion in you, and the strength to be kind to those who are different or less fortunate.

## Peer Pressure

During the fall of eleventh grade, I had finally gotten my driver's license and bought my first car: a 1984 cherry red Ford Pinto. I was extremely psyched to at last have the freedom I so yearned for. One day, I was on the way home from school with my buddy Drew and two new friends I really wanted to impress. It was unseasonably cold for November, and it had been sleeting all afternoon, making the roads quite treacherous. My car was an automatic transmission with the emergency brake in the middle of the two front seats. So, to stir up some emotion, I yanked the handle while driving about thirty miles per hour. We caught a patch of ice and whipped into a screeching sideways halt. We all went nuts with excitement. As I began to drive again, the new guys started to scream for more, only faster this time. Without giving it much thought, I stomped my little four-cylinder to the floor and the speedometer surpassed sixty miles per hour. I remember thinking at that moment that I was about to make an enormous mistake. Yet, the chant of "E-brake, E-brake, E-brake!" completely took over and I lost all control.

Again, all I could think about was being cool and a reckless wild man. So I pulled it up with all my might, closed my eyes, and prayed. At break-neck speed we spun across the ice-covered street in two full rotations, all screaming in unison. Then, in what seemed like slow motion, we smashed passenger side door into a massive oak tree. After losing consciousness for a few seconds, I came back to the sounds of cursing from the backseat. Other than a few bumps and scrapes, we were all okay. Everything appeared to be fine, until I looked over at Drew and saw him hunched forward with blood covering his face. His head had gone through the side window and split open; he was unconscious and we were all panic stricken. It felt like a dream as other cars started to pull over to try and help us. By the time the ambulance arrived, reality had set in and I started to realize the severity of what I had done.

The next few hours in the emergency room with Drew's parents felt like an eternity. All I could do was lie and tell them it was a freak accident, and being the amazing people that they were, they believed me. It turned out that Drew had suffered some pretty serious head trauma. After a plethora of stitches, a concussion, and a brief hospital stay, he would eventually recover. This ordeal left me traumatized and unable to get behind the wheel for months. I could have killed my best friend that day, all because I was too weak to withstand the perils of peer pressure.

Why is it so difficult to resist the temptations to please our friends? Why do we constantly have to pretend to be someone we are not just to make people like us? From what I've seen, it all has to do with your clique selection. While peer pressure exists in every group to a degree, it is the level of popularity that is the deciding factor. Just how high profile do you need to be in the social spectrum? Because, as the coolness of a crowd increases, so does the pressure. Hip crowds relish in their exclusivity; they will constantly be testing your limits to see if your membership is well deserved. "Here drink this." "You wanna hit?" "Come on, one little snort won't kill ya!" "Just stick it in your bag, nobody's looking." Or, the old stickler, "I can't believe how prude you are!" Just how far will you go to prove that you belong? It can be an exhaustive battle.

This is when you have to ask yourself what your core values are. What is your definition of right and wrong? Only your heart knows the answers. Are you doing things you always said you would never do when you were younger? When you get dropped off at the end of the night, how do you feel about yourself? Do you feel appreciated and giddy, or beaten down and cheap?

Having a group of friends that enjoys your company and just likes you for you is what you should be striving for. A Saturday night at the movies, followed by cheese fries and ice cream, can be just as fulfilling as running around town eating ecstasy, having promiscuous sex, and drinking till you pass out. Adolescence is hard enough; the last thing you need in your life is people who will try to control your every move and completely disregard your values.

## Overcoming the Angst

Let's see what we've learned so far. You take about a half cup of puberty, a quarter cup of peer pressure, toss in some self loathing, insecurity, and a pinch of parental rebellion, and you've got yourself a pretty reliable recipe for some good old teenage angst. Now before you lose your mind over this, you have to think about it logically. Puberty doesn't last forever; before you know it you'll be older, more confident, and a successful independent woman. It's just a matter of getting through this little spat of uneasiness, and it will soon become a distant memory that you can share with your children someday.

There are many ways of overcoming this troubling stage of your life. The most accessible approach is to just stay active. Your Aunt Christine has three of the most grounded and levelheaded teenagers I know. Ever since these kids could walk they have been involved in every sport, club, and activity you could imagine. Not a night goes by in their house that someone doesn't have a game, lesson, concert, practice, or club meeting. Sure, it's a pain in the ass for the parent who has to play chauffeur, but it's a welcome trade-off to having kids slipping off the adolescent deep end.

The easiest way to feed into the angst is by spending too much time alone, thinking. This is when your mind can become your worst enemy: watching TV, staring in the mirror, wondering, wishing, and obsessing. Get involved in after-school activities; join the chess club, band, volleyball team, theatre, or art club. This will not only keep you busy enough to avoid peer pressure, but it will also engage you in many different social circles and free of the clique routine.

Confidence is another highly effective way of rising above the angst. Being self-assured can almost guarantee you a successful life. When you truly believe in who you are, it speaks bounds about you. People will look at you differently, have utmost respect for you, and will secretly envy your positive attitude. Something I learned much later in life is that nobody is 100 percent confident. Even the most secure person you know is merely acting the part. It's all a perfectly orchestrated front to appear like everything is fantastic, but in reality they are just as self-doubting as the rest of us. We are all scared shitless inside, adults as well. Just pretend that you are confident and no one will ever know the difference.

To take pride in yourself, you must first discover what your strengths are. Find a hidden talent or an interest that you possess and run with it. The most confident time of my life was when I was singing in a band. Every time I stepped off that stage I felt like I could conquer the world. It doesn't matter if it's baton twirling, race-walking, or playing the triangle, just do it and give it your all. This will not only increase your self-worth, but it will also keep you from obsessing that boys and popularity are everything. Furthermore, you must always try to avoid showing the three signs of an insecure person:

1. **Nervous talking**. Just like I said with your boyfriend, you don't have to say every thought. When things become silent between you and other people, it may feel like something has to be said to break the ice, but ignore the impulse. Keeping your chin up and a smile on your face will make people wonder about the interesting things that are going on inside your head. Being silent can also give off an aura of mystery about you that people will become quite taken with.

2. **Allowing people to mistreat you.** This has forever been my downfall. You know when someone insults you and you just walk away saying nothing, and then twenty minutes later you are bursting with anger and witty comebacks? This is the story of my life. For some crazy reason, I will go to the ends of the Earth to avoid confrontation. So much so, that many times I let people walk all over me without even a word. Lately, I have made a conscious effort to thwart this problem, but it still happens to me occasionally. I'm not saying that you have to unleash a cursing tirade every time someone mistreats you. However, a dirty look and a firm, "Please don't talk to me like that!" will almost always do the trick. Most assholes only want to abuse the weak. As soon as they detect a backbone, they will more than likely move on.

**3. Body language.** The way you hold yourself in public says more about you than any SAT scores, college degrees, or lifetime of achievements. It can be as simple as having good posture, keeping proper eye contact, and giving a firm hand shake. For most of my life I couldn't even look people in the eye. I was so insecure that I didn't think it mattered, or that I mattered. As a teacher, I now see that the kids who possess self-belief are also the ones who succeed at everything they do. Although, I'm sure it has much to do with their parents' coaching. Every kid would turn into a slouchy mess with poor eye contact if they weren't constantly corrected. So the next time you're scrutinizing your physical attributes, forget about which jeans make you look fat, and concentrate on your poised attitude and power stare, because ...

*Life Rule #9: Nothing is sexier than a girl who is comfortable in her own skin.*

# Chapter 3:
# Nobody's Perfect

If there's one thing in this world that I know for sure, it's that nobody's perfect. While some may be able to hide their imperfections better than others, deep down everyone has defects and abnormalities that they are ashamed of. And no one on Earth is better at detecting these imperfections than kids. They dig deep and viciously attack insecurities at the root, not letting up until you are completely defeated. These imperfections can be insignificant and barely noticeable, like a hammer toe or a slight lisp, to something more severe, like a birth defect or permanent disability. For some reason, these can be the only things we see each time we look into a mirror; the things that define us in our own minds.

My older sister, your Aunt Joy, was born with a horrible birth defect called a cleft palette. This is when a baby is missing part of the roof of their mouth, and the top lip is completely split down the middle. She was born in the 1960s when plastic surgery wasn't the cutting edge miracle work that it is today. After several traumatic surgeries, she was left with a deformed upper jaw and a severely scarred top lip. And if to make matters worse, the doctors couldn't fully repair her teeth until she was much older and her jaw stopped developing. My sister was five years older than me, so naturally I idolized her. I followed her around the house and neighborhood every waking moment. Watching Joy's life unfold because of her disfigurement was my first glimpse into the cruelty of humanity.

When Joy hit junior high, I can remember her becoming adamant about not wanting to go to school and complaining that the kids teased her with horrible names. I was a first grader when A. J. Flemming moved into the neighborhood. This kid was evil incarnate. He was my sister's age and he had no mercy, calling her disgusting names everyday including his favorite, "Scar Nose." One time at the bus stop, he taped his upper lip to his nose and incessantly mocked her to tears. I wanted to help her so badly and smash his punk face in, but I was much too little and afraid. Joy's persecution continued throughout her childhood, only getting much worse in high school. Try to imagine for one moment being a fifteen-year-old girl with one front tooth, scarred lip, and slurred speech.

This was about the same time when our relationship went sour. Joy began locking herself in her room day after day. Sometimes I would listen by the door and hear her muffled sobs beneath the stereo. Every so often, I would sneak a peak into her diary, and even though my prepubescent brain could barely comprehend such emotional distress, I was deeply saddened by how badly she yearned for acceptance. She became so withdrawn that she could barely function, and we didn't speak one word to each other for seven years. Although we were hostile to one another on the surface, there was still a distant feeling of closeness between us. Since then, Joy has undergone several successful surgeries. Her current smile is beautiful, she is married to an awesome guy (husband #2), and they have an adorable baby girl. Even though her physical scars have been remarkably concealed, the psychological scars will forever be part of her life.

When I was growing up, I used to tell myself that God purposely gave everyone imperfections so that they could learn humility and empathy. In fact, throughout my life there were many sayings like this that I would tell myself to try and make sense out of my own imperfections, especially one that I have been struggling with for over twenty-five years.

It was the Friday before winter vacation in 1982, and Pine Street Elementary School was having its annual Christmas pageant. A few hundred people were crammed into the cafeteria to view Mrs. Henderson's fourth grade class perform the holiday classic, "Frosty the Snowman." The room echoed with yuletide piano licks, and the smell of freshly brewed coffee and sugar cookies permeated the air. The students were acting their little hearts out amid flashing cameras and the murmur of boastful parents. All of the children were gathered around Frosty in amazement as he walked and talked like a real person.

"It must be this magic hat that has brought him to life, but whoever does it belong to?" exclaimed Suzy Goldman with perfect clarity. Sergeant O'Malley appeared from stage left and stepped under the spotlight; he was frozen in fear and noticeably trembling. After several moments of uncomfortable silence, from his quivering lips a garbled mess of sound was released. "P-P-P-P-P-P-P-Pardon- M-M-M-M-M-M," a line he rehearsed over a thousand times to perfection simply would not come out of his mouth. Chills ran down the spine of everyone within an earshot, as the echo of a horrendous stutter resonated off the cafeteria walls. Beads of sweat began to pour from the sergeant's brow as he frantically wrestled with the opening sounds of his only line. Mrs. Henderson tried to regain order by silently mouthing to other students to begin their lines, but our hero would not relent, "P-P-P-P-P-P-P-P-P-P-P-P," like a flooded lawnmower.

The audience began to break out into nervous laughter, as did the children on stage. The curtain was drawn and the young actor was anxiously led off stage by a parental volunteer. Yes honey, our hero was Daddy and every holiday season without fail, the memory of that fateful night is reenacted in my mind like a scene from a low-budget horror movie.

For some, stuttering is a childhood speech impediment that is outgrown during adolescence. For others, it can be a lifelong debilitating demon that decimates you on a daily basis. What began as infrequent stumbles in childhood, soon evolved into tongue twisting and face-contorting blocks that sometimes lasted several seconds at a time. My peers attacked me with a callousness that I had never known, mimicking me, laughing, ignoring, finishing my every sentence, and assigning me a nickname that would stick for years to come: P-P-P-Peter.

The most difficult aspect of my disorder was that I had all this amazing stuff going on in my head, yet no one would give up a second of their time to listen. Teachers would call on me in class and my mouth would completely lock up. I'd be trembling and drenched in sweat as the rest of the class laughed themselves silly. I was an outcast; every morning I just wanted to stay in bed and hide under the covers until it was night again.

Around the neighborhood, I was fine; the girls all thought I was cute and the boys accepted me for who I was. However, each day in school it became a frantic race to make it from class to class without being abused. Life was as bad as it could get, until one day when I met a very special person: my tenth-grade speech therapist Mrs. Boone. I had seen many therapists before, but none that ever showed genuine concern or did anything more than just tell me to "slow down" over and over again. This lady was different; she listened with her heart and offered eloquent advice.

One day she informed me that her husband suffered from the same affliction, and she knew how difficult it could be. I was speechless; not only was someone interested in my feelings, but she was married to a stutterer! I couldn't believe that there were ladies out there that could actually love someone who spoke like this. Until then, I hadn't known any other stutterers and believed that I was part of a rare breed of misfits. Mrs. Boone informed me of an organization that her husband belonged to called the N.S.A. (National Stuttering Association). It was a national support group with chapters in almost every major city with thousands of members. She gave me a pamphlet and I quickly attended my first meeting a few days later.

When I arrived, to my surprise there were people of all walks of life in attendance: doctors, lawyers, business people, moms, dads, and little kids. I was overwhelmed to tears. I couldn't believe there were all these people out there whose lives were just like mine. Some could barely say their first names, or even get a single syllable out of their quivering mouths. My soul ached as I listened to a nine-year-old girl struggle for three minutes simply to introduce herself.

In one hour, I was completely reborn. I learned different breathing and visualization techniques that actually helped me control my erratic speech patterns. But most of all, these people taught me that everyone in this world has a cross to bear, and you have to stand tall and believe in yourself. No one is ever going to have an ounce of respect for someone who constantly mumbles into their hand as they stare at the floor in embarrassment.

As the months passed, I began to loosen up and believe in myself for the first time. While I still stuttered, it was less severe and I didn't want to jump in front of a bus after every instance. I kept up with my meetings, made some wonderful friends, and even met my first serious girlfriend. Kate was the older sister of a member who I met during Family Night. Not only was she a total knockout, but she was kind, patient, and supportive. She had watched her brother struggle through life and truly understood my plight; plus she was two years older!

I was finally able to talk to someone from the heart without fear of being laughed at or interrupted. Being with Kate helped my self-esteem soar and my speech problem became almost livable. This was about the same time I got the braces removed from my teeth, joined the wrestling team, and starting developing a quiet confidence about me that my peers began to notice. Suddenly I had a girlfriend, a few friends, and a belief that I could actually become something more than a mute homeless guy walking around the city with a squeegee.

After thirteen months together, Kate went off to college in North Carolina and our relationship ended. Although the break-up was less than amicable, in that time I gained tremendous confidence and started viewing myself as a person with much to offer. And best of all, once word got around that I was dating an older woman, some of the girls started looking at me differently.

Today at thirty-three, my stuttering is still with me everyday and sometimes it knocks me flat on my ass. Nevertheless, I always get right back up and say to myself, "Screw you. You don't define me. I'm much more than my stuttering!" I even went on to become a school teacher, and I must say a pretty damn good one at that. Sure, the kids chuckle occasionally when my tongue becomes tied, but I get revenge later with my "silent but deadly" farts as I pass by their desks. Still, most are able to look past the stammering and recognize that I sincerely care about them, and just may be able to teach them a thing or two about the world.

### Life Rule #10: Learn to see the positives in even the worst situations.

I do believe that every dark cloud has a silver lining, and that stuttering has given me a few positives in my life. One is the ability to empathize with people's pain. I have been hurt so much in life, that I have developed a sixth sense for detecting heartache. I guess you could say it's my super-power. I always do my best to comfort people and offer an unbiased ear to listen. Secondly, it's become a great people gauge, or what I like to call my "Asshole Detector." When I speak and people laugh or finish my sentences, I can immediately tell what kind of person they are and that they are probably not worth my time or friendship. Lastly, I was able to accept my stuttering as the sole reason for my extreme introspective abilities. It has forced me to become a deep-thinking intellectual. This can be a burden at times, but in the long run it's something I'm very proud of.

Who knows, if I would have had perfect speech as a kid, I could have turned out to be an arrogant jerk-off with the personality of a wet mop. I had to accept the fact that I was never going to be that power-talking guy who commanded the room, or the one who told hysterical jokes to crowds of people. Regardless, I was secure in the thought that, if given a minute of time, I could comfort and enlighten those who were hurting.

Even though your mother was voted homecoming queen of her high school, had tons of guys after her, and was very popular amongst her peers, she still suffered greatly for years with her own insecurities. Mommy and I first met while moving into our dorm at college. She lived down the hall from me and I was smitten at first glance. Yet, it would be weeks before I could even get her to look me in the eye, let alone utter a word of conversation. She avoided me like the dentist, snubbed me in public, and barely even acknowledged my existence. When I was finally able to break through, I realized that she wasn't a bitch after all, just unbelievably shy. This was her demon, something she had been battling with most of her life. On the outside she was a beautiful young woman envied by many, but on the inside she was a frightened little girl petrified to look anyone in the eye, or partake in any conversation.

It plagued her life; she constantly had to rely on friends to meet people and be social. She would actually have these panic attacks where her heart would palpitate and she'd begin to tremble while talking to people she wasn't comfortable with. She used to cry in her car everyday when she went to community college without the comfort of her friends to help her in social situations. She has tried medication, therapy, and several new-age techniques to try to deal with this problem, and in recent years has come to grips with who she is. Now she's an amazing kindergarten teacher, and even better wife and mother. Her shyness still peaks its head out every now and then and grabs hold of her, but now she comes out fighting.

## Supermodels

I would imagine that one of the toughest parts of being a young lady must be seeing those ninety-eight pound flawless supermodels everywhere you look. Every time I see a ripped male model in a magazine I feel like a grotesque troll for the rest of the day, so it must be much worse for girls. There will always be the few girls in school with the perfect skin, amazing hair, beautiful bodies, and the hottest boyfriends. The mere sight of these freaks of nature must make you nauseous and frightfully insecure. But as I said earlier, everyone has imperfections, some just manage to hide them better than others. Just because you can't see them on the surface, doesn't mean they don't exist. You never know the pain that lies within a person's soul.

Do yourself a favor and check out the book *She's Come Undone* by Wally Lamb. I don't think there's a book out there that does a better job of capturing the sheer desperation of the teenage mind. We all wish for unattainable perfection: "If only my ears were smaller," "I wish my eyebrows weren't so close together," "Why is my nose so pointy?" The list goes on and on. Some girls starve themselves to death, forcefully vomit after meals, or even cut their arms and legs, simply because they hate the fact that they will never be perfect.

I used to squeeze pimples all over my body with such force that I would mutilate myself with horrible bruised blotches. I was obsessed; even those dreaded under-the-skin zits would get brutally crushed until I saw blood. Even to this day, I cannot pass a mirror without doing a detailed surveillance of my nose and forehead.

***Life Rule #11: "To wish you were someone else is to waste the person you are."*** *~Helen Keller*

An excellent example of a pseudo-perfect society is Hollywood, California. This is the home of celebrities; a magical realm where everyone is beautiful, fabulously wealthy, and completely happy, or so it seems. Beneath the surface, this is a land of self-absorbed phonies who truly believe that the world revolves around their fame. I spent a summer there after graduating from college and could not believe what it was all about. Everywhere I went was filled with the most unblemished human beings plastic surgery could create. I don't remember ever feeling so ugly and out of style before in my life. Even the biggest dive bars in the city felt like a red-carpet event strewn with paparazzi.

While these people had looks, money, and constant recognition, were they truly happy? Their whole lives are one gigantic race against the inevitable: the aging process. The appearances that they strive for are only temporary, until the next wrinkle or love handle appears, and then it's back to the carving board. We will all grow old and flabby one day, and all the surgery, Botox injections, and tanning booths in the world can do nothing to prevent it. The few years that you have on this planet should be spent living, loving, and experiencing, not scouring the tabloids yearning for perfection.

My advice to you, Lilly, is to fully embrace your youth; travel, surf, sky dive, climb a mountain, learn an instrument, write a book, run a marathon, watch a sunset, or sculpt a masterpiece. Don't spend one more minute wishing for superficial things that will never bring you happiness. Consider this: Which would you rather become someday, a respected musician, author, college professor, or physician? Or a bulimic, drug-addicted model whose career comes to an abrupt end at the decrepit age of twenty-seven?

# Chapter 4:
# Drugs and Alcohol

This chapter should only be one sentence long: Messing with drugs and alcohol will ruin your life! But I'd have to be an idiot to think that a ridiculous "Just Say No" slogan would be enough to satisfy a teenager's insatiable curiosity toward the affects of mind altering substances. Besides, it would probably have the adverse affect and give you more of an incentive to "Just Say Yes" when the time comes.

In the ninth grade, a police officer came to my school with samples of every drug imaginable in little glass jars. He lectured us for hours and explained the damage that each drug could do to your body, mind, and life. After leaving the assembly, I remember the biggest question on my mind was: why do so many people take drugs if they are so bad for you? Why would they lie, steal, kill, risk death, or even sell their bodies for something so harmful? I finally came to the conclusion that any chemical that could bring a person to the depths of hell and still leave them yearning for more, has got to be pretty amazing stuff! It was this notion that would eventually lead me to the darkest period of my life, and also my lowest point as a human being.

In my early teens, I shunned any and all mind altering substances, claiming they were only for dirt bags and losers. Fast forward ten years, and I would find myself drowning in a sea of addictions and partaking in despicable behavior on a daily basis. My story is just like the countless teenage stories before me.

An overabundance of self-loathing, insecurity, and depression, coupled with a troubled home life, left me on a constant search for a way to escape my reality. A few moments of carefree feelings were all I wanted, and felt it was well deserved.

After joining the high school wrestling team, the parties I started attending were insane. Everyone was out of their minds, drinking their faces off, smoking pot, laughing, and dancing around without a care in the world. I was sick of being a worried mental case all the time, and wondered if maybe more people would like me if I loosened up and partied. I thought I was too strong willed to ever become addicted to any drug, so I took my first hits of marijuana during the summer of tenth grade.

At first nothing happened, it took a few "toking sessions" before I even felt anything besides a foggy headache. I had heard many stories about the wonders of being high, so I didn't know what to expect. Then, one night I was riding in the backseat of my friend Greg's Camaro, a joint was passed around, and it finally hit me. I remember the stereo sounding incredible and being completely captivated by a song I had heard a million times before, "Lay Down Sally" by Eric Clapton. The music washed over me like a spring rain, followed by intense feelings of relaxation, excitement, and euphoria all at once. I suddenly didn't care about being liked anymore, or how I looked or how I talked. All was good in the world and my insecurities just melted away. All I wanted to do was laugh, sing, converse, and live in the moment. It was the most surreal experience of my young life.

Lying in bed that night with an ear-to-ear grin still plastered on my face, I remember thinking, "How can feeling this amazing possibly be bad? What the hell was all that "Just Say No" crap about? Why was I lied to about drugs being the evilest thing a person could do? Spending everyday feeling nervous, depressed, and lonely, now that's evil; this feeling was wonderful." After that night, I finally felt accepted by my peers and I believed that I had discovered the true secret to happiness. "Life is a party, stop worrying and just have fun!"

It can be pretty mind-blowing when you first experience life in the fast lane. However, only possessing genuine psychic abilities can help you foresee the dangers that lurk ahead if you continue to use. There isn't a parent, teacher, movie, book, or catchy anti-drug slogan out there that could ever teach you the hazards that could follow that first amazing night.

***Life Rule #12: With every incredible high must come a devastating low; this is the law of the universe.***

## Alcohol

I don't care how much of a goody-goody someone claims to be, everyone has their vices: coffee, cigarettes, chocolate, pornography, television, shopping, drugs, gambling, sex, booze, or even pulling your own hair out. It's just our nature as human beings to try to escape our feelings of emptiness with activities that can cause an emotional stir. My life of escapism began at fifteen with a warm twelve pack of Milwaukee's Best.

After lifting them from his garage, my buddy Drew and I got stinking drunk in the woods behind his house. Although the taste was so vile, the effects they had on our minds were profound. We jumped around like maniacs, climbed trees, wrestled, mooned passing cars, puked our guts out, and eventually passed out on lawn chairs in his yard. This was the beginning of my journey into distorting the senses and my quest for the eternal buzz.

For me, the seed was planted as a little kid sitting around at family functions watching the adults get royally smashed and having the time of their lives. I remember hiding under the kitchen table at my Nana's house, listening intently to their every word, giggling, and wondering why they were acting so bizarre. They would ramble on for hours telling dirty jokes, explaining the same stories they had many times before, and even busting out into vicious screaming matches. I was very intrigued by the way these drinks made them act so completely different from how they were in everyday life. My most reserved uncle would become a belligerent lunatic after a few scotches, and my loud-mouth aunt would just sit quietly sipping her Chardonnay, chain-smoking, and staring into a candle flame. Occasionally curiosity would get to me and, when nobody was looking, I would steal a few sips from abandoned glasses and induce my gag reflex. It would be years before I would ever figure out the lure of this mysterious potion known as alcohol.

During the later stages of puberty, my friends and I would sneak into the woods every weekend with bottles stolen from our parents' liquor cabinets and any female we could round up. We'd light camp fires, crank the tunes on a boom box, and lose our minds. It was such a grown-up feeling. Sometimes it was beer, other nights it was liquor, champagne, or cheap wine. Yet, every party seemed to end the same way: with me waking up in a puddle of my own vomit and not knowing where I was. At first it was quite disturbing, but after a few instances it sort of became my signature move.

Every Monday morning, kids I didn't even know would give me high fives and congratulatory slaps on the back saying things like, "Dude, you were so wasted Saturday night; it was awesome!" My party invites started to intensify and from that moment I had graduated from, "P-P-P-Peter" to "Pukeman," after a popular 1980s video game of a similar name.

I can't even count how many times I passed out at a party and was drawn on with permanent markers, duct taped to a lawn chair, or had some of my body hair shaved off. It just became part of my persona. At the time it didn't bother me, I enjoyed the attention and it was the easiest way for me to make friends without having to talk much. This reckless behavior would continue throughout high school and into college. They were some of the happiest times of my life. I wish they could have gone on forever.

Super Bowl Sunday 1992, three of my best friends left a party after a night of drinking and good times. Moments later, the driver fell asleep at the wheel, veered off the highway, and smashed into a tree at sixty miles per hour. Jimmy and Greg were thrown from the vehicle and killed; the driver escaped with only minor injuries. As word of this awful tragedy spread throughout the phone lines, countless lives were about to be shattered. Two of our brothers were taken out in the prime of their lives without notice. These were kids we grew up with since grade school and would have done anything for; now we had to say goodbye forever.

The viewings and subsequent funerals were horrific scenes, full of hundreds of colorless faces all asking the same question, "How could this happen?" Words cannot express how devastating it was weeping over their lifeless bodies, or having to restrain Greg's distraught mother from lifting her only child out of his casket. It's an image that will forever haunt me. I didn't know I was even capable of such sorrow. I cried until I ran out of tears.

Out of compassion from the victim's families, Tim, the driver, avoided serious jail time, but in return received a life sentence of guilt and horrible memories to torment the rest of his days. Months later, he would describe to me in graphic detail how he repeatedly tried to give Greg CPR, yet he died eyes open in his arms.

Nobody could even blame him, for it could have been any one of us behind the wheel that night. If the game of pool I was playing had ended a moment earlier, I very well could have been the driver or another passenger. Drinking and driving was just part of the good times for our crowd. We all knew it was dangerous and illegal, but when you're nineteen you don't think about the consequences of your actions. It's not until something terrible happens and you're forced to live with hurt that you learn the truth. Life wasn't supposed to be this way. What happened to, "No worries; just have fun"?

You'd think a traumatic experience like that would've taught me a lesson. But I'm afraid my ignorance runs pretty deep. The following spring after a fight with my girl friend Jenna, I drove home an hour from her college drunker than I had ever been. Most of this occurrence is a complete blur, but I do have vague recollections of nodding off at the wheel and throwing up in my mouth while driving seventy miles per hour down the highway. I woke up at five in the morning in the bed of my pick-up on my parents' lawn. It was an absolute miracle that I did not die, get arrested, or, even worse, kill an innocent person on the road that night.

This is what happens when you drink. You lose all of your ability to reason and make rational decisions. I hear sober people say all the time that they would take the keys away from a drunken friend without a doubt. Yet, I can't remember ever seeing this happen successfully. Sure, people try, but it doesn't work. Everyone is "fine to drive" by night's end, or they use the old, "I'll just sleep in my car for a while," or, my personal favorite, "Don't worry, I'll take back roads home." At four in the morning, all anyone cares about is getting home and passing out. If someone says they're alright to drive, you believe them.

I know it sounds cliché, but drinking and driving can end you in an instant. Sometimes I feel like a paranoid freak worrying about my three-year-old daughter drinking and driving, but that's just how my neurotic mind works. I just love you so much and when I think of how reckless teenagers can be, I shake with fear. What I do promise is this: if you are ever in need of a ride home from anywhere, I'll come out at any hour and drive your whole crew home with no questions. I've never been more serious about a promise in my life. Please take me up on this without one second thought, and never ever get behind the wheel or be a passenger after drinking. For my life would be over if anything ever happened to you.

## When It Isn't Fun Anymore

The crazy thing about drinking is that it's so difficult to realize when it's becoming a problem. It's such a gradual process. One moment you're the life of the party that everyone wants to hang out with, and the next your loved ones are organizing interventions to tell you to get help. Beers on the weekend, wine after work, mixed drinks for happy hour, shots at the bar; alcohol is such a part of the fabric of our society that it's almost impossible to avoid. As you age and begin to struggle through life, a career, relationships, and financial independence, drinking becomes your only sanity after an unbearable week. Before you know it, you can barely make it through one day without a drink, and you begin shaking for that drink during your commute home.

Alcohol is a sinister drug; when you become hooked it will consume your every thought, until just the idea of being sober becomes an intolerable nightmare. Your health will deteriorate and your relationships, career, and family life will all suffer incredibly. Mommy was rushed to the hospital in the fall of 1999 for what turned out to be a pretty severe case of pancreatitis. This was before we were married, when we shared an apartment in Queens and I was a complete alcoholic. Instead of being by her side during this ordeal, I used it as an excuse to get wasted every night. She was in constant agony, and had to endure a week in the hospital with endless tests and blood work. After going on a three day bender with my friends, I only managed to visit her for two of the six days. I was so humiliated when Uncle Sal called to ask how his sister was and I answered the phone drunk with my friends laughing in the background. Just the thought of her lying in that hospital bed wondering where the man she loves was makes me sick with remorse.

As I write this book to you, I am in the early stages of alcohol recovery. It is one of the most difficult things I have ever had to face. Saying, "No, thank you," when someone offers you a frosty beer on a sweltering summer afternoon, is almost like saying no to a slice of your favorite pizza after you haven't eaten in days. The first thing I learned in recovery is that you can't get someone to quit an addiction; they have to be ready themselves. Everyone needs to hit their own rock bottom before they can accept that they have a problem and need help. I knew I was steadily approaching mine one day when I was home watching you while Mommy was attending a baby shower.

After you had gone down for your nap, I started popping prescription painkillers chased with red wine to calm my nerves. I had built up such a tolerance for these chemicals that I was able to ingest absurd amounts. Needless to say, I passed out on the couch completely dead to the world. During my self-induced coma, I kept dreaming that you were hysterically crying in your crib for what seemed like hours, but I couldn't regain consciousness.

When your mother came home, I was startled awake to the sound of both you and her screaming in unison. I opened the door to your bedroom and you were standing in your crib, red-faced, shaking, and exhausted. Your diaper was ripped off and there was poop smeared everywhere, including your face and hair. As I stood there in shock, your mother slipped into a rage that I had never before witnessed, "What kind of a father would neglect his one-year-old daughter to get wasted? You're a pathetic loser!" These were the words I heard as I ran out of the house, hopped in my car, and headed straight for my dealer's house.

I returned home sometime after midnight filled with booze and pills, packed a suitcase, grabbed some cash, my guitar, and left my wife and infant daughter behind me. It was three days before my second wedding anniversary. Although Mommy pleaded uncontrollably for me to stay and offered to get me help, I told her I was in a horrible place with my addictions and needed to go away to get sober. I left Florida on May 29th, 2004, and headed north to Atlanta to try and clean up my act. I almost never made it back.

# Drugs

I abused just about every drug in the book for over fifteen years. In the beginning, I thought I had uncovered my true personality and could never even picture life without them. But towards the end, I would come within inches of losing everything: my sanity, my family, my friends, my dreams, and even my will to live. Drugs are a game that you can never win. Eventually you will become a shadow of your former self, living on lies, and hating every waking moment. I'm going to try and provide some insight into the drugs that almost ruined my life, and also the ones that I have witnessed destroy the lives of others.

The drug world can easily be broken down into two main categories: up drugs and down drugs. While the uppers make you feel energized, border-line psychotic, and all-powerful, the downers make you feel numb and almost nonexistent. Although I tended to dabble in both categories, my drugs of choice were always the downers. As I mentioned earlier, my particular tale of addiction would begin rather innocently with a little green plant called Cannabis sativa.

## –Marijuana (pot, weed, grass, Mary Jane, chronic, ganja, bud, green, trees, monkey paw)

One of the true loves of my life. When marijuana came into my world, I thought I had discovered what I was born to do. Like alcohol, weed was so socially accepted in my crowd that you were considered a freak if you didn't smoke it. Aside from puking and passing out at parties, I figured out that another way to make friends was through this seven-leaved plant. After realizing that pot was the ultimate ice breaker, I made it a point to always have my own stash and rolled fat dubies wherever I went. This plan had tremendous results. It even furthered my social evolution, helping me graduate from "Pukeman" to "Pete the Good Time Guy." I was psyched; a few years ago I was the stuttering reject, and now people really appeared interested in me.

If I had to describe marijuana with one word, it would have to be "enhancer." It enhances everything you do and intensifies your senses to almost superhuman levels. When you're stoned, life is an adventure, music sounds incredible, people watching is mind-blowing; sunsets, sex, and movies can all be orgiastic feasts for the senses. Some of my most memorable moments have been after smoking some killer greens at a concert, social gathering, or a natural wonder. It's an ultra-mellow drug, one that makes you giggly, euphoric, extremely introspective, and, oh yeah, crazy hungry! Canned cat food on Ritz crackers can become fine cuisine when you're in the throes of a munchie binge.

I always rationalized my weed consumption with thoughts like, "If it grows from the Earth, how bad can it be? Maybe we were meant to smoke it?" The catch is that everyone and their mother will tell you that pot is not addictive. I have learned firsthand that this statement is a huge crock of shit. While pot may not be physically addictive, I have never had anything take such complete control of my mind as this drug. In the course of a decade, pot totally changed my personality, my beliefs, and my aspirations for the future. It made me unmotivated and unbelievably paranoid. I can't even count the number of girlfriends, family functions, and jobs I've blown off to get high. Which I'm ashamed to say includes my first few years as a school teacher. I even dropped out of college in my junior year so I could smoke pot, eat, sleep, and play guitar all day in my boxer shorts.

My life became a joke. I actually had these ludicrous delusions that I was going to become a famous rock star and live the party life forever. Weed made me believe that I didn't need love, family, an education, a successful career, or money. All I needed was my dreams, my guitar, and my stash. I lost touch with reality and slowly became a reclusive shut-in who barely answered the phone or the doorbell. The amazing highs I so lived for started to become shorter, and the lows started to become longer and much deeper. This is when the "Pothead Blues" began to set in, where everything is awful when you're not high.

So I came up with a brilliant idea, "Hey, I'll just live my life high!" Yeah, that was a real "Eureka!" moment for me. Things got so bad I couldn't go to work, school, or even out in public without blazing up beforehand. The sooner you understand the following statement the better, because it took me over sixteen years to come to grips with this simple notion:

## Life Rule #13: Drugs make regular life suck!

There were many times when I would preach the wonders of marijuana and how, if given the chance, it could bring an end to all of the injustices in the world. I couldn't have been any further from the truth. Like every other mind-altering substance, weed is just an escape mechanism from reality; a dark room in which to hide from your worries and insecurities. The truth is it doesn't matter how much you consume, your problems will always return in full force. You could smoke an ounce of pot a week for ten years, and when you eventually return to earth you'll be older, fatter, dumber, and those same worries and insecurities will be waiting for you.

When people call pot the "gateway drug," they couldn't be any more on the money. It removes all of your inhibitions, so that you'll try whatever drug is put in your face next. When weed just isn't doing it for you anymore, you'll move on to something stronger to help you regain the beautiful feelings from that first magical high. This is when you start wondering, "Hmmm, I wonder what _____ feels like?" Now that same person who said that one little toke couldn't hurt is dropping acid, smoking PCP, and snorting lines in public bathrooms.

I tried quitting many times, once for a whole year, but it always made its way back into my life. While you don't physically withdraw from weed, you do have mental breakdowns and reoccurring attacks of paranoia. They call this phenomenon "hardcore fiending," and the only way I can describe the feeling is that it's kind of like starving, but food will not satisfy, only the drugs. Every little aspect of life becomes overwhelming; a flat tire can mean the end of the world. Nothing is fun anymore. The best foods, funniest movies, inspiring music, or even sex is now a bore. Getting high is your last activity at night, part of your dreams, and first waking thought in the morning. It even gets to the point where just a few sober days can cause the most erratic mood swings, insomnia, and depression.

In the end, I became a compulsive liar and degenerate thief. I secretly hooked up with my buddies' girlfriends, stole from family members, and even resorted to thieving car stereos to support my pathetic habits. I looked in the mirror one day and could not believe what I saw. I had raccoon eyes, pale wrinkled skin, yellow teeth, and more chins than a Chinese phone book. I was twenty-eight, completely broke, and scraping my empty pipes for resin balls to get high. A change was long overdue.

## –PCP (angel dust, diesel, wet, devil dirt, dips)

Known on the street as angel dust, this is hands down the most disgusting drug I have ever tried. It's classified as a dissociative anesthetic, and for a while was used in the medical field to kill pain and create numbness. PCP comes in both liquid and powder form, and can cause feelings of invulnerability and out-of-body experiences. Although dust was around in the 60s and 70s, its popularity sky-rocketed in the 1990s with the emergence of the rave scene. Raves were all-night dance parties where people took massive amounts of drugs and danced their asses off until the sun came up.

Always up for anything, I went to my first rave in the summer of 1993 at an abandoned warehouse in Manhattan. After a few drags off a cigarette dipped in liquid dust, I thought the walls were closing in on me and I wanted to jump off the nearest bridge. The high was so intense and confusing that I didn't know what to do or how to control my body. Almost immediately, my thoughts started to get psychotic and suicidal in nature. It felt like I was detached from my body and drifting somewhere between reality and the afterlife. I remember repeatedly punching my fists into a concrete wall, just to prove to myself that I was still alive.

On the ride home, I was in the back seat of my friend's car, sweating, mumbling, and bloody-knuckled. I had to physically restrain myself several times from pulling the door handle open and jumping out. Upon crawling in bed, I stared at the ceiling twitching and convulsing like an epileptic for the rest of the night. For days afterward, my brain felt like oatmeal and I couldn't process a single thought. I would go on to try dust a few more times and each instance was shittier than the last. I didn't have one bit of enjoyment. This drug is an absolute nightmare, and if abused can cause dementia, coma, and even death. I wish I could forget ever trying it.

### –Psychedelic drugs (acid, shrooms, mesc, boomers, doses, trips, blotter, tabs)

Dabbling in the hallucinogenic drugs is by far the most mentally-exhausting experience a person can go through. In my wilder days, I would ingest these chemicals quite often and had some pretty life-changing experiences to say the least. The legend of these crazy chemicals goes something like this: In the 1950s, the U.S. government was supposedly conducting secret experiments on the possibilities of mind control and the boundaries of human consciousness. However, the subjects who had volunteered for these bizarre tests started smuggling chemicals out of the lab for recreational use with their friends. This was the beginning of the "Psychedelic 60s," a period when a generation of young people decided to "turn on, tune in, and drop out" of society.

At this time there was a horrendous war transpiring in Vietnam; the youth movement was disgusted with our country's involvement in this foreign affair, and wanted to foster a better way of life. The entire nation was in disarray; people were questioning the government, the war, authority, and even their own existence. It was out of this social unrest that experimental music was born and drugs like LSD, mescaline, magic mushrooms, and peyote were embraced as the ideal paths to freedom. Something about how these drugs interacted with the brain seemed to break down walls in the subconscious mind, and opened doors to a new way of life through free love and communal living.

The affects that psychedelic drugs can have on you can be both enlightening and terrifying within moments of each other. These chemicals speed up your thoughts and brain processes to unimaginable rates, so that you start to hear, see, think, and feel things that aren't real. These surreal occurrences are called hallucinations. The high can last up to twelve hours or more, and sometimes can result in shocking experiences called bad trips, where you spin into a frenzied panic and nothing can calm you down. This is when psychedelics can get extremely dangerous. I've personally witnessed people who truly believed they were having a heart attack or nervous breakdown, to the point where they would freak out and put themselves in grave danger trying to get to safety. There are even stories of people being so tripped out of their minds, that they jumped from buildings or moving cars believing they had supernatural powers.

One of the most frightening and humiliating nights of my life took place after I had eaten magic mushrooms at a friend's block party, and believed that the mafia was planning to kill me. I know it sounds ridiculous, but there is actually a back story here that puts it into better perspective. I was renting a house in a primarily Italian neighborhood in the summer of 1998, and one day got into an argument with a neighbor about my dog pissing on his lawn. Usually I would've just apologized and walked away, but this day I was in a crappy mood and chose to go at it with this guy. As I hurled expletives and flipped him the bird, he replied by yelling things like, "You don't know who I am!" and "You better watch your back punk!"

The next day, one of the neighbors who I had become friendly with told me that he noticed I was having words with Frankie Spinelli, and he just wanted to let me know to be careful because,

"He has a lot of clout, if you know what I mean." These were his exact words. This statement sent chills down my spine, so much that I obsessed over it for the next few days. I had always been a huge fan of organized crime movies, so this news left me imagining one outlandish scenario after another.

That weekend came the block party; my friends and I were ingesting mushrooms, dancing to a band, and getting crazy. Out of the corner of my eye I noticed somebody watching me. I took a quick glance over my shoulder and saw Frankie Spinelli and two of his guinea T-shirt-wearing friends standing there talking and smiling at me. My heart leaped into my throat, I broke out into a cold sweat, and started trembling. This is right about when the mushrooms really started to kick in and my mind suddenly became a war zone with paranoid delusions. I actually believed that these guys were coming to "whack me" as they say in the movies. I was frozen in fear; as I looked around it now appeared that everyone was watching me and also secretly involved in the plotting of my death, even my own friends. On pure adrenalin, I bolted from the scene and started running barefoot through traffic, narrowly avoiding being struck by several cars. I lived about a mile away, so you can imagine the ten minutes of hell I endured on that run.

When I got to my house I barricaded the doors, shut the blinds, turned off all the lights, and began sobbing violently on the floor. The thoughts were eating away at my clenched eyes like vultures, and in sheer desperation I reached for the telephone as my only salvation. In the next few hours, I would call every important person in my life hysterically crying, and insisting that the mafia was coming to rub me out.

As I hid behind the couch and prayed, distraught loved ones began showing up at my door: my parents, Mommy (my fiancé at the time), friends, Uncle Sal, and even random neighbors who heard me screaming. And this was all at two in the morning. They rushed in the house to a puddle of nerves cowering in the corner. For hours they tried to talk me down by telling me it wasn't real, but I would not relinquish my position. As morning approached and the effects of the shrooms started to wear off, my thought patterns started to change and the paranoia transformed into overwhelming humiliation. Everything that seemed so real and life-threatening just a few hours ago now seemed exactly like what it was: a drug-induced psychotic episode. Now everyone I knew saw me for what I had become: a mentally unbalanced freak.

Needless to say, I quickly left that neighborhood, afraid to show my face ever again. Every time the memory of that night comes to mind, I want to crawl under a rock and die. A bad trip like that can come out of nowhere and literally bury you in terror. That was the last time I've ever taken psychedelic drugs and would never even consider it again.

From what I know, psychedelics aren't addictive, however the chemicals used to make them can cause permanent brain damage and even mental illness. I've seen this happen first hand. A guy who lived in my college dorm that I had become good friends with took acid one night and completely lost his mind. He started running through the hallway naked, screaming that the government had bugged his room and was monitoring him through satellite technology. Public Safety was called and he was taken away kicking and frothing at the mouth in a straight jacket. He showed up a week later with his dad, packed up his stuff without a word to anybody, and soon became a distant memory. The brain is an extremely delicate organ. Drugs of this nature can have devastating effects on your fragile psyche that you may never fully recover from.

If you choose to ignore my advice and someday find yourself in a precarious situation like this, the following instructions will most certainly get you through the night in one piece...

## The Bad Trip Emergency Plan

1. **Get to a safe and quiet place-** Dim lighting is a must, candlelight if possible.

**2. Ditch any annoying people-** If someone annoys you when you're sober, they will surely push you over the edge in your current state of mind.

**3. Music-** Nothing too up-tempo, we're not looking to rage here. You require sounds that will create a calm atmosphere and soothe your frazzled nervous system.

**4. Engage in a cerebral activity-** You need something enticing to occupy the next 6-8 hours. This calls for a DVD marathon, challenging game, or some amusing conversation.

**5. Avoid non-tripping people-** You're on completely different planets at this point, especially drunkards. They will only flare emotions and worsen your mental state.

**6. No Mirrors-** Unless you enjoy watching your face melt off your skull, I'd listen to this one.

**7. Never try to force sleep-** This one is a biggie, I wouldn't wish this madness on my worst enemy!

Depending upon how much you ingested, this experience can last a lot longer than you think. The chemicals have to run their course until they are absorbed by the body, and you eventually pass out from exhaustion. Keep in mind, a bad trip is triggered by allowing negative thought patterns to take hold and begin the breeding process. One of the most important things I learned from reading Tom Wolfe's psychedelic bible, *The Electric Kool-Aid Acid Test*, was not to accept nor deny your thoughts. Merely allow them to pass through like the air you breathe. Let this be your mantra as you struggle to reclaim your sanity.

If anything can be worse than the horror of a bad trip, it's the severity of being caught by the police with these types of drugs in your possession. The punishments for carrying any kind of psychedelic drugs are quite staggering. In some conservative states it requires mandatory prison time for even first offenses. The prisons of America are full of ignorant kids who made the colossal mistake of carrying psychedelics around with them, thinking that everyone was hip to the party life.

## –Ecstasy (X, molly, rolls, mdma, E, triple stax, vitamins, pills)

Just when I was trying to piece my life back together after college, a new drug burst into my social scene and literally tore me a new one- ecstasy. Better known as X, this drug had been around since the 1950s, but only recently began popping up in mass quantities on college campuses and in suburban America. You have to hand it to these chemists; they really know what they're doing when it comes to screwing with your head. X works off of a chemical called serotonin, which is naturally synthesized in your glands and responsible for your moods and emotional stability. Well, some genius figured out a way to open the flood gates to these glands and unleash all the serotonin in your body at once, leaving you engulfed in utter joy and sensual pleasures not of this world.

During the two or three-hour high your body actually hums with electricity and you feel like you're going to explode with excitement. You are bombarded with feelings of openness, empathy, energy, and have amazing realizations, like, "Life is great, people are awesome, everything makes perfect sense, and I will never be sad again!" The mere touch of someone's hand on your neck is enough to make you melt in elation.

After a few hours of sweating, grinding your teeth, and smiling so hard that your cheeks are bleeding, from out of nowhere comes the biggest crash of your life. Like someone pulling a rug out from under your feet, X leaves you just as quickly and powerfully as it arrived. You begin plummeting toward the Earth at astonishing speeds, your smile disappears, and your insecurities pull you into a deep depression that you never knew was possible. With your serotonin supply completely exhausted, you are now left with an inescapable emptiness. Apparently, serotonin isn't something that the body can remake quickly. In fact, it can take months or even years to get back to the normal levels your body needs to function properly. Recent studies also suggest that with continued abuse, the serotonin neurotransmitters may be permanently damaged, therefore making it much harder to feel happy naturally.* So basically, you just sold your soul for three hours of happiness, a false happiness that was completely imagined.

I've spent many a Saturday night rolling to the heights of ecstasy, and many a Sunday hopelessly crying into my pillow. This feeling is so common that it has been aptly titled, "Suicide Sundays" among club enthusiasts. I'm extremely lucky that I got out of the game before any permanent damage was done. Several friends of mine abused the hell out of this drug for years and now resemble the walking dead, unable to smile or enjoy the beauty of a sunset.

Ecstasy is illegally manufactured in secret underground labs by criminals who mix it with deadly chemicals like heroin and cocaine to increase potency. One time I took a pill and it must have been cut with something nasty, because I sat on the couch under a blanket shivering for five hours, and was unable to move any part of my body. Horrid tales of this drug are heard everyday on the news. Some high school freshman from a loving family, straight-A student, and an outstanding athlete dies after their first X experience. The human heart is far from indestructible. Between all the harsh chemicals, the dehydration, and over exertion from dancing, it can be too much to handle and it just stops beating—game over.

If you want my advice, ecstasy is not worth it. I'm sure your peers will preach about how wonderful it is, but all you have to say is, "No thanks, my dad said ecstasy made him depressed for years and almost ruined his life!" Get your smiles the old fashioned way, go to the mall, flirt with boys, dance, sing, or start a band. Don't sell your soul for a phony happiness that will only break your heart in the long run.

## –Cocaine and crack (rock, nose candy, powder, booger sugar, blow, base, yayo)

Cocaine is pure evil. It might be the one drug that I've seen destroy the most lives. Derived from the coca plant in the jungles of South America, it can provide the most intense rush and send the user on a rocket ride into the stratosphere. Cocaine is the powder form that is usually snorted, and crack is the solid form after it's mixed down with various substances to smoke. The many tales associated with these drugs are so appalling that it sickens me to even mention them, such as the Mastic, Long Island grandmother. Apparently, a sixty-four-year-old, crack-addicted woman "lent" her twelve-year-old granddaughter to a local dealer for twenty bucks worth of the drug. The girl was almost unrecognizable when the police rescued her hours later. Another story that comes to mind is of my cousin Matt who lost his house, law career, wife, and three kids due to his coke addiction. He's now forty-one, unemployed, and residing in his childhood bedroom.

The cocaine high is so compelling that you become powerless to its urge and will lie, steal, kill, give up children, or even prostitute oneself for just a taste. One day you're harmlessly experimenting with your friends, and the next you're an addict. And once you're hooked it usually ends in one of three ways: death, a prison sentence, or a miserable life of squalor—take your pick. Every race, age, and socio-economic class can fall under its power. Even doctors, politicians, teachers, and police officers can turn into homicidal addicts overnight.

With my first taste of cocaine, I knew that I had made a terrible mistake. My heart felt like it was going to come bursting through my chest, and my whole face went numb. I chewed a hole in my cheek and babbled on incessantly to complete strangers about my deepest fears and desires. I came home so wired and strung out that I was literally clawing at the walls. I gobbled down some Valium and woke up hours later soaked in my own urine with a hangover that lasted for days. Yet, every time someone offered me a "toot" I could never say no. Even though I knew of the hell I would face at the end of the night.

Cocaine is only fun for about twenty minutes. The rest of the night you spend chasing that initial high, grinding your teeth, and falling deeper into despair. Every one of my close friends from high school was either a dealer, an addict of some sort, or both. It got to a point where I couldn't leave my house without someone offering me cocaine, and when I joined the band it got much worse. This drug would linger around my life for years, continually rearing its head in times of vulnerability.

I tried crack once. I know—what a scummy thing to admit. When I worked as a waiter, I went through a short phase of hanging out with a few of the degenerate line-cooks. These guys took their partying rather seriously. One night after a few beers at this guy's apartment, they called me into the bedroom for what I thought was going to be a smoldering spliff; it wasn't. After just one puff, the rush came on high and mighty, gushing with intensity. As I exhaled, my chest filled with warmth and my heart began pounding with the excitement of a first kiss. I remember having the terrified feeling of, "Oh no, I kinda like this!"

Then, in what felt like seconds it was all gone, and I had a ravenous craving for more. I couldn't believe that something so powerful could possibly be so brief. I took another hit and made note of the time. Within four minutes, I was up, down, and on my knees digging through the carpet for another speck of the drug. There just happened to be one hit left in the vial, and we all stared at each other with hateful eyes, wanting it for ourselves. I left the room in disgrace and desperately tried to drink myself to sleep. I never felt so dirty in my life. It was now quite apparent to me why this drug was known as the lowest of the low, and people quivered at its mere mention. I made myself a promise to never go near it again, and I haven't.

Nowadays, crack is everywhere and no one is safe from its clutches. One of my friend's younger brothers recently became addicted while attending the prestigious Princeton University. We went to visit him in rehab and were astonished by both his physical and mental decay. He said after only one try, he simply could not stop. Even ivy league rich kids are smoking this trash, and once you're an addict there is no limit to the depravity that you will subject yourself to.

## –Methamphetamine (meth, crank, ice, crystal, speed, tweak, glass)

Every addict has one drug that they brag about not using, "Hey, at least I never tried _____!" Well, mine was methamphetamine. While cocaine stimulates you for an hour or two, meth can keep you out of your mind for days on end. One of the bands that we used to open for had a horn player named Dennis, who was a complete meth-head. He was one of the messiest guys I've ever known. He would fight constantly, crash cars, get arrested, and his teeth looked like rotting corn kernels, but he could blow a trombone like nobodies' business. Denny was a tremendously talented kid and deep down a kind hearted soul; he just got involved with the wrong chemicals.

After a gig one night, I mistakenly offered him a ride home. He torched up right in my passenger seat and became a raging lunatic, screaming to the radio, and punching my dashboard. He was living in a dilapidated shack on his grandmother's property with two other black-tooth junkies. The place was a cesspool, with rotten food and garbage piling up ankle high. It was three in the morning when we arrived, and the house was full of tweaked-out people sucking on pipes, twitching, and talking super fast. Although I was slightly tempted, my disgust overwhelmed me and I headed for the door. After five minutes in that house, I had gotten a firsthand perspective into the seedy existence that is crystal meth, and was completely scared straight. Denny would eventually disappear into the depths of the drug world, never to fulfill his musical potential.

Meth is made from chemicals you can buy right from the shelves of your local Mega-Mart; things such as battery acid, drain cleaner, and fertilizer. Everyday, people find out how to make it on the internet and begin concocting deadly batches in their own bathtubs. Supposedly, the high is stunningly powerful. I've heard of people binging on crank and not sleeping a wink for five days straight. When your body is deprived of sleep for that long you begin to go insane. You can become paranoid, suicidal, delusional, and even the mellowest person can go on a meth-induced murderous rampage. Like ecstasy, meth can cause irreversible damage to a person's brain chemistry, causing severe mental psychosis and long term depression.

This drug has been sweeping across the country like wild fire, even in rural Midwestern communities. I recently viewed a documentary about a thirty-five-year-old Missouri man who wanted to chronicle his meth-addicted demise on film. Watching this guy literally fall to pieces in a matter of a few months was startling. In the end, he died a ninety-pound toothless bag of bones, clutching his heartbroken mother from his hospital bed. That image alone is enough to send the most hopeless addict running to the nearest treatment center.

## –Heroin (dope, junk, smack, yam yam, black tar, skag, China white, Persian)

The king of all street drugs; while coke, crack, and meth send you on a nerve rattling thrill ride, heroin will send you on a spiraling descent into the cushions of your couch. This chemical is the complete antithesis of the upper drugs. It is also one of the most physically-addictive substances known to man. Heroin is a yellowish powder that is derived from the opium poppy plant. People take it in a variety of ways, including sniffing, smoking, or "shooting up" with a needle. Being a tremendous music fan I always had an insatiable curiosity with this drug. I kept reading about all of the rock and roll legends who died as a result of heroin abuse. While it was disturbing, I couldn't help but be intrigued by the powers of this chemical. It must be an unbelievable high if all these people would risk their lives, fame, and vast fortunes. Every night I would stare at the posters on my walls of Jimmy Hendrix, Jerry Garcia, Janis Joplin, and Jim Morrison, and I began to believe that maybe heroin was some kind of magical short cut, or right of passage into musical brilliance.

One of my fraternity brothers at college was way into heroin; he even dealt it on the side for a semester. At this point in time I was completely lost, alienated from my family, and searching for anything to bring me out of my lifelong depression. When heroin was offered to me, I didn't care about the dangers, I just wanted to stop feeling. Being deathly afraid of needles, I chose to snort a few bumps while others smoked or injected it into their arms. Like a punch in the face, the effects hit me immediately and pulled me to the floor. It was not what I expected at all. Within seconds my eyelids weighed a thousand pounds each, and my clothes felt like one of those lead suits that you wear during a dental x-ray. I was totally paralyzed in a foggy haze and every blink of my eyes became a forty-five-minute black out.

For the next six hours, I laid there motionless, drifting in and out of consciousness. I learned later these are called "the nods." Several times I tried to free myself from the clutches of the sofa, but was unsuccessful. When I had to throw up (a natural side effect), I merely leaned over and chucked on the floor without care. The hours flew by like milliseconds, and each time I came out of my coma there would be a different bunch of people in the room getting high, watching a different movie, and drooling like myself.

After sleeping it off for fourteen hours, I awoke itchy and confused. I couldn't form a thought or figure out what day it was. I tried to make it to my afternoon classes but only made it as far as the library, sat down at a study cubicle, and drifted back into oblivion. When I woke up, it was night and the library was closing. I staggered back home wondering if I would ever regain my sanity.

After complaining to my friend about how much I hated the high, he said, "Yo, it gets better bro!" I would try heroin two more times with the same ill affects. I just couldn't understand the extreme fascination with this drug; for me it was like a complete forfeit of life. Then I realized why so many people get addicted to this junk. The answer was so simple. It takes away reality; all your worries, anxieties, and physical pains completely vanish as though they never existed. Life can be tough; people die, relationships sour, careers end, and dreams get shattered. Heroin takes all of these negative feelings and purges them from your mind, numbing you to the point where nothing matters and the high is all there is. I finally knew why so many musical icons were killing themselves with this stuff. The pressures of fame were too much to handle and heroin became their medication. They simply surrendered.

There isn't a drug out there that possesses as treacherous a reputation as heroin. I've often heard the withdrawals compared to being eaten by ants or set on fire, followed by a three-day puking session, shakes, night terrors, and cold sweats all in one. Furthermore, this stuff is so strong that it can stop your heart after just one try. Every dealer has different batches of potency. What took a whole bag to get high from one guy, could kill you with one snort of another guy's stuff. Also, heroin addicts often share needles to shoot up, causing the spread of such deadly diseases as AIDS and hepatitis C. Next time you see a homeless, emaciated street beggar, and wonder how they got that way, this drug just may be your answer.

## –Prescription pills (pharmies, oxies, vikes, zannies, perks, vallies, o.c.)

This nightmare began with a routine dental visit and ended with an opiate addiction of immense proportions. Prescription pill addiction is one of the strongest around, and also the easiest to slip into. These drugs were created by scientists with the sole purpose of numbing your body from any form of pain and suffering. "Pharmies," as they are affectionately known, are meant to ease physical pain. However, they relieve mental anguish just as well. Within minutes of ingestion, your whole body becomes engulfed in a sea of warm fuzziness, all your anxiety is gone, and you feel like you're on top of the world. Drugs of this nature are so easy to abuse. Doctors prescribe them without hesitation for even the slightest pain, and they are virtually undetectable by other people. It's not like weed where you're glassy eyed and stinky, or coke where you're wired and sniffling. On pharmies you seem perfectly normal and relaxed. Some might even say, "Hey, you look great!"

I began taking them recreationally long after the pain of my oral surgery had subsided. Just for kicks with my friends at first, but pretty soon I was popping multiple pills three or four times a day. The human body builds up a tolerance to prescription drugs very quickly, and before long, one pill has no affect anymore and your body begins to crave the high with a passion. If it doesn't get what it needs, vomiting, stomach cramps, suicidal thoughts, hallucinations, chills, and fever may occur. Picture the worst flu you've ever had, then multiply that by fifty and you won't even be close.

When one doctor wouldn't prescribe anything for me anymore, I simply went to another and complained of pain from a previous injury. Nobody's bathroom was safe. I ransacked any medicine cabinet I could get my hands on, and eventually met a guy with an endless supply. At my lowest point, I was taking up to twenty pills a day and teaching middle school completely zonked out of my mind. If I would have gotten caught, I would have lost my job, my teaching license, and any possibility of a secure future for my family. But I didn't care; I was a stone-cold junky. I was even high on pills for my wedding. The most memorable day in a person's life and I was totally out of it. This battle would go on for over two years, and finally end one night in an Atlanta housing project.

While your mother cried herself to sleep every night, trembling at the possibility of becoming a single mom, I was drinking and drugging myself into a stupor with one of my old college roommates in his roach-infested apartment. My addictions were running rampant. I had once again fallen in with the fast crowd, and had now added cocaine to the daily mix.

The sixth of June was a rainy Sunday. Dave had gone away for the weekend and I was left to fend for myself in an unfamiliar town. I was playing guitar completely wired out of my mind, and every chord I struck sounded like the screech of an alley cat. My voice was shrill, my hands were shaking, and my mind was racing at a maddening pace. I caught a glimpse of myself in a mirror and was aghast by my seething, almost demonic appearance. The rage boiled over inside me, and in one violent act of frustration I smashed my guitar on the floor into splintering shrapnel, and collapsed in despair.

In the ensuing minutes, my whole life came unraveling; my dreams, family, friends, future, and past were all before me. At that moment without any consideration at all, I decided to end my life. I was a complete waste of a human being and saw not one reason to go on. I reached for my little brown bottle and poured the lot into my mouth, and with one retching swig of cheap vodka the deed was done. Calm came over me as I lay there, my tears stopped and my mind came to a peaceful state. I thought of you and all the people who would be greatly affected by this tragedy. I actually believed that after the initial shock wore off, you'd be better off without me. And eventually Mommy would marry a man who could provide you with a better life than I ever could. Besides, I was a piece-of-shit addict who ran out on his family and was physically incapable of normalcy. The world would be a better place without me in it.

As I tried to compose my apology letter on the back of a paper plate, I had several visions of you: when you were born and I held you for the first time, when we used to slow dance every night before bed, splashing in the tubby, and the last one was of a time I did not recognize. You were standing alone at my grave, clutching an aged photo of us together. You appeared to be in your twenties, yet your weathered complexion resembled that of an unhinged forty-year-old woman. You then began screaming, "Why, you bastard? How could you do this? You had everything!" The pain in your voice echoed through the cemetery, and as you kicked dirt on my headstone I began to realize the severity of my actions. I had taken your daddy away; in one selfish act your beloved playmate and protector was ripped away from you forever.

I was fooling myself into thinking that my death was best for you. When, in reality, it caused you to have to live with grief, and the unbearable questions as to why your own father would end his life. Seeing the anguish on your mascara-streaked face was something that my soul could not bear. I reached out to you begging for forgiveness.

Suddenly, I found the strength to crawl to the toilet bowl, jammed my fingers down my throat, and heaved for all I was worth. The poison gushed from me like a breached levee, and with each convulsive spasm, I promised you that I would never leave again. I prayed to God to just bring me through this one, and I swear I'd mend my ways.

I awoke several hours later on the bathroom floor covered in dried vomit mixed with bits of pills. I cleaned myself up in the shower, packed my bags, and headed south on I-95 immediately. I had come within minutes of becoming another junky found dead of an overdose, leaving behind a shattered wife and baby daughter to struggle through life without me. This was my rock bottom; all I could go was up.

## Getting Clean

There are millions of alcoholics and drug addicts in this world who are simply trying to fill a void in their soul. But this void can only be filled with love and nothing else, God knows I've tried. The true struggle in overcoming addiction is being able to harness that compulsive behavior and focus it on something healthy, something from within. For me, the most difficult aspect was that I felt like I wasn't cool anymore. I was no longer "Pete the Goodtime Guy" and my identity was completely lost. I wasn't funny, my phone stopped ringing, party invites diminished, and I felt like a stuttering loser all over again. I had to rediscover who I was sober, something I hadn't been since tenth grade.

After returning from Atlanta, I was determined to get help and begin a chemical free existence. I knew I needed a rehab facility, but most of them cost a small fortune and we were completely broke, so it was out of the question. I opted for Narcotics Anonymous and a miracle drug called suboxone. In recent times, methadone was the only cure for opiate addiction, which is also quite addictive and only available in clinics. Suboxone can be prescribed by a doctor and self-administered at home. Within just a few weeks, it can assist in a safe detox with minimal discomfort. It was amazing, whenever I felt that evil itch, I just popped a tablet under my tongue and the urge would disappear. Now I just needed to find people to lean on, friends who might possess a map of the dark roads ahead.

Narcotics Anonymous is a support group for people who are addicted to various kinds of chemicals. The one common thread that binds all the members together is that everyone has come to admit that they are powerless to drugs, and cannot maintain sobriety alone. They have meetings everyday of the week at all hours to assist people whenever they are tempted to use. The organization is built around a philosophy known as the "Twelve Steps to Recovery," which is a lifelong process of maintaining a healthy mind and body through spiritual understanding. In my case, it was the convictions of the other members that really hit home. Hearing their personal stories of heartbreak and addiction made my emotions flutter with familiarity. They were all just as messed up as I was if not worse, and I found strength in their truthful accounts.

Not a meeting went by that I didn't break down and gain some sort of insight into my self-destructive personality. I met convicted felons, homeless people, ex-prostitutes, and even regular Joes like myself. And they all had the same story: it started as innocent teenage fun and eventually spiraled out of control in later life. I learned that addiction of any kind is usually masking deeper mental or emotional problems such as depression, anxiety disorder, or unresolved psychological trauma. In my case, it was all of the above. However, the most important thing that any kind of support group can teach you is that you are not alone.

My next step was to completely cut myself off from my social circle. Most of my friends were selfish addicts who didn't care if someone was trying desperately to get sober. They'd cut up lines right in front of me, blow smoke my way, or offer me pills after I begged them not to. They'd call me high all the time, pressure me into partying, and even involve me in their legal troubles. Finally, I had to change my phone number and lay low for a while. At first, it sucked; some of these guys had been great friends of mine for years and it was very painful. But it was either cut them loose or have constant relapses; I chose the former.

I had no social life for a while, but eventually made a few friends in my meetings and just took it from there. One guy in particular, my sponsor Phil, has been a great friend and a true lifesaver. I call him almost every day for guidance and he's inspired me on many a dark night. At times when sober life has seemed unattainable Phil would say, "Just hold on Pete!" and with those simple words I'd find my strength.

## "Run, Forrest, Run!"

One of my all-time favorite movies is *Forrest Gump*. It's about a mentally-challenged guy who lives a truly remarkable life. During the climax of the movie, Forrest is forced to deal with the death of his beloved mother, and the abandonment by his lifelong sweetheart Jenny. One day while sitting on his porch in despair, he stands up and begins running. He runs across America back and forth several times, and not only cures his broken heart, but inspires an entire nation. Now, I know it's the movies, but this idea still made perfect sense to me. Every time my urges were eating away at me and I felt like my skin was crawling, I ran. Sometimes I ran three times a day until almost passing out from the nausea and blistering side cramps. Yet, little by little my endurance grew stronger.

After six months, I was running like a champ, feeling a natural high like no drug could ever give, and finally getting my flabby body back into shape. Every facet of my life started to come together. My addictions were in remission and I even began training for my first marathon, which I still haven't done.

## Hopes for a Better Tomorrow

They say that ignorance is bliss. I could easily become one of those parents who lives in denial thinking their kid would never get involved in mind altering substances. However, it is often these same people who have to endure the agony of finding their child dead from an overdose. How could I possibly tell you to never experiment with drugs and alcohol? This would only make you lie to me and turn our relationship into one based on deceit. During my downfall, there were many times when I wanted to collapse in my father's arms and beg him for help, but I chose to shoulder the burden alone. In your case, I don't care what physical or mental state you may be in, my arms will always be open.

I've been clean now for thirteen months and three days, and it's been the happiest times of my life. Now when the urges come over me, I just give you the biggest squeeze and tell you I love you over and over. In the last few months, I feel like me again. I wake up with childhood joy, eager to seize the day, and not just in search of my next fix. By the time you read this, I'm sure they'll be many more drugs than the ones I have listed, but they are all essentially the same: soul crushers, ambition killers, dream spoilers, and potential life-enders. I pray that you can learn from my mistakes, and when you come to that inevitable fork in the road, choose life my darling.

## Cigarettes

I cannot end this section on drugs without discussing one more insidious addiction. The other day I was at a street fair and noticed a very pregnant lady smoking a cigarette. I almost had to restrain myself from strangling her. Cigarettes are so deeply embedded into our society that one often forgets they are drugs, but they most certainly are. Nicotine is a very powerful stimulant that gives users an immediate rush of energy, followed by a mellow calming effect. Nicotine addiction starts out slowly and it can take years before you consider yourself a smoker. In the beginning, it's only one or two at parties, then you have a few during the day, then you buy your own pack so you don't have to bum them anymore, and before you know it you've become a wrinkled-faced, yellow-toothed, hacking old geezer.

The smoking statistics are astounding: close to five hundred thousand Americans die from cigarette-caused diseases every year, and studies show that one in five smokers are teenagers who begin by age fifteen.^ I believe the reason for these alarming numbers goes back to our good old friend teenage angst, and the desire to rebel against authority and be accepted by the cool crowd.

Growing up, almost everyone I knew smoked: both my parents, sister, neighbors, relatives, and when I became a teenager, all of my friends. I tried it many times, mostly in social situations to fit in, but I always looked like a fruitcake smoking. I held cigarettes like a girl and practically fainted with every drag. Your mom was much better at smoking than I was; yes, even she caved to the pressure. She could puff convincingly with the best of them. Thank goodness for her superior maternal instincts, because as soon as she became pregnant with you she never touched them again.

When I was a kid my house had a perpetual cloud of smoke wafting above. My parents were prolific smokers filling ashtrays by the hour. They ashed in everything; in my house you couldn't put a drink down for a second without getting a lit Parliament flicked in it. Cigarettes just weren't for me. They made me sick for one, but mostly because I witnessed one of my uncles die a slow painful death from lung cancer. I watched this cheerful old guy go from a 210-pound Italian firecracker to a one hundred-pound withering skeleton in a matter of months. Seeing that kind of suffering had a major impact on me, and the memory of his disease ravaged body will always be with me.

The tobacco companies prey on kids, getting them hooked at an early age so they will become lifelong addicts. Nicotine addiction comes on hard and you can forget about the easy quit. My dad tried to stop smoking unsuccessfully for twenty-five years, and it took a pretty serious health scare before he was finally able to put them down for good, after four decades. Many of my friends smoked behind their parent's backs and they never suspected a thing. Telling you never to smoke would be a waste of my breath, and I'm not going to play detective and secretly rummage through your bag or smell your dirty laundry. I just hope you can use your head and see that these things will only lead to disaster. Don't let cigarettes capture you like the millions of other stupid teenagers out there.

* National Institute on Drug Abuse, InfoFacts: MDMA (Ecstasy), May 2006.
^ National Center for Health Statistics. National Health Interview Survey, (Cigarette Stats) 2005.

# Chapter 5:
# Abuse

Human beings have been abusing each other since the dawn of time, and they will always continue to do so. For some unknown reason we are subconsciously drawn towards dominating those who appear weaker or different than us. Look at the greatest story ever told for instance, a peaceful and compassionate man was tortured, nailed to a wooden cross, and bled to death in front of hundreds of cheering onlookers, simply because of his religious beliefs. Suffering is all we know. Each night the newscasters speak of the most heinous crimes one could imagine, without an ounce of emotion, and plastic smiles on their faces. Rapes, murders, babies found in dumpsters, domestic abuse, and yet we sit back in our easy chairs and absorb it like mindless zombies, becoming desensitized to it all.

This is so prevalent in our society that it even exists in children's movies. Notice how the plots always have someone or something being unjustly abused, yet they find the strength to overcome it. Even at this tender age we are trying to prepare them for the harsh realities of the world. We sit our three-year-olds down to watch these movies without one thought of the messages they contain; stories such as *Cinderella*, with the abusive family who enslaves her in a tower, *Snow White*, who gets drugged into a coma by an evil witch jealous of her beauty, or your favorite as a toddler, *101 Dalmatians*, starring Cruella Deville the malicious puppy killer.

Just flip through any school history book and you'll see endless tales of abuse: war, social injustice, oppression, and genocide.

During World War II, Adolf Hitler and his Nazi army set out to extinguish the Jewish race throughout Europe and eventually the whole world. They hunted them down, bashed in their doors in the middle of the night, rounded them up like animals, separated families, and then systematically murdered them in some of the most brutal methods imaginable. The Nazis used firing squads, lethal injections, and even gas chambers big enough to kill dozens of people at one time.

When this nightmare was finally over at the end of the war, more than six million people of all ages were savagely murdered. This dark period in history was named the Holocaust and it would go down as one of the greatest human tragedies of our time, one that people can barely speak of to this day. Could it be possible that this Hitler guy was a demon spawn from the depths of hell, and merely a one time freak of nature? I think not. Things like this happen all the time, maybe not in those numbers, but definitely in severity.

Many would like you to believe that despicable crimes of this nature have taken place everywhere but our own soil; this is not true at all. In fact, two other disgraceful acts against human beings occurred right here in the United States: the abduction and enslavement of the African race, and the premeditated slaughter of the Native Americans. Each one of these atrocities takes up about one page in any American history book that I've seen. This is because it's an embarrassment for our children to discover that their own ancestors may have taken part in such actions.

Imagine learning that your great-great-great grandfather had sailed to Africa to kidnap innocent people from their villages, forced them to become slaves, bought and sold them, raped, beat, and murdered them. Or, that he may have been involved in the annihilation of a peaceful race of people living on this land when Christopher Columbus supposedly discovered America in 1492. Next time you read that the Native Americans were all barbaric killers, don't believe it. These people were massacred, driven off the land they had lived on for hundreds of years, and forced to live on reservations located primarily in uninhabitable desert. Many of whom still live there today, grasping at the few shreds of dignity and tradition that once withstood this proud people.

We'd all like to believe that we have evolved as a species, and that these tragedies are merely a dark part of our past. However, present-day tales of detainee torture at Abu Ghraib, along with the attempted genocides in Bosnia and Darfur, bring us back to the cold reality that people may never change. Why we do this to each other is one of the greatest mysteries of the human condition. In my opinion, it is due in part to a set of traits within our genetic code, dating back to the age of primitive man, when the mentality was "kill or be killed." Medical experts say that the human appendix is a useless organ left over from eons ago when we used to eat bark and other indigestible things. So if this is still inside us, who's to say that some of our primal instincts aren't still within us as well? These are the same traits that make a child burn ants with a magnifying glass, pour salt on a slug, or pull a fly's wings off; a smidgen of sadism present in us all.

People of all ages are abused everyday. Even as you read these words countless human beings are being physically, sexually, or psychologically abused, maybe even all three. You'd be amazed at how many people you know that are living with the pain of an abusive past or present, including your dear old dad. I know with all my heart that the root of all my psychosis, addictions, obsessive compulsiveness, speech disorder, and general distrust of others is a direct result of the severe childhood beatings from the hands of my emotionally unstable mother. The memories of the abuse I withstood are so harsh, that I still wake up shaking in terror some twenty years later.

Your grandma wasn't always the pleasant old woman you see before you. She was raised the eldest daughter of two Hispanic Americans in an impoverished section of the Bronx, New York. Her mother ruled the roost with an iron fist, showing no mercy when any of her three children showed disrespect or unruliness.

Her father was a distant deceitful man who womanized behind his wife's back, and would even spend several years in prison for selling cocaine out of his business. My mother was more or less raised on the streets of her unforgiving neighborhood, developing a tough as nails attitude, truck-driver mouth, and an extreme physical prowess.

My earliest recollections of my mother are ones of love. I remember never wanting to leave her side as a small child. It wasn't until I was nine years old that I noticed profound changes in her personality and behavior. My father was constantly working at one of his three jobs, so mom had to raise us kids practically on her own. At this time she also began driving a school bus to make ends meet, and to ease the stress of her hectic life she turned to alcohol for comfort. Many a night I drifted to sleep to the sounds of bottles clanking in the kitchen, ice hitting empty glasses, and screaming matches between her and my dad. This began the period of my life when the beatings began and my childhood would be ripped away from me.

Her attacks were vicious and without remorse. Picture a seventy-pound, spaghetti-armed boy backed into a corner weeping mercifully, while an enraged wild woman with hate in her eyes, flared nostrils, and snarled lips unleashes a barrage of flying fists, slaps, and kicks. I once had a friend who would laugh in his mother's face and grab her puny wrists when she tried to hit him; I wish my life was that easy. My mother would actually hold down my defensive arms with her left hand, while repeatedly landing brutal face shots with her right. All the while screaming, "Don't you dare cover up you worthless piece of shit. I'll give you something to cry about you son of a bitch!" I'd run to my bed, my only sanctuary and hide under the covers, only to be followed by her with the leather belt in hand and the stench of spiced rum on her breath. With each lash, she would rip the blankets from my clenched fists to reveal bare skin; pleading was my only defense, "Please, Mom, I'll be good. Please stop!"

My extreme punishments were for actions that in most households would go completely unnoticed: syrup on the counter, mud on the carpet, a snide comment, or sometimes just a look I gave her. I was once pummeled clear out of my chair for telling a dinner guest that her highly regarded spaghetti sauce was from a jar. In hindsight, I don't think the physical pain of these beatings was what damaged me, for the psychological abuse that this woman dished out was far greater. After a while she actually had me believing that I was a worthless piece of shit, and that I deserved everything I got.

I can still taste the sheer terror of each afternoon as her car pulled into the driveway. I'd peak through the curtains to catch a glimpse of her face to try and gauge her mood. This was about the same time I noticed myself stuttering excessively. My mind was in such turmoil that my mouth would no longer respond to my commands. There's an instinct that all living things possess called, "the fight or flight" reaction. This is a feeling that naturally comes over you in times of imminent danger; life or death situations when your body tells you, "Okay, time to fight or run. Choose one or you will die!" Your adrenaline rushes, logical thought shuts down, and suddenly you become a deer in the sights of a hunter's rifle. While most experience this reaction a few times in their whole lives, it is my opinion that abused children live much of their existence in this heightened state of panic. I also believe this to be a major contributor to the abundance of depressed and mentally disturbed people in the world.

Most of the time people turn a blind eye to this type of child abuse, mainly because parents have been raising their kids this way for generations. My whole neighborhood knew I got the snot beat out of me on a regular basis, but no one ever helped, not once. Even my own father looked the other way many times when he could have intervened. He was hardly ever home to witness much, but when he did he was much too subservient to my mother to stand up to her. He made the money, and disciplining the kids was her job. To this day he is in absolute denial as to the frequency and severity of what went on, and I feel he is scared to death to admit that he could have somehow married a person with such violent tendencies.

One time I found the courage to tell my sixth grade teacher that my mother was beating me. After a face to face conference, she realized that my mom was "Deb, the beloved bus driver," so my complaints were brushed aside as much needed discipline for an unruly boy. In those days, child abuse was breaking bones, burning, and throwing kids down stairs. For me to complain of beatings was silly.

After being betrayed by my teacher, I gave up the fight and just became a nervous, stuttering, emotional basket case with more pain than I knew what to do with. I started believing that I was a horrible person and began acting out by vandalizing, running away from home, setting fires, killing woodsy creatures with my B.B. gun, and abusing the weaker kids in the neighborhood, including once when I knocked a kid's front teeth out by throwing a snowball with a rock inside. My life was turning out to be a self-fulfilling prophecy. Tell a kid they are nothing enough times, and that is exactly what they will become.

My last beating came two days after my seventeenth birthday. For some reason, Mom came home from work an hour early and caught me in bed with my girlfriend Kate. As we wrestled with our clothes, my bedroom door burst open and I was immediately grabbed by the throat and slammed into the wall. After two lightning-fast rights to the face, I caught an open handed left directly to the ear. Like a jet engine, a deafening roar engulfed my whole body and I collapsed in agony. In slow motion, I watched Kate cowering in fear as my mother shrieked the psychotic statement, "I told you to stop coming on your God damn blankets!" with exposed teeth and spit flying from her mouth. At that very moment an indescribable rage came over me, and for the first time in my life, I wasn't a frightened little boy anymore.

I sprung to my feet, and in one swift action shoved her in the chest with eight years worth of fury, sending her flying across the room into my dresser and shattering the mirror. Then from the darkest corners of my soul came the primal scream, "If you ever touch me again, I'll kill you, you crazy bitch!" As I stepped over her disheveled body, there was a look in her eyes that I had never witnessed before; it was one of utter bewilderment. I spent that night at Kate's recounting the disturbing events that unfolded and wondering what my future would bring. When I returned home the next morning, my broken mirror was by the curb and neither of my parents mentioned a word about it. To this day, I have no idea if my father was even told.

Since then, Mom began trying to piece her life back together by getting much needed therapy and even rediscovering her faith. She is now retired from bus driving and desperately searching for the loving family that she let slip away. I will never be able to comprehend how a parent could possibly cause harm to their own child. When the doctor first placed you in my arms minutes after you were born, all I could think about was loving you forever.

The main reason that people abuse their kids is because of something called, "the cycle of abuse." This is when parents mistreat their children because that's the way they were raised, and it's all they know. This style of parenting gets passed down through generations like a family heirloom or piece of property. It's almost inborn, like some uncontrollable urge to act out violently in times of great stress. The only way to end this cycle is to stop reacting to those inner feelings of rage. All it takes is one set of parents to break the chain and then it ceases to exist.

With you and your brother, I know from the bottom of my heart that this evil thread that has been in our family for many years will no longer haunt us. I will never lay a hand or harmful word on my children for as long as I live, therefore ending the cycle forever. There is so much pain in the world, the last place it should be is in the home. Home is a place that should give you a safe and fuzzy feeling every time you think of it, not the cold and nauseous one that I had for most of my childhood.

***Life Rule #14: The true cure for an abusive upbringing is to be an amazing parent, and relive childhood through the eyes of your children.***

This is the reason why I am the thirty-three-year-old goofball who adores cartoons, burps at the dinner table, and bites your belly. I am reliving my youth vicariously through you. With each smile, laugh, and discovery that you make, you are unknowingly silencing the demons of my troubled past. And I thank you for that.

## Sexual Abuse

There are tales of abuse however, that make my own experiences look like a sunny day at the beach. Being a young woman, it is imperative that you have an understanding of the evils that exist in our world. For how else could you know the dangers that may lie ahead? There are men out there who are so completely deranged, that they will go to any means to get their hands on a defenseless female in which to perform unspeakable acts. They are lurking in alleyways, driving around in cars, and even trolling the internet posed as fifteen-year-olds with the intent of satisfying their disgusting sexual urges. And to make matters worse, these maniacs are not always strangers. They can be close friends, teachers, neighbors, or even your own relatives. The thought that someone of this nature could ever get hold of our precious children, is the unbearable horror that leaves parents lying awake at night unable to rest their minds.

Having been a physically abused child with much psychological baggage, I cannot even imagine the devastation that sexual abuse can have on someone's fragile psyche. While sex can be the most beautiful thing two people can share, unwilling sex can be the most traumatic experience a person can go through. It can leave a victim emotionally hollow and never able to truly love again.

Rachel was the sweetest girl in my classes at college. We student taught together and became the best of friends. One night after drinking at the bars, she broke down and started crying on my shoulder. She then told me the awful story of her tenth grade volleyball coach. In the beginning he was the nicest guy in the world, a respected teacher, husband, father of two, and the person who single-handedly helped her get through the death of her father. After a Friday night game, Coach O'Brien dropped all of the girls off at their houses until only Rachel remained in the van. He then proceeded to pull down a darkened dead end road, held her down, and raped her amid the sporting equipment and scattered gym bags. This man who she trusted like a father was now hurting her in the worst possible way.

Like the many rape victims before her, she let the incident go unreported. She was afraid of the repercussions it would cause, and also the misery it would bring her newly widowed mother. Instead, she buried the pain deep down and forced herself to live with the horrific memory of the loss of her innocence. Rachel wept on my shoulder that night harder than I have ever felt, deep belly sobs as her tears flowed like a river of despair. I told her I understood, but I could never truly understand that type of pain. We still keep in touch. She married her high school sweetheart and is now pregnant with her first baby, a little boy. After each conversation she thanks me for my friendship and support; it's the least I can do.

I remember once my grandma told me to be careful of strangers because they could do bad things to me. In my naivety I asked, "What could they do to me? I'm a boy." I'll never forget her reply: "You know where you make cocky? Well, that's where they stick it!" My grandmother was a very crude lady, and from that moment I have been petrified by the evils of man.

## Date Rape

In the animal kingdom, male wants female, male takes female, and that's that. In the human world this is a reprehensible act, one that even prisoners consider the vilest of crimes. So instead, men must use their devious minds to conquer their prey. When you hear the word rape you probably picture the horror of being attacked by a lunatic, dragged into the woods, and barely escaping with your life. Can you even imagine being attacked by a boy that you know very well, or after a wonderful date with the most popular guy in school?

Date rape is becoming more and more common in this dangerous world. Guys learn at an early age that drugs and alcohol usually equal easy girls. There are chemicals on the street like Rohypnol (roofies), Ketamine (special k), and GHB (gook) that if secretly sprinkled in your drink, can leave you unconscious and defenseless for several hours. Some of the fraternities and sporting teams at my college were famous for this. At least once a semester some freshman girl would wake up naked in a strange bed, completely void of the last ten hours. The police would be called, arrests made, and it would shock the community, yet they never learned.

Some guys don't even bother with drugs. They firmly believe that the movie and Taco Bell they just bought you gives them every right to have sex with you, and sometimes the word "No!" doesn't mean a thing.

## Where Can a Girl Turn?

First of all, keeping an assault to yourself is never the answer. No matter how much it hurts, it must always be revealed to a loved one and eventually the proper authorities. Allowing someone to get away with such a crime means that they will only do it again, and it is also putting many unsuspecting females in future danger. God forbid, you or anyone you know should ever need assistance with something of this nature, come to us immediately and we'll try our best to make it better. There are people out there who specialize in situations like these and who have the knowledge to help victims reclaim their lives. One of the most reputable rape hotlines in the country is 1-800-656-HOPE. They are available every day of the year at any hour.

The absolute destruction caused by a sexual assault is one of our most primal fears; it doesn't matter whether it was perpetrated by a stranger or a trusted acquaintance. The key here is prevention. You must be constantly aware of your surroundings and every situation that can arise from your decisions. Always be mindful of the following suggestions:

1. **Never go anywhere alone.** Whenever I see young girls walking alone after dark, I always feel scared for them. Are they really that clueless to the dangers, or are they just on some sort of rebellious quest? An abduction can take place in the blink of an eye. Such as the 1997 case of beloved Long Island teacher Cynthia Quinn, who was raped and murdered while jogging in the light of day, minutes from her home.

2. **Never chat with strangers online.** There's a disturbing new television show called *To Catch a Predator,* where a network news team partners with law enforcement to lure internet predators to the home of an underage child. Time after time men arrive with the full intention of committing a lascivious act with a minor. They come bearing such gifts as condoms, alcohol, and, in one instance, a roll of duct-tape. We're not talking the scum of the earth here either, these are doctors, politicians, teachers, fathers, grandfathers, and in one episode, a well respected rabbi from a local synagogue. You never know who's on the other end of that connection. No matter how tempting, avoid this for all you're worth.

3. **Practice cautious dating.** Most date rapes occur when lone couples get together for a night on the town. Everything was wonderful, the conversation was fresh and chemistry was in the making, until the young lady tried to end the night early with just a kiss. Organizing a group date, or public dates in crowded places, can really relieve the pressure for unwanted intimacy. Avoiding the car ride altogether is an even better way to assure your safety in the dating game. As cheesy as it may be, consider being dropped off and picked up by a loved one. I'd even drop you around the corner and duck down as I drove away if you preferred.

4. **Don't ever leave your friend's sight when you go out.** Your mom and her best friend Jess have had a pact since they were teenagers, to never allow each other to go somewhere alone when they are out. Whether at a bar, club, or party, they always stuck by each other's side and watched closely when guys were involved. Under no circumstances could this pact be broken. Activities like going to see a guy's room, taking a ride, or the old stand by, "You wanna get outta here?" can mean disaster for a young girl.

5. **Always watch your drinks like a hawk.** All it takes is a split second for someone to slip something in your drink. Whatever it may be, always pour it yourself, and never accept something that was prepared out of your sight. And when you go to the bathroom, bring it along for the ride.

## Abusive Boyfriends

I student taught in the most charming mountain town imaginable, Skaneateles, New York. It was like a fairy tale; everyone knew each other, no one locked their doors, and kids rode their bikes in total safety. In October of 1998, I arrived at school and was notified that the principal had called an emergency faculty meeting. We were informed that there was a severe incident of domestic violence in one of the student's households. One of the dads had beaten his wife into a coma with an aluminum baseball bat. If that isn't horrifying enough, after being released on bail this maniac snuck into her hospital room wearing janitor's clothing and poured a packet of cyanide poisoning on her face, killing her instantly. This community was rocked to its core. The story made national news, and suddenly this quiet little town was a media circus with children of all ages swept into the frenzy.

Whenever a young girl hears a story of an abusive relationship such as this, her first thoughts are usually, "Why would anyone stay in an abusive relationship?" or "That would never happen to me!" I've heard these exact words from countless middle schoolers in my classes. Do they really think that the millions of abused women in the world just decided one day to hook up with someone who would eventually turn their lives into a torturous hell? Remember when I told you about first-date behavior, well this is exactly how they get you. He plays you perfectly, and you actually start believing he can do no wrong. Once a guy coerces you into a physical relationship and he knows that you are hopelessly in love with him, three things will happen:

1. They know they've got you wrapped around their finger for a long time.
2. They get all of the power in the relationship.
3. They become their true selves.

Once a girl makes a sexual commitment they are in it for the long haul, through whatever horrible conditions that may come. Now that he has you under his spell, you will start to notice slight changes in his once perfect demeanor. Suddenly he's paying less attention to you, offering fewer compliments, giving less phone time, and complaining he doesn't see his friends enough. The relationship turns into a constant argument. He becomes jealous and controlling of your every move, how you dress, who you see, and what you do in your free time. Then it happens: he gets rough with you for the first time. Maybe just a light shove, arm grab, or a hair pull, something minor, but it happened and this is the beginning of the end.

Nevertheless, he apologizes, cries, and swears on his life that it will never happen again. You want to believe that it was just a one time thing, so you take him back and it only gets worse. The violence increases and the mind games get malicious. "Nobody will ever love you like me; you're fat, ugly, stupid, and good for nothing," reducing you to an empty shell of a person. This is how most abusive relationships begin, and why they are so difficult to escape. Now just imagine adding kids to the equation.

I started dating Jenna the summer after high school graduation. She was a raven-haired beauty one year my junior, with the greenest eyes I had ever seen. After meeting her through a mutual friend, I was determined to make her mine. Although she played hard to get in the beginning, eventually I won her over with my charm and endless compliments. With our one year anniversary approaching, things were still as strong as ever. We even talked about getting married one day. However, once college came around it all went in the crapper.

She was going away to school, while I was attending a local college as a commuter. Her school of choice was only an hour away, so we hoped for the best, but it was doomed from the start. She began living in a coed dorm at Hofstra University, partying her ass off on a nightly basis, while I spent every spare moment waiting by the phone for her call (this was before cell phones by the way). When I would visit her on weekends, I couldn't believe what was going on: guys and girls walking around the halls in towels, drinking, drugs, and everyone randomly hooking up with each other. It was something I had only seen in the movies and I was sick with jealousy.

One Thursday night, I went to the local pub with Jenna and her roommate. This place was a zoo, hundreds of people were packed shoulder to shoulder, making out, dancing on the bar, and spilling pitchers of beer on each other's heads. I didn't know anyone so I proceeded to get royally smashed. Just past midnight, I came out of the bathroom after throwing up, and spotted my lady on the dance floor with her arms behind her head getting grinded from the front and back by two goons, making a Jenna sandwich!

With adrenalin in my veins and my heart pounding in my ears, I became an enraged psycho. Without a moment's thought, I charged onto the dance floor and dragged her out of the bar by the arm like a rag doll. When we reached the street she tried to break free from my grip, so I grabbed a fistful of hair and vigorously threw her into a parked car. Next thing I knew, I was on the ground in the fetal position being pounded within inches of my life by an incensed mob.

All I remember is endless fists and boots stomping me into the pavement, and the echo of Jenna's hysterical wail. It just so happened that the guys she was dancing with were neighbors from her dorm, who also happened to be in a local fraternity. When they saw what I did to her, about eight of them fled the bar and began to beat the living crap out of me. When I regained consciousness, my shirt was ripped from my body, both of my shoes were off, one of my front teeth was knocked loose, and I was lying in a puddle of blood. Believe it or not, it was Jenna who pulled them off of me and saved my drunken ass; that's how loving she was. She scraped my lifeless carcass off the curb and carried me back to the dorm. Neither of us said a word.

I couldn't believe what had just transpired. I had actually become something I swore I never would be: an abusive boyfriend. After two bruised ribs, a split lip, and a fractured nose, I was more ashamed than I had ever been. From that night on, our relationship was permanently severed and it would never be the same. She tried to break up with me many times, but I always manipulated my way back into her life. A few more months of jealousy and distrust would eventually tear us apart for good, after two tumultuous years together. Even though I was only an ignorant nineteen-year-old, I don't know if I could ever forgive myself for that disgraceful lapse in judgment. What could possibly bring a person to the depths of abusing someone they love with all their heart?

The best way to avoid a hellish experience like this is to learn how to detect any abusive tendencies a guy may possess. You must develop a foolproof screening process, and be extremely cautious before you allow a guy passed your defenses and into your comfort zone. Here are four tips that will surely assist your efforts:

1. **How does he treat his mom and other female family members?** You can tell so much about a guy's disposition by this. Not only does this tell you about his true self, but it is also a great indicator of his family values. Although they may mean little to you now, they will be vital if there is to be any future with this guy. A guy who is loving and respectful to the women in his family, is most likely going to continue this behavior with his girlfriends. Sure, every girl loves the loner and the mysterious bad boy, but you have to ask yourself: Why are they a loner? What kind of emotional baggage are they carrying? Do I want to become part of that baggage?

2. **How does he treat kids?** A guy who genuinely adores kids is a guy who enjoys living. No one is more honest or zestful of life than little people. They tell it like it is and if your guy can get along with them, he may be a keeper. Kids have a built-in "jackass sensor." Let a bunch of kids give you their opinion of a guy, and you will gain tremendous insight into his true character. Also, teenage guys who are great with kids usually possess the ability to become the great dads of tomorrow: the soccer coaches, tree-house builders, snowman makers, and Sunday-morning egg scramblers. So invite Mr. Wonderful to a kid's party or a babysitting gig and see how he responds to the chaos. Does he resemble a caged tiger dying to escape captivity, or is he laughing, smiling, and playing around in good spirits?

3. **How does he treat animals?** A guy who loves animals will almost always have a soft heart. He doesn't have to be an animal fanatic or anything; many just didn't grow up with pets, so this one isn't foolproof. Try to gauge his demeanor when he comes upon animals. Is he unaware of their presence, cruel, or annoyed? Or is he friendly and inviting? What does he do when you bring up the death of a pet you had in the past? Does he laugh or give you a hug? It's little inconspicuous tests such as these that can help you catch a guy totally off guard, even one on his best behavior. If someone you're dating treats his pets like his children, or stops his car to help stray animals, chances are he's got a heart of gold and his intentions are pure. Furthermore, a guy that is nurturing to animals is actually capable of caring for things besides himself. This quality is a true example of a selfless person.

4. **Investigate previous relationships.** This will take your best detective work. I don't care if it takes being so bold as to calling ex-girlfriends or grilling family members, but find out whatever you can. Why did they break up? How long were they together? How did he treat her? This will give you a revealing look into his past and, more importantly, his future.

## Verbal Abuse

After thirty-five years of working his ass off, my dad finally retired from his career with the county highway department. He was now ready to enjoy his twilight years puttering around the garden, and recapturing his inner passions. He began seeking spiritual introspection through yoga, meditation, tai chi, and reading hoards of new-aged books about the meaning of life. One of these books was *The Four Agreements* by Don Miguel Ruiz, a Mexican medicine man. This book had such a tremendous impact on him, that he insisted I give it a read. I'm so glad he did, because the book was life changing. It's basically about different methods of ridding your life of negative energy, which I am aware has been done many times before. However, Don Miguel utilizes the ancient wisdom of the Toltec civilization to provide his insights. Looking at the world from this perspective creates a brilliant portrait of existence, one that can be easily achieved, yet totally against our traditional American values.

My favorite part of the book tells the story of a middle-aged mom coming home from a stressful day of work, her head splitting and body aching for the quiet comfort of her living room. She collapses on the sofa with pounding temples, wondering if life ever gets easier. Upstairs in a distant bedroom, the woman's young daughter is standing in front of the full length mirror, microphone/brush to her lips, singing her favorite song in full bravado, dreaming of future stardom. All of the sudden, the performance is abruptly cut short by the exhausted woman, screaming at her daughter to cease the infernal racket. The door slams, the brush hits the floor, and the young girl jumps head first into her pillow, sobbing hysterically, never to sing again.

Everyday, the things we say to each other without a moment's thought can potentially have devastating affects on our lives. You know how adults are constantly telling kids that, "sticks and stones may break your bones, but names will never hurt you"? Well, that might be the biggest lie we ever tell them. While physical abuse damages the skin, verbal assaults go right to the core and damage the soul. For thirteen years, my mom came home every night like the woman I just mentioned. I wouldn't call my worst enemy the names she called me during one of her psychotic episodes. Calling me a "good–for-nothing son of a bitch" as a child, was now what I saw when I looked in the mirror as an adult. Though, as I matured, I started to realize that her attacks on me were in no way personal, but more a part of her battle with her own demons. I was merely an innocent civilian who had gotten caught in the crossfire.

Every generation hopes for a peaceful world for their children to live in, but could this ever really happen? One logical place to start making renovations would be with our words. Wars are fought, families are divided, and people die because of harmful words. For the better part of my life, I would say horribly offensive things to people and then cover it up with, "Oh, I'm only kidding!" I passed it off as my weird sense of humor, but in reality it was my feeble attempt to redirect some of my insecurities and self-loathing outward for others to share.

In my first year of teaching, during my druggie days, I actually thought that using humiliation as a motivational tool with my students was a good idea. There was one kid in particular named Rahim, who was one of the worst students I have ever met. His aloof attitude, defiant behavior, and complete lack of the most basic of skills would send me into a boiling fury on a daily basis. In my extreme ignorance, I would constantly bring attention to his shortcomings, calling on him when I knew he didn't know an answer, forcing him to complete difficult problems on the board, and even announcing failed test grades.

One day, after discovering that he had copied his research report verbatim from an encyclopedia, I completely lost it. I tore into him like he had just slapped my grandmother, screaming in his face and eventually bringing the boy to tears. As soon as that first tear hit the desk, I felt like the biggest dick in the world. I envisioned myself as a child plagiarizing numerous school assignments, and couldn't believe the shameless hypocrisy I was exhibiting. I was too blind to see that maybe all this neglected kid needed was a positive male influence in his life, instead of a malicious drill sergeant. After that he never opened a book, picked up a pen, or cracked a smile for the rest of the year. He just sat there like a statue.

One of my biggest fears is that my behavior could have somehow ruined this kid's life. It's mistreatment like this that causes kids to shut down, give up, and eventually quit school altogether, being forced into a life of hardship. To think that I could be the catalyst for something like that makes me deathly ashamed. I pray he has long forgotten me.

## Life Rule #15: "Be impeccable with your words." ~Don Miguel Ruiz

The only way to combat the misuse of our words is by constantly trying to improve ourselves, and by spreading positive vibes with our actions. You don't know how much a compliment like, "you look amazing," or a simple, "great job!" could brighten up a person's day. People's energy can be quite contagious if you spend a lot of time with them. I work with people everyday who are constant fountains of negativity. They talk badly about others, put people down, offer back-handed compliments, and revel in the pain of co-workers. I wanted no part of this anymore, so I cleaned up my act and started applying the principles in *The Four Agreements* to my career. I stopped counting the seconds until the school day was over, and began cherishing the amazing opportunity I had to shape children's minds in a positive way. I realized what a privilege it was to be a teacher, and I wanted to be one that kids remembered with a smile rather than a grunt.

I began to utilize my talents as a musician, confidant, and even hack comedian to make each day something they would always remember. I gave extra help every morning, volunteered for field trips, chaperoned dances, organized talent shows, and started an after-school guitar club. But most importantly, I offered heartfelt encouragement to every kid. My classroom became a place for fun and interactive learning, with a teacher who was fair and approachable, rather than an unstable jerk-off. And let me tell you, watching those inner-city kids raised on hip-hop music, hold a guitar in their hands for the first time was one of the most rewarding experiences of my career. It didn't make up for the way I treated Rahim, but it made the memory a tad less brutal.

Abuse is one of the evils of this world that unfortunately we all must learn to deal with. Yet, when I look back on my childhood, I can't help but wonder how I would've turned out if I was never beaten. This is one of the many irritating thoughts that disrupts my every attempt at peaceful slumber. Nevertheless, with a rosy past I probably wouldn't have been able to express myself to you in this way. As you read my words, I hope that they will enable you to have a better understanding of your Daddy. For I wouldn't change a single thing about my life; I'm now very proud of who I am. Still, having been on both ends of the abusive spectrum, there is but one undeniable fact that I have come to realize …

**Life Rule #16: Everybody hurts.**

# CHAPTER 6:
# DEPRESSION

There's an incredible song from the early '90s by the band R.E.M., called "Everybody Hurts." I always took notice whenever I heard it, but one day I saw the video and my whole outlook on life was changed. It's a sorrowful tune about being overwhelmed by life's hardships, and how one should never give up the fight. The video takes place within stand-still traffic, and people of all sorts are shown sitting in their cars staring hopelessly out the windshield. The intriguing aspect of this scenario is that everyone's thoughts are in subtitles as they flash from car to car. Each vehicle is the same: people with miserable looks on their faces, obsessing over their troubles, and wondering why life has to be so hard. The one scene that always gets me is of an old man sitting alone, with tear-filled eyes, and a melancholic facial expression. His caption simply says, "She's gone forever."

During the song's climax, the people begin abandoning their cars and fleeing the scene as if to say, "Who needs this shit? I'm outta here!" As the anthemic chorus of "Everybody hurts, Everybody cries, So hold on!" is repeated, hundreds of people are seen walking away in unison. I get chills just thinking about that song. For one, it helped me realize that maybe other people felt as helpless as I did. It also showed me that I wasn't a complete mental case, and that my incessant feelings of impending doom were just another part of being human. It was a moment when I saw the light at the end of a dark tunnel. One I had been in search of for many years.

If you asked anyone who knew me, they'd probably say that I'm one of the most laid-back and happiest guys they ever met. I wish that was the case, but it couldn't be any further from my true feelings. I have had a shadow of sadness following me around for as long as I can remember. As early as third grade, I would hide in the bathroom stall and silently weep, sometimes multiple times a day. I was always one of those kids who could be sent into hysterics with so little as a dirty look or passing comment. These feelings lingered throughout my adolescence and into adulthood. Yet, I developed a very elusive front to hide my problems from others.

Not until my mid-twenties did I even know what depression was, or that it was a real disease that affected millions of people in the world. In case you don't know: depression is feelings of helplessness, hopelessness, overwhelming sadness, and even physical pain that can infiltrate one's every thought. It can reduce the most secure person into a blubbering mess, afraid to leave the safety of their own bed. Once depression sinks its claws into your heart, escaping its grasp can become a never ending battle. It can hit anyone at anytime, even those who appear to have the world on a string.

I would tell myself constantly that I had no reason whatsoever to be depressed. I had my health, family, education, and was loved by many. But this disease has more to do with what you don't have, than what you do. It's a question of the stability of your foundation. What kind of ground were you built on as a child? Was it solid rock or unstable swampland?

No one knows for sure what causes depression. Some say it's inherited from your parents and passed on through your DNA, while others say that traumatic experiences may be responsible for its onset. It could even be the horrible diets and sedentary lifestyles that Americans have become so famous for. Personally, I feel it's a combination of all of the above, with one being the most prominent for each individual person. After numerous therapists, medication, and endless research into the causes and treatments for depression, I came to the conclusion that there were two possible paths toward recovery. One was years of therapy, which was lengthy and expensive. The other path was easier and the most direct route with almost immediate results: prescription medication. I read somewhere that antidepressants are the most prescribed drugs in the world, with millions of people relying on them everyday. However, happiness in a bottle comes at a cost, and I don't mean the thirty dollar co-pay.

After complaining of constant sadness to my doctor and the briefest of examinations, I had a prescription for Lexapro in my hand and was out the door. My rationale was that I'd been self-medicating unsuccessfully for years with illegal drugs, so maybe someone with a medical degree could do a better job at controlling my wacky mind. I always suspected that I needed medication, but I was avoiding them because of the vast side effects they were associated with. While the majority of them sounded like a minor nuisance, there was one that scared the hell out of me: diminished sex drive. This had never been a problem for me before, and the thought of becoming disinterested in the bedroom was something I wanted no part of. Nevertheless, I decided to try it anyway, opting for happiness over studliness.

## Happy Pills

Before I took my first pill, I searched the internet for any information on this type of medication. I stumbled upon a ton of message boards pertaining to this topic and was surprised by how informative they were. Most of the people wrote that antidepressants worked great, but the side effects were sometimes too hard to handle. Some of the most prevalent were insomnia, fatigue, nausea, diarrhea, headaches, spacey feelings, and of course the dreaded limp noodle. I wanted to be happy at any cost, so I just went for it and gulped down my first pill with a swig of orange juice.

The side effects kicked in right away. I was completely exhausted all day, yet stared at the clock all night. I was practically glued to the toilet seat for days, and waves of nausea rolled over me like a pregnant woman in her first trimester. I definitely felt overwhelmed by all of this, but everything I read said the medication could take up to eight weeks before the negative effects would subside.

As the tormenting weeks passed I started noticing subtle changes in my daily mood and attitude. I was becoming less agitated by things that would normally send me through the roof. I was also less preoccupied with the negative thoughts and rituals that once plagued my life. Like clock work, at eight weeks I was a completely different person and suddenly found myself smiling regularly and whistling "Zippity Doo Dah" like a 1950s mailman. I felt relaxed, comfortable in my own skin, and able to get through my day without a depressive episode. Life was good, very good!

These kinds of pills affect the brain chemical serotonin, the same one I mentioned in the Ecstasy section. Anti-depressants regulate the body's supply of serotonin, so you don't experience the drastic emotional peaks and valleys associated with day-to-day life.

After a solid year on the medication, I was very satisfied with its affects, although I was becoming concerned about a few things. I know there's nothing more grotesque than the idea of your parents being intimate, but I promised full disclosure remember. My libido had become one of a sixty-eight-year-old Medicare recipient. I just wasn't ready yet to give up on my youth and become one of those guys who looks at his wife with minimal interest. Mommy actually couldn't have been more understanding and supportive; my happiness was always her first concern. Secondly, my life had become totally void of any emotional highs and lows; I was a "Steady Eddie" 24-7. I was never super happy, nor was I extremely sad either. This was quite strange because I was always a super-sensitive person who wore his emotions on his sleeve.

The weirdest thing for me was that I was physically incapable of crying. My tear ducts were completely dysfunctional for the entire time I was on Lexapro. I've always tended to cry much more than the average guy; movies, TV shows, books, commercials, weddings, songs, you name it, I've cried during it. I remember balling like a pre-schooler when you were born. Yet, when your brother was born I wanted to, but couldn't bring it on. It doesn't mean I loved him any less. The medicine simply wouldn't allow me to become emotional enough.

In addition, I didn't want to become dependant on medication for the rest of my life. One weekend away I forgot to pack my pills and almost had a nervous breakdown from the withdrawal symptoms. For once in my adult life I wanted to be free of any and all mind-altering chemicals. I wanted peace and happiness more than anything, but I wanted it naturally. Was it possible for me to be 100 percent drug-free? Although the question terrified me, I had to take the chance.

I decided to wean myself off the medication and try to cope with my depression head-on. I split my pills with a razor blade and took smaller doses less frequently, until I was finally ingesting crumbs and specks of dust. At first it was like a horrible acid trip. As my body withdrew from the chemicals, I had to recalibrate all over again, leaving me paranoid and delusional. The insomnia, night sweats, and nausea returned with a fury, and sometimes I went three days without sleep. The madness slowly diminished after a few weeks and once again I was greeted by my old friend depression, and he was anxious to continue where we had left off.

Feeling completely helpless, I took the recommendation of a good friend and decided to seek professional therapy. Throughout the years I've seen several therapists. Some were pompous windbags who offered no help at all, yet still wanted to see me three days a week, while others were very caring and insightful. One in particular helped me tremendously. She listened intently, shared personal stories from her life, and offered inspiring advice. In fact, much of this chapter is based on information and literature given to me by her, including the unbelievable book *A Child Called It* by Dave Pelzer.

In one of the most horrific child-abuse cases in recent history, this true story chronicles the life of a man who was brutally beaten and psychologically tortured by his alcoholic mother as a young child. I ached with each page as buckets gushed from my tear ducts, my first cry in thirteen months. This man's amazing will to survive gave me the courage to continue treatment and try to overcome my past.

I saw Dr. Gadsen off and on for two years and she genuinely helped me through a very rough stretch. However, my problem was I always felt enlightened after our sessions, thinking more clearly and promising myself a better outlook on life. But after an hour or two my depression would return, and the negative thoughts would again flood my mind. A few times I even called her late at night out of desperation, pleading for help. I realized that she was becoming just like the Lexapro, pot, Vicodin, and alcohol—a crutch to save me from myself. I had now become addicted to therapy and couldn't live without it. If I ever wanted to be normal, I would have to handle my problems alone: no doctors, no pills, no drugs, no nothing. I couldn't spend the rest of my days clinging to a life line, there had to be a better way.

In order to fight a goliath like depression, it was going to take a lot more than a quick fix or weekly counseling sessions. I was going to have to change everything about myself, from who I hung out with, to what I ate, to how I lived and thought. My plan was to try and combine bits and pieces of all the different self improvement techniques, and create a whole new me. What I came up with was something that I like to call, "The Soul Enema." It's an aggressive purging of everything your life has become, a holistic method that rids your mind, body, and soul of negativity. However, this time it would be much more difficult than swallowing a pill.

## The Soul Enema

### –Step 1: Take Back Your Health

When I was on anti-depressants I became horribly out of shape. As I said, there were no extreme highs and lows, no moments of energy and excitement, no inspirational bursts where I wanted to climb a mountain or write a song. Extreme moods can be debilitating on one hand, yet very motivational on the other. I basically became satisfied with doing nothing; just sitting on my ass, eating crap, sleeping, and staring at the idiot box. I became lethargic, unmotivated, and for the first time in my life—fat, this from a guy who weighed 118 pounds when he graduated high school. I was always one of those kids who could eat junk food everyday and never gain an ounce. I was now developing a pot belly, love handles, and was pushing 185 pounds on a 5' 8" frame.

While the medication made me lazy, it was the food I was eating that was making me fat. A lifetime of shoddy eating habits had finally caught up to me. My metabolism had slowed down to the point where if I didn't make a drastic change in my diet, I'd soon be one of those dudes you see hanging out at the mall food court with the huge belly, man boobs, and a carpenter's crack.

Believe it or not, but the food you eat is directly related to how you feel. Normal everyday food is loaded with preservatives, pesticides, and many other harmful chemicals that not only wreak havoc on your body, but can destroy your mind as well. Changing your diet is by far the most difficult component of the holistic cure for depression. Poor eating habits start in childhood with fast food and sugary snacks like candy, cake, and soda. These foods taste so damn good it's hard to imagine that they are harmful. Who doesn't love a Whopper, French fries, ice cream, and candy? Eating is one of our most primal and pleasurable urges. Certain foods like chocolate trigger natural chemicals in your body called endorphins, which are the same feelings you get when you are in love.

When I first found out that fast food was harmful, it was almost as awful as discovering there was no Santa Clause. Why do you think America is the fattest country in the world? Because we have such a "time is money" attitude; so when hunger calls, all we have time for is a quick bite and then it's right back to the work. Also, our whole concept of nutrition is completely ass-backwards. We eat tons of sugar, dairy, fried food, fatty meats, and little or no fruits and vegetables. Let me ask you this: when was the last time you saw an overweight Asian person, besides sumo wrestlers, who purposely get that way? Probably never, because they understand the essentials of a proper diet. The major portions of Asian meals are usually vegetables and rice with a little bit of meat on the side for protein.

I recently read about a race of people from the Himalaya Mountains of northern Pakistan called the Hunzas. These people were extraordinary human beings with amazing strength and longevity of spirit, often living in excess of 120 years. Because of their extreme isolation from the world, they were forced to be a completely self-sustained society. They lived on organically-grown produce and the healthiest free-roaming live stock on earth. They walked everywhere, worked hard in the sun all day, and led a life completely void of stress, disease, and depression. After spending several years studying the Hunza population, one anthropologist described them as being the happiest people he had ever met, and a true testament to a healthy lifestyle.* I guarantee that if a burger joint was to be erected amongst these people, they would become extinct in no time.

Fast food is a billion dollar industry. They actually have scientists working in labs creating this food, making it taste so good that it is impossible to resist. There's a phenomenal documentary made by a guy named Morgan Spurlock that everyone should see. This wacko ate nothing but McDonald's for breakfast, lunch, and dinner for thirty days straight, and caught it all on film. He wanted to prove to people that this food was having a devastating effect on our society, and you know what? His little experiment almost killed him.

Watching this marathon runner in optimal health, literally fall apart physically and emotionally was quite eye-opening. Almost immediately, he began feeling depressed and constantly craved the fast food. His body had become addicted to it like the millions of uninformed teenagers out there. When the thirty days were up, his doctors were astonished at the nearly irreparable damage to which his body had succumbed.

## Health Tip #1: Stay away from fast food

I'd be lying if I said I didn't still indulge in this garbage. It's such a difficult habit to break. Sometimes I feel like a strung out junkie cruising the streets after midnight, in search of my Big Mac fix. I go to the drive-thru alone, order my meal in shame, inhale the food like water, and then drive away feeling disgusted with myself and wanting to puke in the nearest dumpster. The other day there was an awesome article in the newspaper about Spain. It was about how their society has completely abandoned the age old tradition of the "siesta." This is when people would go home every afternoon to have a hearty lunch and a refreshing nap before returning to work. Since this way of life has been disregarded, they have now adopted the American work ethic of long hours and fast food. Interestingly enough, the rates of anti-depressant medications have sky rocketed as well in their country. I thought this article was quite revealing about the dangers of fast food.

I'm not saying that you can never eat this stuff. If it's in moderation it can be tolerated. There are times when eating fast food is unavoidable, such as when you're traveling or pressed for time. It is possible to find things on the menu that are less damaging. Try to avoid fried foods at all costs: French fries, fried chicken, onion rings, etc. This greasy crap will not only add inches to your waist-line, but also demolish your complexion. I never had more zits than the summer I worked as a fry cook at a chicken wing joint.

## Health Tip #2: Avoid dairy

Milk, cheese, cream, and butter are all extremely fatty, can cause cardiovascular disease, and are loaded with harmful chemicals. Dairy farming is a highly competitive business these days, and usually the farmers with the biggest cows make the most money. With this in mind, they pump the cows full of steroids such as RBGH, a bovine growth hormone. It's the most inhumane thing you can imagine. I went to college in cow country, so I've actually seen cows with udders so big they looked like they were sitting on a small car. These harmful drugs get passed on to us through the dairy products we ingest, and who knows how much damage they cause. The farmers also want their cows to be healthy and disease free, so along with the steroids they shoot them up with antibiotic medications, which also get transferred to us. The dairy industry spends millions in advertising to brainwash people into believing that cow's milk is a necessity for survival. I think it's a travesty that the government allows this to happen.

Sometimes your body can even lose its ability to digest dairy products. Right after college, I started having these unbelievable stomach pains and long bouts of irritable bowl syndrome, which is basically just a fancy name for "trouble on the bowl." My farts had become weapons of mass destruction, and I couldn't get through one day without a bathroom incident. With my neurotic mind, I pictured the worst and immediately sought out the best internal doctor in my insurance booklet. Within a week a doctor would be inserting a three foot long camera up my butt during a sigmoidoscopy examination. I didn't even know I had a sigmoid.

After many more painful and degrading tests, Dr. Keller was without cause to my digestive distress. On a whim she suggested I try cutting out all dairy products from my diet, for I may be unable to digest them or "lactose intolerant," in medical terms. At twenty-three, my whole diet consisted of pizza, chocolate, cheesy tacos, and ice cream, so it was very possible she was onto something. After my first dairy-free week, my stomach felt amazing and I had finally received some much needed regularity. Although it was extremely difficult to avoid my favorite foods, the pros significantly outweighed the cons.

There are many healthy alternatives to dairy that can give you all the nutrients that you need to stay healthy, such as milk derived from soy, rice, or almonds. These products are organically made, drug-and chemical-free, and way healthier than the crap from the dairy farms. I know this is a lot easier said than done, but try to limit your dairy intake. Just be careful around your mom, she's a hopeless ice cream addict always on the prowl for someone to indulge with.

## Health Tip #3: Limit your sugar consumption

Being that diabetes runs in our family on both sides, be extra cautious here. We all have a sweet tooth, some more than others. Some people ingest so much sugar that their bodies lose the ability to break it down any longer. They have to give themselves needles every day, monitor their sugar levels, and maintain a very strict diet. If not, the disease can progress, possibly causing blindness, amputation of extremities, or even stroke. Diabetes is a killer; millions have it and it seems to run in certain families and races.

Sugar should be eaten in small doses. Overindulging in soda, candy, cake, ice cream, and syrup for many years can not only lead to diabetes, but can wreck your body and rot the teeth right out of your mouth. In sixth grade my teacher asked us to bring our baby teeth to class. We placed them in glasses of soda and put them on the window sill. As the weeks passed we watched the teeth completely disintegrate until there were none at all. I still think about that experiment every time someone offers me cola and I opt for water.

## Health Tip #4: Drink plenty of water

The human body is made up of 75 percent water. This stuff is the life blood of our world and every living thing on it. Choosing water over sugary drinks can mean all the difference to your health and state of mind. Water flushes out all of the toxins in your body, aids in digestion, and cleans out your pores, keeping your skin looking healthy and clear. However, the water that comes directly out of the faucet is something to be very cautious of. It can be riddled with chemicals, pesticides, pollution, and whatever else seeps into our water table from the environment. It may look clean to the naked eye, but there are chemicals galore in that simple glass of tap water, some that can be very dangerous to your body. It's sad to say, but bottled water may be the only way to go these days. Twenty years ago if you were to buy water in a bottle, people would have called you crazy. Now you're crazy if you drink the free stuff. I just hope we don't have to pay for oxygen someday; yet with the direction this world is heading, you never know?

## Health Tip #5: Limit your medications

I saw a commercial the other day for a medication for AADD (Adult Attention Deficit Disorder). The ad said something like, "Are you easily distracted, disorganized, and unfocused? Well, we've got the pills for you!" I couldn't believe my ears. Could it be possible that my fifty-hour work week, two kids, excessive mortgage, and boatload of stress may be causing these symptoms? Nah; now even being preoccupied is a freakin' disease.

The drug companies are making billions off of our hypochondria and obsession with medications. I'm convinced that they all get together at conventions and conspire on what illnesses to make up next. They take a symptom that everyone has to a degree, such as obsessive thinking or restless legs, and then make some pill to combat this pseudo-disorder. When you see the ads for these new drugs you say, "Hey, that's what I have!" No shit, so does everybody else.

Medications can make you very depressed, and even more importantly weaken your body's immune system. If you are constantly taking medications for every ailment, then you are not allowing your body to fight them naturally, therefore the system becomes vulnerable. Just like an unworked muscle gets flabby, an unworked immune system gets weaker. Your body was built to fight off germs and establish a healthy balance. Give it a chance and stop running to the pharmacy every time you have a symptom. Eat healthy, exercise, and take a ton of vitamin C. You can never have too much of that stuff and it builds up your immunity big time.

## Health Tip #6: Limit your red meat intake

Just like I mentioned before about the chemicals in the cows milk, well, it's also in the meat. Too much meat of any kind is not good for you, but too much red meat can have disastrous consequences. This stuff is terrible for your heart and extremely difficult to digest. It literally sits in your intestines for weeks and putrefies before it's excreted. A friend turned me on to this guy named Howard Lyman. He was one of the most successful cattle ranchers in the state of Montana for over forty years. After a serious health scare, he began investigating the dangers that were associated with tainted meats. What he discovered not only caused him to convert to a strict vegetarian diet immediately, but also inspired him to become one of the leading advocates in the fight against the corruption of the meat industry. Mr. Lyman now has web sites, news letters, and seminars where he preaches the dangers of factory farming and healthy alternatives to beef. Although not perfect, turkey, chicken, and certain types of fish tend to be much safer than red meat.

Many people go vegetarian for the right reasons and then totally go about it the wrong way. My friend's sister gave up meat and her new diet consisted entirely of pizza, French fries, and chocolate, causing her to become sickly and chronically-fatigued. If researched and done correctly, a vegetarian diet combined with the proper nutritional supplements can be extremely healthy.

## Health Tip #7: Exercise, exercise, exercise

I can't stress this enough: one way to ensure that serious depression will come knocking on your door someday is to submit to a sedentary way of life. Lifetimes of television, couch surfing, and junk food will not only destroy your physique, but eventually gain control of your mind as well. One effective way to combat this is through exercise. Whatever it may be; running, swimming, dancing, biking, skating, or anything else that gets your heart pumping. Nothing fights off germs like a healthy body.

Sunshine can also be a great mood elevator, so when you're exercising get the hell out of the house. I never understood how people could spend hours a day on an exercise machine staring at a wall and counting the seconds until it's over. While too much ultra-violet light can be harmful, a little in moderation is actually quite beneficial. Vitamin D is an essential nutrient that is in sunlight and can help fight off Seasonal Affective Disorder (SAD). When I lived in New York my depression would always peak right after New Years, and by spring I'd be practically in the psych ward. Moving to the sunshine state did wonders for stabilizing my mood and increasing my motivation to get healthy. Too many people want the easy way out when it comes to health: shakes, pills, creams, surgery, and fad diets. Believe me; nothing works better than a nice bone-rattling jog in the sunshine. After a strenuous run and a shower, I feel like a man with a plan.

## –Soul Enema- Step #2: Be Passionate about Life

There's a famous saying, "An idle mind is the devil's playground." The human mind is an extraordinary machine, yet it can also become your worst enemy. The brain is on a continuous quest to analyze every impulse, and contemplate infinite thought patterns. During the day we are so preoccupied with our hectic lives that we are able to ignore it, but at night when the lights go down and your head hits the pillow, let the battle begin. Trying to stop a racing mind at night can drive you insane; thoughts overwhelm, emotions heat up, questions arise, and it becomes a struggle to regain control.

Your brain is much like a computer attempting to crack an unbreakable code, like trying to unlock the secrets of the universe. That's why human beings are able to accomplish amazing things, because our minds never stop striving towards the unknown. The problem is the brain just doesn't know how to stop processing information, so when you want to relax it continues to analyze like a mad scientist. This is another reason that people drink and do drugs. It's a desperate attempt to silence their minds from self destructive thought patterns.

Even when you are sleeping, the mind is still hard at work creating outlandish dreams that leave you waking up completely befuddled. The restless mind is one of the main contributors to depression. To prevent this you must find positive things in your life in which to focus and channel your cerebral energy towards. You must be passionate about activities that give you intrinsic enjoyment and can allow you to stop thinking. This is why you always hear those stories on television about people with wacky or dangerous interests, like collecting bottle caps, sculpting out of garbage, ropeless rock climbing, or naked hang gliding. My passions tend to change with the seasons. Lately they have been running, traveling, and something that I've picked up quite recently, reading.

Until my late twenties I only read out of necessity and never for enjoyment. One day I was bouncing around a book store looking for guitar tablature, and I overheard people discussing the book *The Celestine Prophecy* by James Reddfield. On a whim I picked it up, read the first few pages, and was immediately captivated. This book opened me up to a world of intellectual thought that I never knew existed. I tore through it like a tray of fudge brownies and it inspired me to try and figure out who I was, and what the world was all about.

I took a night job at a Barnes and Noble bookstore and completely ensconced myself in literature. I talked to everyone who worked or hung out there, picked their brains, and wrote down as many authors and titles as I could. Being a slow reader this was no easy task. There were many books that weren't for me and others where I had to re-read the same pages several times to grasp. I just went along at my own pace and tried to really identify with the author's voice. The perfect remedy for a restless mind is a challenging book. Instead of flicking on the television before bed, I started reading biographies of inspiring people, self-help books, and tales of historical fiction. Not only did this help me fall asleep without the aid of drugs, but it also taught me a very valuable lesson …

### *Life Rule #17: Knowledge is power.*

It was during this time that I realized I wanted to become a reading teacher and show children that reading isn't a dreaded chore, but a way to bring your imagination to life. I enrolled back in college and received my masters degree in literacy instruction, in less than two years. It's amazing what you can accomplish with a sober mind and a sincere passion for succeeding. Everyday I see the positive results with my students from immigrant families. Some of which couldn't speak a word of English a few years ago, and are now enjoying some of the best-known children's literature. These are the ideals that I would like to pass on to you and your brother. Developing a love of reading will open up endless doors throughout your entire life, both physical and mental.

My next passion is traveling. There's nothing in the world that can teach you more than the experience of visiting new places. There's a whole planet out there to explore, and your hometown is but a mere speck of dust in comparison. I can't tell you how many people I went to high school with who still live in the same neighborhood they grew up in, and aside from the occasional weekend getaway believe the whole world is Long Island, New York. In many countries it's customary to take a few years off after college to travel the world, before settling in on a career.

My friend Doug and I traveled cross-country by car in the summer of 1999. For three months we trekked thousands of miles in a huge triangle across America. I learned more about the world and myself on that trip than I did in seventeen years of schooling. While school may be important, "the school of life" is education for the soul. Now I'm not claiming to be Lewis and Clark, discovering uncharted territory here. The places I have seen are frequented by millions of people a year, but until you set your own eyes on them you have no idea what true beauty is.

The first time I witnessed the Rocky Mountains and the great western plains, I felt like I had caught a glimpse of heaven. The views were spectacular; nothing but open land, blue skies, and picturesque scenery. I felt completely connected to nature for the first time. After riding mules down the awe-inspiring Grand Canyon, we ventured west through the desert, and discovered the nirvana that is California. Cali has a vibe that cannot be explained in words. It's a compilation of the people, the beaches, the weather, and the over-all laid-back attitude of the locals that is just utterly entrancing. As we ventured north on the breathtaking Pacific Coast Highway, it was soon apparent why many people feel that northern California should be a state of its own. The trees in this area are called Redwoods, and they are gigantic with some being as tall as a thirty-story building. It made me realize how insignificant I really was.

We then hit Idaho and camped in some of the most pristine forests in the country. Who knew this forgotten state was such a natural paradise? While driving through northern Montana we encountered Glacier National Park, 1.5 million acres of the most amazing landscape imaginable, and one of the last places in America where nature still rules. Animals I had only seen in zoos and on television were suddenly ten feet from our car. I could write an entire book on the enchantment that is America, but there simply aren't enough adjectives to do it justice. Someday you will see it with your own eyes and understand exactly what I mean.

Traveling is such a liberating experience; if done the right way with a compatible partner; it can become a defining moment in your life. Mommy did the whole European train thing with her friend Jess, and when she returned from her six-week expedition, she was a completely changed person. The debilitating shyness and insecurities of her past were finally put to rest and she felt reborn.

My last passion is something I mentioned in the drugs chapter: running. Again, after you get beyond the first few weeks of nausea and cramping, this activity can be the ultimate weapon against depression. There's this feeling that runners get called the "runner's high phenomenon," where endorphins flood your body and you begin floating on air. You feel no pain, your feet are no longer pounding the pavement, and you fall into a harmonious balance with the circadian rhythms of your body. After eight months of relentless running, I finally experienced a runner's high and I knew I'd never need drugs again.

I remember riding my bike as a child and wanting to keep up with the older kids so badly that I would push my body to extreme limits of human endurance. Like some hidden gear inside my soul, I would keep pumping the pedals as my leg muscles burned and lungs gasped for oxygen. As we get older does this gear get lost, or is it merely stored away? Any endurance junky will tell you that when every cell in your body is begging you to quit, yet you continue to press on, there is no greater personal triumph. While your body and mind are engrossed in a fierce battle for survival, suddenly that crappy job and endless debt mean nothing. It's just you against the road. I recently caught the interview of an eighty-four-year-old marathon runner on the news. When asked to explain his secret he simply stated, "Where most people give up, I'm just beginning." I guess he found his hidden gear?

There are so many things to be passionate about in this world. You'll never know what they are or how much they can change your life unless you go in search of them. My friend Luke discovered his life changing passion in something that no one ever thought was possible. He was always a strange guy, tall, lanky, quiet, and kind of awkward in public. One day he informed us that after only a few years of martial arts training, he wanted to try out for an Ultimate Fighting competition. Ultimate fighting is a barbaric sport in which boxing, martial arts, wrestling, and street brawling are all used concurrently during combat. Opponents are pit against each other in a fenced in octagon-shaped ring, until only one remains standing. However, unlike professional wrestling these guys are not acting. Although everyone told him that he'd get killed, he was fully determined on achieving this unbelievable goal.

To everyone's sheer amazement, not only did he excel in the sport, but he also landed a highly coveted spot on the cable television show, *The Ultimate Fighter.* After an astounding second-place finish in the tournament, he was signed to a professional fighting contract and is now known as Luke Cummo, "The Silent Assassin," inspiring thousands with each gutsy underdog victory. I think what we can all learn from this story is to never let anyone tell you that you can't. Can you even imagine becoming a thirty-five-year-old slouch someday, sitting around the house, watching mindless sitcoms, and eating potato chips? It is imperative that you get out there and discover what your passions are. If you do, you may never experience another gloomy day.

## –Soul Enema– Step #3: Spiritual Healing

Now that we've talked about healing the mind and body, let's discuss the last piece to the puzzle—healing the soul. There comes a point in everyone's life when you have to start accepting the past and begin to move on to the future. Most people have had turbulent childhoods, traumatic experiences, and possess painful memories. I don't think I know a single person who hasn't had rough patches in their life. The question being: how long do we remain slaves to our past? When is it time to let go and become who we are supposed to become?

The only two things that can heal you from psychological trauma are acceptance and forgiveness. Hating can be a full time job, one that can tear you apart and make you feel like the ugliest person alive. Getting hurt by someone either physically or mentally can be extremely painful. You may feel like vengeance is the only answer, but you couldn't be any further off the mark.

Hate is an emotion that I have been struggling with since I was nine years old. There were many times when just the thought of my mother would make me explode into a psychotic rage. I so wanted that woman to experience some of the suffering she had put me through. I looked everywhere for solace: alcohol, drugs, meaningless relationships, and therapy. But I was still lonely and living a hollow existence. I sought answers from family and friends on how to overcome my rage, and they all offered the same advice- forgive and forget. This notion seemed so foreign to me. On my best day, I couldn't imagine being able to achieve either one. I soon found the answers I was searching for in a place I never even thought to look: church.

I was never a super religious person; to be honest there were many times in life when I was a serious doubter. My main gripe was always: if there was a God how could he allow such tragedies and suffering in the world? Religion seemed much too rigid and difficult to understand, and the fact that the Bible was written by ordinary men made me distrustful of their intentions. Although I was always captivated by the story of Jesus Christ, the tale that is the basis for Christianity. At one of the Catholic schools I taught, the principal decided that the upper grades should go see the movie *The Passion of the Christ*. I was hesitant to see it at first, but I'm so glad I chose to chaperone.

I'm sure you know the story by now. Jesus believed that he was the son of God and that his mission was to save mankind from self-destruction. For these beliefs, he was horrifically tortured in a public forum. Amidst this tortuous onslaught, Jesus looked toward the heavens with blood pouring down his face and said, "Forgive them, Father, for they know not what they do." I quivered in my seat as I watched; here's this guy bleeding to death, beaten, whipped, and nailed to a cross, yet still he could not hate. This scene moved me to tears, not only for the graphic violence, but because it was the first time in my life that I realized what true forgiveness was.

People do horrible things in this world, no question. But is this because they are inherently bad, or because they are not strong enough to fight their evil impulses? My mother didn't sit down one day, pen in hand, and plan my abuse and eventual demise. She was simply overwhelmed by the struggles of life, driving obnoxious teenagers around on a yellow bus for twenty years, and raising two kids practically alone. All of her bottled up frustration needed a way to be released. How could I wish suffering on a weak person like this? It was something I could no longer do. I had to have pity on her because, she knew not what she did. These are the same words I think about every Sunday at church. While everyone else is reading their Bibles and fussing with their kids, I'm usually staring at the cross and thanking Jesus for teaching me to forgive.

A few months ago, a deranged man walked into an Amish schoolhouse in Pennsylvania, armed with a gun, and started randomly shooting innocent children. The parents of the murdered children completely forgave the killer and even attended his funeral. Although so difficult to comprehend, I was inspired by this story and even envious of the Amish people's simple and spiritual convictions.

Now I don't claim to be the holiest guy on the block; but I do believe in God, Jesus, and Heaven. Not because I have overwhelming scientific proof, just because it makes me feel secure knowing that something is watching over our family as we sleep at night. It also gives me great pleasure knowing that after we all die, there may be a place where we can be together again, but this time for eternity. You don't have to stand on the street corner with a wooden cross and a megaphone to be a believer. It really is a wonderful feeling when you can let go and have trust in something much bigger than you.

When Mommy was pregnant with you, doctors informed us that you might have a choroid plexus cyst in your brain. This is a chromosomal abnormality that can result in Down Syndrome and severe brain damage. It turned out to be a false alarm, but I never prayed more in my whole life than in the weeks before the final tests. When you were eleven months old, you swallowed a watch battery and Mommy and I completely freaked. I put the remaining battery in a glass of water, and watched in horror as greenish acid poured out of it. We prayed non-stop. Two days later I finally dug it out of your diaper with a pair of chop sticks and again was truly grateful to the man upstairs.

When you have nowhere else to turn, God is always there, that's why you need spirituality. Give me any non-believer and put their child in a hospital bed, and watch how quickly they convert. I would never tell you what to believe. Your mom and I were raised Catholic as were you. When you become an adult and have done your share of soul searching, I will respect whatever spiritual decisions you make. But always remember, whether it's Christianity, Buddhism, Islam, Judaism, Hinduism, or even Scientology, they all share the same essential values: love one another, have mercy on the weak, and forgive others. How could you ever go wrong with ideals like that?

## Controlling your Inner Voices

My cousin Josh has been living in a mental health facility suffering from schizophrenia for the last thirteen years. This is a mental disorder where you have split personalities, paranoid delusions, and constantly hear voices in your head. Although I was quite shocked when I found out he was going to be committed at twenty-two, I remember thinking, "Doesn't everyone have those symptoms to an extent?" I hear voices (most call them thoughts), feel paranoid, and sometimes feel like a completely different person, and I know many who would say the same exact thing. Does this mean that we all have traces of schizophrenia?

Maybe everyone does have those feelings, but while most of us choose to keep busy and ignore them, others give in and spend all day alone, obsessing and regretting until they eventually drive themselves crazy. I'm in no way saying that Josh and the millions of others diagnosed with this disorder aren't legitimately ill. I just can't help but wonder if these kinds of illnesses can be perpetuated psychosomatically? Regardless, why are our inner voices so impossible to control? Learning to control our thoughts and ignore these inner voices is a huge part of curing depression and healing your spirit.

There are methods of doing this very thing that have been successfully practiced for thousands of years around the world. Exercises that if done correctly can help you win back your mind. Meditation and yoga are two amazing ways to change your life and help you become the optimistic person that you always wanted to be. They were both derived from the same school of thought: clear your mind, get in tune with your body, and release your negative energy.

One of the songs I wrote for my band had a great opening verse:

> Oh the sun came up this morning,
> and it got me out of my bed.

> Millions of thoughts and worries
>     were running through my head.
> I went into my backyard,
>     and I laid down in the grass.
> Started thinking about the world,
>     and how it's goin' by so fast.

For me, morning has always been the most stressful part of the day. The moment my eyes pop open, my brain immediately begins racing through the many things I must do that day, deadlines, bills, appointments, work, phone calls, etc. By breakfast I'm already exhausted, and ready to crawl back into bed and die. This is the perfect time to do some stretching and clearing of the mind. Yoga and meditation can both give you the power to unlock your inner strength and establish balance. It takes months of practice before you can actually assume the difficult body positions and set the mind at ease, but if you stick with it and believe, it can have an incredible impact on your health and peace of mind.

Another great way to control inner voices is through writing. Whether it's a journal, diary, memoir, fictional tale, or true-life story, everyone should put pen to paper and just let it rip. Writing helps you interpret your thoughts and discover who you are. I never wrote anything longer than a paragraph until college. I hadn't the faintest clue how to even form a coherent sentence for most of my life. I knew that I had stuff going on in my brain, but how to get it on paper completely boggled my mind. Then I realized one day that writing my feelings, no matter what pathetic drivel it may be, really made a difference in my emotional stability.

Bruce Lee, the famous martial artist, once said that he wrote his negative thoughts on pieces of paper and then threw them into a fire, being rid of them forever. If you saw this guy fight, you'd believe every word he said.

## Life is Tough

It's not like you can defeat depression and be done with it forever like the chicken pox. This is a battle that people fight continuously for their whole lives. The only way to prevail is to be the complete opposite of everything that depression represents; be loving, forgiving, merciful, sympathetic, generous, and, most of all, optimistic. The world is full of pessimists. Everywhere you go you can just see the "life sucks" expressions on their faces. Then, before you know it, you look in a mirror one day and you've got the same face. It's as contagious as the Ebola virus. Pretty soon you're avoiding social gatherings, screening phone calls, screaming in traffic, and full of rage on lengthy grocery lines.

While researching for this book I was introduced to the compelling works of Elizabeth Wurtzle. She has written several books about depression, addiction, OCD (obsessive compulsive disorder), and troubled relationships, all from a firsthand perspective. After reading three of her books, I came to understand her work as a testimony to the unrelenting pain that comes with being a female: menstruation, asshole guys, feelings of inadequacy, sexual pressure, the list goes on and on. Elizabeth provides superb clarity into the hopeless mind of a young girl coming of age. Her words will help you understand that every minute you spend hating, brings you one minute closer to dying a miserable person.

So the next time you feel yourself getting aggravated and overwhelmed, just take a few deep breaths, count backwards from ten, and try to laugh at something. Whether it's at a cute baby in a store or a slothy guy picking his nose in the car next to you, laugh. Depression is a part of life, but if given the proper tools it can be kept at bay. Although the Soul Enema may be difficult to abide by, I'm living proof that it can work miracles.

* Rodale, J. I. 1949. *The Healthy Hunzas*, (Emmaus, PA: Rodale Press).

# CHAPTER 7:
# THE THREE KEYS
# TO HAPPINESS

As I write these words, countless human lives are being senselessly taken in the country of Iraq. What began as a brief invasion to free an impoverished country from an oppressive regime, has now become an incomprehensible bloodbath spanning over four years. Our country has become divided, and there is a general distrust in the air that it is reminiscent of the Vietnam era. While the U.S. government pledges to be out for the benefit of the Iraqi citizens, and remains determined to establish democracy in this chaotic country, Americans simply want their loved ones back. With the scores of oppressed nations in the world, it is preposterous for me to believe that this is still our goal. It is the suspicion of many that we continue to send our young soldiers to the slaughter because of one thing and one thing only: the overabundance of "black gold" that flows beneath this country's desert landscape, also known as oil.

One of my childhood neighbors has been serving his second tour in Iraq for the last nine months. We email each other regularly, and with each heartbreaking letter I can sense that he is beginning to lose his will to live. Every day, soldiers are gunned down by attacking insurgent forces and blown to pieces by suicide bombers. Unlike wars in the past where the soldiers were fired up, patriotic, and focused on victory, these troops have no idea what they are fighting for and just want to make it home alive.

With death looming around every corner, Ronnie wonders if he'll ever see his wife and twin daughters again. In one letter in particular, he told me that the only things that get him and his fellow soldiers through the agony of each day are: the friendships they have forged with each other, thoughts of loving family members, and listening to tunes on their iPods.

These words spoke to me. Here are these soldiers, most of them practically kids who are scared to death, and they aren't even the slightest bit concerned with the things that the rest of America is fixated upon. Cars, houses, sex, technology, sports, careers, money, and fame all mean nothing. It's just family, friends, and music, for these are the three keys to happiness.

## Family

The first thing that Mommy said to me when I returned from Atlanta was, "Pete, you are my family and family doesn't give up on each other!" This concept was so foreign to me. For most of my life I was about as anti-family as one could be. As a teen, I barely ever went home except to sleep or take a shower. I avoided endless family functions, shunned the idea of marriage, and couldn't even imagine being a loving member of any family. I turned to my friends for family love at an early age; they were all I needed.

Every night I'd pass out on a different couch, wake up, and search out the next gathering I could take part in. Soon enough, I started to realize that no matter how much you believe you know someone, the majority of people are out for themselves, and even the best of friendships can sour. Whether it's an argument over money, a love interest, difference of opinion, or an un-kept secret, friendships end; people move on and start new lives, sometimes without notice. Without a family to love, you can look forward to a lifetime full of betrayal and abandonment.

It wasn't until I met your mom in college that I finally discovered the true meaning of the word family. Your mother comes from a big loving family of seven siblings, twenty-one nieces and nephews, and countless extended relatives. However, the story of how her family was born is an amazing testament to the will of the human spirit. Grandma and Pop were both married before, with three small children a piece. Grandma's first husband was stricken down at an early age with heart disease, and Pop's wife was tragically killed in an auto accident; leaving them both brokenhearted and a struggling single parent. Unwilling to give up on life, they would eventually cross paths at a Parents-without-Partners meeting and fall deeply in love. They were married within a year and had Mommy as their seventh child combined. Grandma always told her that she was the glue that made two separate families become one.

I will never forget my first Phelan family experience. It was Thanksgiving night about three months after we had met. I was invited over to Aunt Donna's for dessert, and more importantly to be examined by the family. Until then, all Thanksgiving meant to me was: get wasted the night before, sleep until noon, watch football alone in my room, come out for some turkey amid the usual dinner table bickering, and then retreat back to my dungeon. When I arrived this night, I was quite taken back. There were about thirty people crammed into a tiny two-bedroom cottage, little kids climbing the walls, and adults telling dirty jokes and fondly reminiscing the past. You could tell that everyone was totally enjoying the moment and relishing each other's company. I can't remember ever feeling so out of place. I didn't know how to act or even where to look.

As the night progressed, I loosened up a bit. They didn't grill me with questions or make me feel uncomfortable in the slightest, but rather treated me like one of the clan. After a few slices of pie and a heated game of Pictionary, I left feeling in awe of the closeness I had just experienced; something I thought existed merely on television. As Mommy and I grew closer, I became even more enamored by her dedication to her family. She talked to them on the phone daily, and yearned to go home for visits on every long weekend. Whenever she spoke of her parents, a sparkle of loving adoration would appear in her eyes. I envied this bond so much that I would constantly mock her with names like, "Mama's girl" and "Daddy's little angel," and tell her to "Cut the cord already!" I began to imagine what my life could have been like with such endearing family values. Would I have still been such a selfish, pessimistic, and neurotic adolescent? Who knows?

Your family is the only constant source of love and stability you will ever have in this crazy world. Everyone needs a rock to cling to when the flood waters rise; without it you would wind up drifting into oblivion. Family is the key. While they can be as bothersome as a stiff tag in a T-shirt, you always know deep down that you have a group of people who would literally die for you. This is the one essential element that many human beings are lacking, and why so many of us are lost and depressed.

For years I was convinced that I had some serious mental illness, like portions of my brain weren't working properly. "Why can't I just be freakin' happy like everyone else? Why can't I like me?" In hindsight, it is apparent that all my years of loneliness and substance abuse were because I never had the stability of a loving family in my corner. I never knew my dad, my mom used me as a stress-relieving punching bag, and my sister despised me with such a passion, that when I was younger I thought my real name was "GET OUT!" This negativity skewed my vision of what a family could be. If you build a house on unstable ground, how long will it stand?

After being so blown away by Mommy's family, I decided to partake in a little sociological experiment. A quest if you will, to discover all there was to learn about loving families and what they had to offer. I had developed a theory and wanted to test it out. My hypothesis was that people with awesome personalities came from strong loving families. My plan was to seek out the most confident, self-assured, generous, optimistic, and friendliest people I could find and establish a friendship with them. Then, once I was a part of their life, I could conduct my study in a natural environment and gain unbiased results. Could other families be as closely knit as Mommy's? I needed more data to figure it out.

My first subject was my mentor during student teaching, an amazing woman named Dannie Thayer. After spending the first eight weeks with the bitchiest supervising teacher imaginable, I was terrified to show up for my second placement. I walked into the classroom extremely apprehensive, and was greeted by the most wonderful person I have ever had the pleasure of knowing. Dannie was a fourth grade teacher in a rural upstate New York town. She was a middle-aged mom with a tremendous heart and a smile that could melt a glacier. The mutual admiration was obvious and we became instant friends for life. Although our difference in age was awkward in the beginning, it quickly disappeared and after only a few weeks I was invited over for dinner with her family. And wouldn't you know, her husband Jim and four kids were just as warm and amazing as she was. They all displayed that same aura of optimism, and once again I was in awe of the chemistry the family shared.

As the weeks passed our friendship grew immensely, and for the first time in my life, I actually felt like I had a mom whom I adored. When the semester ended, we said our tearful goodbyes and I headed back to my regular life at college, dreaming for the first time of someday starting my own loving family. Dannie and I would keep in touch over the years; she flew down for my wedding, and we even visited her picturesque lakeside home many times when you were a baby. She is still one of my favorite people in the whole world.

My next test subject was a college friend named John Hogan. I could tell immediately after meeting this guy that he came from good stock. He possessed a golden heart and many other intangible qualities that I look for in people. He came into my life at a much needed time. I had just re-enrolled in college after flunking out when I was twenty-one. I was now twenty-five and much older than your average college kid. Most of my friends from home had drifted away, my college buddies had all graduated, and your mom and I had taken a break to assess our relationship. Needless to say, I was lonelier than ever. John was a neighbor in my building and after passing one day in the halls, he invited me to a party. This dude was just teeming with life and positive vibes, and from that night on we were inseparable buds.

It was on one of our college breaks that I had the pleasure of meeting his super-cool family. Like Mommy, he came from a large family of the warmest people imaginable. Mrs. Hogan, a saint of a woman made me feel like her seventh child and would eventually help me land my first teaching job. John would become one of the greatest friends I would ever know. Many a night we watched the sunrise over a twelve pack and talked about life, family, and our childhoods. He passed no judgment and only offered a silent ear to my sorrowful stories. I envied his confidence and optimistic attitude, just being around him could improve your foulest of moods. I wasn't the slightest bit shocked when he was recently promoted to principal of a school at twenty-nine years old. His parents must have been so proud of the life he had made for himself. I wanted to be proud of my kids like that someday, and hoped that in turn they'd be proud of me for how I raised them. I came to know John at a time when I was beginning to discover that there was more to life than the eternal buzz and having a hot girlfriend.

Even though the data I recorded from Mommy, John, and Dannie significantly supported my theory, I decided to dig deeper and continue my research. At this time I was a school teacher and in the company of sixth graders all day. They would be the perfect subjects to further my studies. I focused on the kids that really seemed to be confident, grounded, and happy. I would ask them personal questions about their home life: What they did on weekends? Were their parents still married? Did they fight a lot? And, did they ever get screamed at or hit at home? I did realize that I was stepping over ethical boundaries, but I justified my prying by declaring it all in the name of science.

When the parents of these selected students would come in for teacher meetings, I would really get a good feel for who they were. What I soon found was that all of these kids had dynamite parents. This is why their kids were growing up so positive and grounded.

My theory was valid as far as I was concerned; a strong loving family does indeed lead to optimistic and emotionally stable individuals. All families have issues, hold grudges, and say things they don't mean, but the bottom line is they possess unconditional love. This is a true key to happiness. You have no need to look any further my dear, what you seek is right down the hall.

## Friends

November 3, 1990, was a brisk Saturday on Long Island. My parents were on a Caribbean cruise celebrating their twenty-fifth anniversary, and I was left under the supervision of my darling sister. My buddy Steve and I conjured up a devious plan to throw the biggest house party my town had ever seen. As soon as my sister left for work in the morning we were on the phone ordering kegs, finding a DJ, and hiring some muscle to work the gate. Word was on the street and spreading fast.

Our only obstacle was a rather dismal weather forecast of unseasonably frigid nighttime temperatures. As I stood in my backyard thinking of ways to make my party unforgettable, I came up with a magnificent idea: "Dude, how about a bonfire in the sand pit where my pool used to be?" Steve's eyes lit up like light bulbs and he began dialing the phone before I had even finished the sentence. In less than an hour, someone with a pickup truck filled with wooden palates backed into my yard. As the wood pile reached ten feet high, the DJ began setting up his equipment, and the many kegs rolled in on hand trucks; it became a harsh reality that this party was definitely going down. I just so happened to go to one of the biggest high schools in the country.

Sachem High School had over a thousand kids in each grade, and by eight o'clock, almost all of them were at my house.

Music pumped from the speakers of DJ Tommy, Miller Light flowed continuously, and my back patio resembled a scene from the 1970s disco era. Just after ten, the temperature started to plummet into the low thirties. I stood at the edge of the sandpit pondering my next move. Hordes of kids were egging me on, fascinated by the excitement of what this fire could do. At that moment, all my apprehension and childhood pain festered up inside and made me dry heave. In one swift action, I dumped some kerosene on the pile, threw in a lit match, and watched my creation come to life. The towering inferno that would ensue would blow everybody's mind, and soon bring me to the heights of superstardom amongst my peers. The fire raged and the backyard climate was suddenly like that of a summer's night. Jackets were shed and hundreds of drunken teens danced around the blaze in a somewhat tribal fashion.

The police raided the yard just before midnight and everyone frantically scattered to the exits. As the last teenagers stumbled to their cars and the embers smoldered out in the fire pit, I tried to comprehend the damage to my house and my extremely grim future. The aftermath wasn't pretty. My dad's canoe was stolen, two sections of fence were destroyed from a brief fight, my mom's precious gardens were trampled, and the houses' vinyl siding was stained in soot. Fortunately for me, the responding police officer was one of my friend's fathers and I got off with a stern warning. But that would be nothing compared to the fury I would face when my parents returned from their vacation. The resulting mayhem culminated with a full-out fist fight between my father and I on the front lawn, for all to see.

I could have burned my parent's house to the ground that night, but I didn't care because the fame I achieved from this event was monumental. My group of four friends had now become twenty, and my phone started ringing off the hook. My dream had finally come true; suddenly people knew my name and I was somebody, or so I thought. Girls were beginning to like me and I now had a posse of cool guys to hang out with. Every weekend we hit the party circuit, and I always got the same emphatic reaction from the crowd, "Dude, that party was killer!"

After a few months of celebrity status, I started to realize that these people didn't really know me, nor did they care a thing about me. They stabbed me in the back, spread rumors about me, mimicked my stutter, hit on my girlfriends, and constantly pressured me into doing things that I knew were wrong. They were merely drinking buddies. When I broke my back in an accident one winter, not one of them came to visit me in the hospital. I actually missed the days when my two nerdy friends and I would go to the mall and gawk at girls that wouldn't even spit on us. The girls I was now dating were so superficial, and these new friends I so cherished would eventually play a key role in my decision to move to Florida. I'm rambling here; what I really want to tell you about is the wonders of true friendship, and the many pitfalls of meaningless popularity.

The year you were born, I was teaching in an upscale community on the eastern end of Long Island. I had such a great group of kids this year, who were all from good homes and very sweet. One kid in particular will forever stand out in my mind as the coolest; her name was Stephanie Harkin. This girl never had a mean thing to say about anyone and was so kind, confident, and sincere. Out of jealousy, the other girls would constantly try to put her down and intimidate her, but it never worked. She just ignored it and always kept smiling. She would ask about you all the time when you were born, and even came to see you in the hospital.

On the last day of school, I told her that I hoped my Lilly grew up to be just like her someday. She cried, gave me a big hug, and an "I put the cool in school" T-shirt. I taught Steph how to multiply fractions that year. However, she taught me that a young girl can be good-spirited and genuinely kind to all, without giving in to cliques and the pressures to fit in. Thanks to my compassionate friend, I learned that for girls there are five laws of friendship:

### Friendship Law #1: Always be honest and trustworthy.

Nobody likes a liar; it's a horrible way to go through life. I've been a liar and I've hated myself for it. Sometimes I lied for the fun of it or to impress girls, but mostly because I was a self-centered drug addict, and I created a sad reputation for myself as a bullshit con-artist. I guess it spilled over from my childhood. My parents never let me do anything as a kid, so I had to constantly lie to them to get my way. As I grew, it became a disgusting habit that I would swear to resolve every New Years. I was the worst kind of liar, too; the one who does it so often that he starts believing his own stories. I knew I had gone off the deep end when lies began spewing from my mouth without a moment's thought, and I would cringe the moment they left my lips.

I took baby steps to try and improve myself and it became easier after a while. Although it's still a daily battle to refrain from lying, this is a fight I won't give up on. Being honest is so important to your self-image and to those who love you. Do you want to constantly be afraid that people will figure out your lies, have to stress over remembering all of your stories, and worry about to whom you told what? It's a dreadful existence. Be straight with your friends and only associate with those who are straight with you.

Being trustworthy can be the one difference between being a good person and a complete loser. This one thing will be the true test of what kind of friend you are and how loyal you can stay. When the juiciest of secrets is revealed to you, or when your best friend's boyfriend secretly makes a move on you, what will you do? Will you opt for the instant gratification and betray the trust of a loved one, or will you bite your lip and remember what friendship means?

There are few things in my life that I cherish more than the twenty-eight-year friendship I have with my buddy Drew. We met on the first day of kindergarten and have been like brothers ever since. Although we've drifted apart and had our battles over the years, trust and loyalty has always been the basis for our relationship. There were many nights when I ran to his house after a beating and cried on his shoulder, or listened to the saddening stories of his agonizing battle with Crohn's disease. This special bond persevered to the moment when he stood next to me as the best man at my wedding. To this day whenever something wonderful happens in my life, Drew is always the first number I dial.

Another important aspect of being a trustworthy friend is to beware of the gossip bug. Whenever you open your mouth and spread rumors about others, it will always come back to bite you in the ass. I have lost many friends and even been beat up a few times over spreading rumors. Although challenging for boys, this is especially difficult for girls because they just love to talk about their peers. But remember, nothing is just between you and whoever, it always gets passed on.

One of my students recently got her period through her white pants and nobody realized. Later, I intercepted a note written by her best friend informing others of this devastating experience. It breaks my heart that kids can get such satisfaction from the pain of others. It's just human nature I guess; we somehow feel better about ourselves when others suffer. If your life suddenly becomes weighed down with rumors and vicious gossip, I'd suggest you find a new group of friends or pretty soon it will be your head on the chopping block.

## Friendship Law #2: Don't judge your friends by their looks.

Every year in my classes, I watch in amazement as the girls establish the social hierarchy according to looks. The pretty ones join forces, alienate all the late bloomers, and eventually leave them in the dust. They parade around singing all these "Best Friends 4 Eva" songs, and then by Christmas they're at each other's throats, bickering, spreading rumors, and stealing each other's boyfriends. From what I've experienced, great looking girls tend to score rather high on the bitch-meter. It's something called the "hot chick syndrome" and it usually starts to show up during puberty. Pretty girls get treated like princesses everywhere they go; this in turn causes them to develop a much skewed perception of the world. They begin to believe that no one is as important as they are and the whole world revolves around them; in other words, Bitch City! I've known so many of these girls in my life and they are awful people to be around. Yet, being friends with them can be extremely tempting.

I would assume the lure of belonging to the "hot chick clique" is that it's kind of like getting a taste of the celebrity lifestyle. It sounds so enticing: hanging out with the beautiful people, the best parties, expensive clothes, new cars, and the hottest guys. However, after a while the girls start to reveal their superficial selves and it becomes an unbearable nightmare. You begin to see yourself as a worthless pawn at the mercy of your alpha-female, living in constant fear of expulsion from the group. While I've never personally experienced such a group dynamic, the enlightening book *Queen Bees and Wannabes*, by Rosalind Wiseman, opened my eyes to the many intricacies of the adolescent pecking order. It's a must read for every young lady.

When scouting out a prospective friend, you want a heart of gold rather than a million dollar smile. Someone who will stand by you for years, not someone who will judge you, betray you, and spread your deepest secrets without care. Respect people for who they are on the inside and what they stand for, not by their looks or what shoes they wear. If you do, you could discover wondrous friendships that can last your entire life.

## Friendship Law #3: Shut up, and listen.

It's amazing how many people suffer from a disease called, "diarrhea of the mouth." These people are so obsessed with the sound of their own voices that they never know when to shut up. You hear them blabbering at movie theatres, concerts, restaurants, and libraries. They are just physically incapable of keeping their gigantic pie holes closed, even for a moment. If you really aspire to be a good friend, you have to learn how to shut up and listen to others. Now I'm not talking about just being quiet and waiting for your turn to talk, I mean really listening with your ears and heart. A true friend listens intently to the speaker's words, and then later offers thoughtful analysis and encouraging advice. This simple act can mean more to people than anything else in the world.

Most of us aren't even looking for advice, we just want to vent frustrations and get worries off our chest without the fear of harsh criticism. Why do you think millions of Americans are in therapy these days? Because they are so desperate to be listened to by a non-judgmental person, that they are willing to pay thousands of dollars for it. This is something I've experienced many times in my life as a stutterer. I've been ignored, cut off, laughed at, and had my sentences finished every day since the fourth grade. However, it has taught me the importance of being a first-class listener. This is something I take very seriously, and I believe it's one of the qualities that make me a caring friend, husband, teacher, and dad.

This trait is also one of the reasons I had many platonic and romantic girlfriends when I was growing up, because there are few things girls love more than a guy they can really talk to. In fact, much of the information in this book was attained from thousands of conversations with females over the years. I learned at a young age that listening to people makes them feel comfortable and trusting of your opinion. So, next time you're around an airhead teenage girl who utters something comparable to, "Oh my God, like, me, me, me, me ...," remember what I wrote and take notice to what a ditz she is.

## Friendship Law #4: Avoid pessimistic energy suckers.

I mentioned a book earlier called *The Celestine Prophecy*. It's a fictional tale about nine insights to life written by an ancient civilization, which are discovered deep in the jungles of Peru. One of these insights has to do with "energy takers" and "energy givers." The givers are people in your life that are positive, happy, secure, encouraging, and generous; the kinds of people that make you feel good just to be around. While the takers are the complete antithesis: negative, miserable, and insecure. These people can suck every ounce of energy out of you and leave you depressed after a mere two minute conversation.

The bizarre thing about these energy takers is that they aren't always assholes. Sometimes they can be extremely kind at first, gaining your friendship, and then when you're hooked, they unleash a tsunami of negativity into your world. I must admit though, this is one of the huge downsides of being a great listener. Suddenly you become everyone's psychologist and begin to lose sleep over their problems. One of the many reasons that we moved to Florida had to do with energy takers, and my realization that I had way too much negativity in my life. My friends with their drug/alcohol problems, money issues, and troubled relationships were beginning to invade my every thought. It got to a point where I couldn't even answer my phone anymore, nervous about who it might be and what misery they would share.

When first meeting someone, be overly skeptical, because once they are inside your comfort zone they can become like an inoperable cancer. Allow new relationships to develop slowly; let people prove to you that they are worthy of your trust. And I don't mean for a few weeks either, I'm talking several months to years of exhibiting a kind and unselfish attitude. You will seriously regret it if you jump into a relationship with someone, and then discover that they are a soul-sucking freak, calling at all hours begging you to fix them. Choosing your friends can be almost as difficult as choosing a boyfriend. It should be easy to hang out with them, not complicated and chaotic. If things always seem to fall apart and get negative when they are around, you should get away now.

## Friendship Law #5: Become an unselfish giver.

I mentioned Ray in the peer pressure section; he was my best friend from age nine until about fourteen years old. His grandmother lived on my street, and he would stay over her house all the time because his single mom worked nights as a waitress. It became apparent to me early on that Ray was hiding something about his life. He never invited me over his house, wouldn't tell me where it was, and would change the subject whenever it was brought up.

After three years of friendship, he finally invited me over for a birthday sleepover, and upon arrival I realized just what Ray was hiding. He lived in a filthy one-bedroom apartment that reeked of cat urine and was crawling with carpenter ants. When I suggested that we play in his room, he sheepishly pointed to a stained pullout sofa in the living room with a few random toys scattered about. There were five cats lounging on the furniture, endless piles of dirty dishes and laundry, and when I opened the fridge there was no cake, just a lone bottle of ketchup.

His wacky mom slept through most of the night, and the more time I spent at Ray's, I realized that's all she did. The only time she stumbled out of her bedroom was to give him money for his nightly 7-Eleven run, to sustain his healthy diet of soda, cookies, and potato chips. Until then, I never even knew that people lived like this. My childhood was rough, but I always had food, clothes, and a clean home to live in. Now I knew exactly why he was overweight and wore the same clothes to school every day.

It was an immense eye-opener for me, and when I left the following morning I was overwhelmed with sympathy for my neglected companion. You never know what someone is suffering through until you see it with your own eyes. I began to invite Ray over for meals, paid for him when we did stuff, and offered my time whenever he needed me. Not only did being kind toward him brighten up his dismal life, but it also made me feel great about myself as a person. I only wish I would have been stronger to continue throughout high school. If you are ever lucky enough to have someone like Ray in your life, be truly giving of yourself and your things, for it will mean more to them than you could ever know.

I find it strange how social lives can come full circle with age. I had four good friends when I was a geeky thirteen-year-old, dozens of "whatever" friends in my late teens/twenties, and now I'm back to four in my thirties. But these four people are remarkable human beings, who constantly lift me up and have proven time and again that I matter to them. Friendship is definitely an area where quality is much more important than quantity.

Out of all the hell that is adolescence, one of its greatest joys is simply relishing in the silliness of your best friends. Next time you're with them and laughing so hard that your cheeks are aching and you cannot breathe, stop and take notice to the unforgettable memories that you are creating. Friendship can be almost as magical as a first love; it is without doubt a true secret to happiness.

## Music

The last key to happiness is something that you hear quietly in the background of your everyday: music. There was a time in my life when this was all that mattered. It was the only thing I knew that was 100 percent positive and could never hurt me. I was either playing music, writing music, listening to music, or highly anticipating a future tour with one of my favorite bands. Music is such an abstract concept that words cannot even fully describe it, kind of like trying to explain a rainbow to a blind person. In essence it's just a whole bunch of noise, but organized and with a purpose. The aspect that makes music so magical is how it is instinctually tied to human emotions. When you were about seven months old, we'd sit you in front of the stereo and turn on the tunes. As soon as the first notes permeated the air, a huge gummy grin would appear on your face, and you'd shake your diaper covered booty in perfect time. The natural affect it had on your mood was amazing. Some things just aren't learned, they are inborn.

Whether it's rock, classical, techno, blues, rap, country, trance, jazz, or whatever the new sound is when you read this, they all have one special thing in common: soul. The passion in the songs comes directly from the musician's soul, and gets transferred into the soul of the listener. Music is a universal language that all human beings can utilize to share their personal understandings of the world we live in. Now don't get me wrong, there's a ton of crap out there too, such as music made for the purpose of monetary gain and superficial fame. However, there is a distinct method of differentiating between the good, the bad, and the ugly; it's called "the chills factor."

When you are listening to music and the hair on the back of your neck stands on end, and suddenly the whole world stops for the song, you have just experienced the magic of which I speak. This is a moment that will be forever etched in your subconscience. One day you'll be driving around in your car and that same song will come on the radio. You will suddenly be transported back in time, and those same emotions will come flooding back as intensely as the first time you heard it. All of the different memories of your life, maybe a sleepover, an exboyfriend, a school dance, a first kiss, a pet, a vacation, a best friend, or a lost loved one, will be attached to certain songs or bands that helped shape those experiences. It is sort of like a movie soundtrack to your own life.

As you age, your musical tastes will change with the tides, constantly evolving with each life experience. It wasn't too long ago, that your dorky dad was a free-styling, Adidas-wearing, "gangsta rap" fan, if you can imagine that. Just embrace it all, Lilly; be open to every song that you may encounter. Whether it's from a homeless street performer with an out-of-tune guitar, or a Julliard trained pianist at Carnegie Hall, if it's from the soul, you'll know and you'll never forget it.

## The Sounds that Time Will Never Forget

Of the countless musicians to come along in the last half century, there have been but a few that have completely revolutionized the concept of what music is and what it could become. These true innovators of sound will never become a mere footnote in some musical anthology. They will rather be eternally regarded for their amazing achievements, and undying devotion to the art of organized noise. I can almost guarantee that hundreds of years from now, people will be sitting around somewhere being profoundly enlightened by the intricate workings of Lennon, Hendrix, and Dylan; much the same way modern-day historians have immortalized the likes of Socrates, Mozart, and Nietzsche.

Since primitive man first banged a hollow log with a rock, enjoyed the reverberation it made, and repeated the process, people have been producing the most mind-blowing sonic creations ever assembled. To scour the hundreds of years of musical geniuses like Beethoven, Bach, and Debussy would be pointless. So I am just going to stick to the last five decades, for these are the years when music became more than a past time and more like a religion. I'm going to try and give you a brief description of some of the most inspiring musicians to ever comprise a tune. These people have not only defined a certain genre, but they have all changed the way people listened to music. I do realize that showing appreciation for your dad's music is taboo amongst people your age, but you must trust me on this one. Listening to these artists will change your life.

## –The Beatles

Hands down, this group of musicians will forever be regarded as the greatest band to ever grace our world. This is not only my opinion, but an undisputable fact that no one in their right mind would debate. The words, brilliant, genius, and prolific, don't even begin to pay proper homage to any of the band's four members, nor to their phenomenal catalogue of songs. What began as a three-chord bar band from Liverpool, England, over fifteen years would evolve into a hit writing juggernaut that would completely change the face of popular music.

Paul McCartney and John Lennon are perhaps the greatest song writing team to ever put pen to paper. Together with Ringo Starr and George Harrison, they would conjure up songs that would speak to the world like no band had before. The Beatles single handedly revolutionized the possibilities of sonic engineering, and gave birth to studio techniques that people still utilize to this day. After breaking up in the early 1970s over creative differences, each band member would enjoy varying success as a solo artist, but it is their collaborative efforts that will always remain relevant in our society. One simply cannot go through life without discovering this band. Their songs will transform you and slice into your soul. If not for the infamous Fab Four, popular music as we know it would not exist.

Must hear album: *Sgt. Pepper's Lonely Hearts Club Band*
Song: "A Day in the Life"

## –Jimi Hendrix

Before Jimi Hendrix came onto the scene in the mid 1960s, the guitar was merely an instrument used to supply a rhythm track in which to lay vocals over. After Hendrix, six strings would never be looked at the same way again. A masterful left-handed blues guitarist as a teenager, Jimi grew up in Seattle, Washington, backing the great rock-and-roll pioneer Little Richard. It wasn't until his journey across the Atlantic to the United Kingdom, that he became an international phenomenon. Upon arriving back in America after a few years, he was nothing short of a guitar god. His blistering speed, bone-chilling tone, and incendiary use of feedback left thousands of awestruck fans standing mouth agape after every performance. To hear a Hendrix solo is to experience aural utopia; it is something not of this world and decades ahead of it's time. These are sounds so primal and mysterious, that even at this very moment someone is lying in bed with headphones on discovering their magical effects. As the Beatles were the greatest band to record sound, Hendrix is by far the greatest human being to ever lay hands upon a guitar.

Must hear album: *Axis: Bold as Love*
Song: "Bold as Love"

## –Bob Dylan and Joni Mitchell

Mentioning Bob and Joni together is nothing short of sacrilege. However, I feel that these two musical icons share the same vision, the same spirit, and have very similar messages to convey. At a time when the youth of America wanted to break free from society's norms and governmental injustice, these two people offered insight and guidance with their music. Their songs possess messages of biblical proportions; lyrics that transcend time, voices so visceral they can induce trancelike states, and stories with such depth they could lead you on a journey into spiritual discovery. Listening to the intricate melodic stylings of these two amazing artists will make you view the world in a whole new way.

Must hear albums:

Bob Dylan: *The Free Wheelin' Bob Dylan*
Song: "A Hard Rain's a-Gonna Fall"

Joni Mitchel: *Blue*
Song: "River"

## –Bob Marley

I knew of Bob Marley as a kid and appreciated his music, but it wasn't until I went away to college that I realized what an unbelievable musician he was, and how many people truly adored him. Almost every room in my dormitory had posters of Bob decorating the walls, and his music blaring throughout the hallways. At first, I thought everyone loved him because he was a huge advocate for marijuana use. But I would soon discover that Marley's music spoke deeply to people of every race, creed, and religion throughout the world. Born into poverty on the island of Jamaica, Robert Nesta Marley would go on to define the genre of reggae music, and circle the globe sharing his inspirational songs. To hear Marley's voice and tender guitar playing is to hear freedom incarnate. After a soccer injury he developed cancer in his big toe, and being that amputation was against his Rastafarian beliefs, he chose to try to heal himself with natural methods. The cancer spread to the rest of his body and he passed away at the youthful age of thirty-six. I read that his last words to his son before dying were, "Money can't buy life." Nothing epitomizes Bob more than that statement. He stood for freedom, sang for truth, and died for a cause.

Must hear album: *Legend*
Song: "Redemption Song"

## –B.B. King

The undisputed king of the blues, born the son of sharecroppers in Itta Bena, Mississippi, Riley B. King was destined for greatness. I once heard an interview where he spoke of his disadvantaged childhood. His musical career began by plucking a wire tied to a nail on the porch of his parent's one-room shack. As a young man, B.B. combined the slave spiritual songs of his ancestors with musical instrumentation, and created "the blues" as a genre of its own. Together with his beloved guitar "Lucille," he's been touring hundreds of nights a year for the last sixty years. I was lucky enough to see him live once and I could not believe the fire that this seventy-two-year-old man possessed, and his innate ability to have people of all races singing together like family. And to this day I've never heard a guitar cry with such a deep mournful wail, and I don't think I ever will again. While today's musicians can make millions of sounds with all their digital effects and synthesizers, when B.B. and Lucille do it, it's just flesh, wood, steel, and tons of soul.

Must hear album: *Live at the Apollo*
Song: "The Thrill is Gone"

## –Miles Davis and John Coltrane

What exactly is jazz? Got me; I don't think anyone can fully answer that question. The only musical genre to have American origins, jazz was born out of the blues, and soon evolved into free-form expression. Many artists would come to define jazz through their uncanny ability to improvise and break down the barriers of musical possibility. Two of the most prominent jazz musicians who shattered the molds were Miles Davis and John Coltrane. Hearing Miles's trumpet, or Coltrane's sax is like stepping into an alternate dimension of weirdness, yet its magnitude is impossible to deny. Jazz is thought-provoking music that can even be scary at times, but it is definitely one of life's hidden treasures. If you ever want to be inspired to create, listen to these guys and you'll want to better the world. Anyone who loves improvised music has these two brilliant men to thank.

Must hear albums:

Miles Davis: *Bitches Brew*
Song: "Bitches Brew"

John Coltrane: *Blue Train*
Song: "Blue Train"

## –Stevie Wonder

The grandmaster of funk, from out of the gospel churches of Detroit, Michigan; a thirteen-year-old true musical prodigy was discovered. Born blind, Stevie embraced music at four years old and would soon develop one of the most amazing singing voices, and rhythmic styles that the world has ever known. He was signed to a professional recording contract as a teenager, and went on to create some of the most endearing songs ever. I'll never forget the first time I heard the tune "Superstitious" and was left speechless by the sound. I would later find out that sound was a clavinet, and as I began to pour through his extensive catalogue, I felt like I had stumbled upon an unknown fortune. Stevie Wonder was my musical coming of age, when music became about listening and nothing more.

Must hear album: *Talking Book*
Song: "Superstitious"

## –Led Zeppelin and Black Sabbath

While not my cup of tea, I cannot in clear conscience list genre-defining musicians, without mentioning the true pioneers of the hard rock or "metal" sound. These two bands ended the "peace and love" generation of the 1960s. Their distorted guitars, ear shattering drum beats, and medieval-like lyrics, would bring upon a musical revolution. Suddenly, the "flower power" songs of love and friendship were being replaced by the head banging sounds of death and black magic. Ozzy Osbourne, Tony Iommi, Robert Plant, and Jimmy Page, along with their band mates, brought their traveling circuses of mayhem and rebellion to endless nations full of troubled youths. It is very rare to find a musician these days who doesn't have these two bands listed as influences. Next time you want to rage against the world, pop on these guys, throw your horns in the air, and get ready to rock.

Must hear albums:

Led Zeppelin: *Houses of the Holy*
Song: "Over the Hills and Far Away"

Black Sabbath: *Paranoid*
Song: "War Pigs"

## –Public Enemy and N.W.A.

If hip-hop is your thing, then you should definitely pay proper respects to the two groups who put rap on the map: Public Enemy and N.W.A. (Niggaz with Attitude). In the early 1980s, a new sound burst onto the scene, one so fresh and angst-ridden that teenagers became completely captivated by its raw power. While from opposite American coasts, P.E. and N.W.A. contained the same messages of urban rebellion and resisting "the powers that be" in their music. With the prolific minds of Chuck D, Flavor Flav, Ice Cube, Eazy E, and Dr. Dre manning the microphones, people of all races took notice to this provocative new groove, and donned Raider's hats in salute. Although these men may not have invented the street sound, they without a doubt legitimized their genre and made it a tour de force in the music industry. Today, hip-hop is king among the younger generation. However, it would not have the same mass appeal or cutting-edge style if not for the groundbreaking methods of these lyrical masterminds. The other day one of my Guatemalan students who barely speaks English came into class and said, "Yo, what up ma nizzle!" to a student of a similar background. If that isn't proof of hip-hop's tremendous cultural significance, then I don't know what is?

Must hear albums:

Public Enemy: *Fear of a Black Planet*
Song: "Fight the Power"

N.W.A. - *Straight Outta Compton*
Song: "Straight Outta Compton"

# –Nirvana

During the 1980s, music took a drastic turn for the worst. Bands were dressing up in women's clothing, slathering on makeup, and performing the most uninspiring songs ever to be written. The entire music industry seemed to become enthralled by this absurd movement of spandex pants, eyeliner, and hairspray. While some of these musicians possessed genuine talent, they chose to sell out and give into the image first MTV generation. This would all change in the early 1990s with a new brand of musicians from the Pacific Northwest. Leading the uprising was a band named Nirvana, with its genius front man Kurt Cobain. With one strum of his distorted Fender Stratocaster, Kurt and his band mates gave birth to the "grunge sound," completely extinguished the dim glow of the hair bands, and sent them running for the hills. Cobain's tragic suicide would stun the world and become a crushing blow to music lovers of all ages. But thanks to Nirvana, "balls-to-the-wall" rock and roll was back again in full force.

Must hear album: *Nevermind*
Song: "Smells like Teen Spirit"

## –The Grateful Dead

Daddy's all-time favorite band! If you asked any group of people who knew of "The Dead" what they thought of them, most of them would say that they were a group of drugged-upped hippies from the 1960s, with tripped-out freaky fans who followed them all over the country. Hell, I would have even said that before I had the pleasure of catching them live in the early 90s. On a crisp spring day in 1992, a friend of mine asked if I wanted to go to a concert at the Nassau Coliseum. Always being up for anything, I jumped at the opportunity without even inquiring about who was performing. Upon hearing that the band was a bunch of fifty-year-old leftovers from "The Summer of Love," I started regretting ruining my Friday night with this poor choice of entertainment.

I tried to remain positive, however, regardless of the crappy music I was about to hear. When we pulled into the parking lot, I was dumbfounded. It felt like I had stepped back in time to a parallel universe full of people who had dropped out of society to live a simpler life. These people were freaks in the fullest sense of the word. They wore crazy clothes, had wild hair styles, multiple tattoos, piercings, and a complete disregard for modern style. I felt like an anthropologist who had just discovered a lost race of people isolated from the rest of the world.

We stumbled inside the arena as the house lights were dimming to ear shattering screams and a party resembling New Years Eve in Times Square. The enthusiasm of the crowd reached fever pitch as the band took the stage, and just like I imagined, a bunch of old men appeared, led by this one fat dude with a heap of white hair and a scraggly beard to match. The band kicked into their first number, and as that first guitar riff hit the air, my life as I knew it would never be the same. Each song they played was more delightful and inspiring than the next. They jammed and sang their aging hearts out, and the twenty thousand fans cheered and rhythmically undulated in a meditative state. The collaborative excitement was palpable, and it was at this moment that I realized music was so much more than I ever dreamed it could be.

Before the Grateful Dead, there were bands that would play upbeat rock and roll songs, and the crowds would lose their minds and jump around like maniacs. The Dead, however, took that simple formula and brought it to a whole new level, creating a sound so experimental and fresh that people would become captivated body and soul. They single handedly invented the notion of the extended jam, sometimes turning a four minute tune into a forty-five minute journey into the depths of psychedelia. The mad scientist behind all of this was a nine fingered guitar virtuoso named Jerry Garcia. Together with Bob Weir, Phil Lesh, Ron "Pigpen" McKernan, and Bill Kreutzman, they would go on to give birth to a generation of "tree-hugging hippies" and invent the genre known as psychedelic rock.

Today there are hundreds of bands of this nature, bringing jams and positive vibes to legions of fans around the world, who prefer to dance and rejoice, rather than sit and listen at a concert. After Jerry's untimely death in 1995, millions of "Deadheads" mourned the loss of a true musical innovator, and a lifestyle that had endured for almost forty years. Nevertheless, the Dead's legacy will forever live on in the live recordings of their approximately three thousand concerts, hopefully bringing smiles to the faces of people who have yet to discover this amazing music.

Must hear album: *Without a Net*
Song: "Eyes of the World"

## *Life Rule #18: Never judge a book by its cover, for that very book may change your life.*

### Becoming a Musician

Some of my earliest memories are of being in my crib, enticed by the infectious grooves and spine-tingling melodies of Stevie Wonder, Otis Redding, and Marvin Gaye. My family's musical taste was very eclectic, so I was exposed to a wide range of sounds. My dad loved Fifties doo-wop, my mother fancied Motown classics, and my sister was into pop music. I just soaked in every last bit like a sponge, listening intently to every note, vocal nuance, and lyric to exit the speakers. The seed was planted early but never watered. I was never encouraged to pursue music, but even more so I wasn't strong enough to face the ridicule at school. I joined the chorus in fourth grade and immediately quit after a fellow student called me a "chorus fag."

My childhood slipped away and my obsession with music would lay dormant inside of me. Until that first Grateful Dead concert, when it would all be awoken. As I listened to their songs, an overwhelming passion for life came over me. It was unlike anything I had ever experienced before. I wanted that exact feeling to continue forever. I decided right then and there that I had to become a musician at any cost.

This began my quest. I bought a used acoustic guitar the next day, locked myself in my room, and began the long arduous task of learning an instrument. I played until my fingers were blistery and worn, desperately trying to make a joyful sound with that hunk of carved wood and steel. Yet, as the months passed, all I could make was dissonant trash, barely being able to pick a buzz-free note. My negative mind was beginning to have its way with me; "Just give it up, you're not cut out to be a musician, your fingers are too short, you have to start this stuff as a kid, you have to be able to read music, you're not smart or strong enough." But I tried to remain optimistic and focused on my goal, telling myself that nothing great is ever achieved overnight.

Every night at sunset, I drove to the beach to practice my instrument in search of inspiration. One random Tuesday amid the buzzing frets and botched barre chords, I heard the most beautiful sound. It sounded like hundreds of angels singing in unison from the heavens. I looked down at my hands and I was holding a C chord in perfect formation. After almost a year of torture I had finally made a joyful sound!

With that one chord, my obsession grew at an enormous rate, the hand positions started coming easier, and I was actually beginning to play the guitar, not great but listenable. While strumming along one day in my bedroom, I opened my mouth and out came a passionate voice in perfect tune. The voice had fire and purpose; it was the one from my youth that had been buried deep within for the last ten years.

I began writing my own songs and playing for handfuls of people at small parties and barbecues. It was all I thought about every second of every day. My style was simple: write from the heart, play from the gut, and sing from the soul. I never really cared much about fame. I was happy just putting a smile on one person's face when I played, helping them forget their troubles even if for a moment. To my sheer delight, this happened time and time again.

It is simply indescribable, the unbridled elation that comes from performing music in a live setting. I've often heard it compared to the joys of sex and I must say its pretty damn close. Like making love, you find yourself having this conversation inside your head, saying stuff like "Oh my God, this is so unbelievable; I can't believe this is happening!" As the music emanates from your body, you feel like an all-powerful being that is connected to the whole universe. This exhilarating emotion is the single reason why people practice their instruments thousands of hours for many years.

My friends and I used to go see this kick-ass band every weekend. We became close with the members and after a while I started taking lessons from the lead guitarist. Hank was an awesome teacher; he taught me some valuable lessons that opened many musical doors for me. One day after complimenting me on my progress, he asked if I wanted to open for his band with an acoustic set at a Fourth of July party. Without a moment's thought, I jumped at the opportunity and was informed that I had two weeks to put together a set list. As soon as he left that night, I immediately regretted my impulsive decision and started to tremble already at what I agreed upon.

After a few sleepless nights, I came to the conclusion that I was going to go through with it; get on that stage, close my eyes, and just sing from my toes. I already had three solid tunes of my own, and with a few covers, I'd be ready to make it happen. At the time, Mommy and I were beginning to take our friendship to the next level, so I invited her to come along. When we arrived at the party, to our astonishment there were at least two hundred people there, with a flatbed truck being used as a stage. After throwing up and the worst case of "Hershey squirts" imaginable, I gave Mommy a hug and took the stage.

I played my freakin' ass off that night and the crowd totally loved it. For the first time in my life, I felt like someone that people admired. It was a high I never dreamed possible. My whole future began to piece together in my head and it made perfect sense. Words simply cannot describe the magnificence of this experience. A few days later, there was this mind-blowing poem written by Mommy in my mailbox. I think it says it best.

**"Always Remember"**

Through your heart and passed your lips
From your soul, out your fingertips
Leaving me breathless and in awe
Of a man's spirit I just saw

I saw burdens rising from your chest
As conquered fears were put to rest
As a fortunate witness to a dream come true
I'd never been so inspired by you

Your voice was strong and full of pride
Allowing kind friends to see you inside
We felt your love and saw your grace
You took us to a higher place

Always remember how you felt that night
Like no wish or desire was out of your sight
And I promise too- to never forget
The magical sounds of your very first set

Love, Gina

And it was this poem alone that made me believe in myself as a musician, and also absolutely positive that I had found my future wife.

The only thing missing was that I wanted to make people dance, for that I was going to need a band. I took out ads in all the local music papers looking for like-minded musicians, and I wound up meeting a group of guys who were already a band in search of a singer. I was a self-taught novice, and they were all products of music school, theory junkies, real pros. They took my simple three-chord songs and transformed them into fifteen-minute orchestral monstrosities, and not to mention they were the coolest guys in the world. We bonded immediately, jammed, wrote, sang harmonies, and of course partied our asses off. We built up a repertoire of original songs and a small following, and started playing the Long Island bar scene and even a few famous New York City clubs.

We were Pangea, a name I lifted out of my sixth-grade science textbook, a rock band on a mission. We really started making a name for ourselves, playing several nights a week to packed bars and parties, all culminating on one summer night in July of 2000. On this night we played an outdoor festival to hundreds of people. As I stood on stage, I realized that my dream had finally come to fruition. I was a musician and people were actually dancing to and calling out the names of my songs. A huge crowd of people cheered us on, and at that moment I could have died a happy man, totally satisfied with my life's accomplishments.

It was an incredible ride; four years of non-stop action and wild memories. I learned more from the band than I could have learned in a lifetime as a solo artist. But as always, every good thing must have its bad and the partying got way out of hand. When your mom came home from work one day and told me she was pregnant with you, although I was ecstatic, I knew my days as a rock and roller were coming to an end. The band tried to make it work for a while, in fact you attended many a Pangea gig in Mommy's belly. But when you finally came into my life, I knew I had to make some serious changes.

I have managed to still keep music in my life though. Now my acoustic is back out of the closet and I've gone back to my folk roots. Today, the only crowds I have dancing are you, Mommy, and Jesse—and that's all the fans I'll ever need.

### Life Rule #19: Everyone secretly wants to jam!

With regards to music, there are only two types of people in this world: performers and listeners. What I've learned is that all listeners really want to be performers, and they don't realize that all that separates them is a little determination and loads of heart. I don't believe there's such a thing as a tone deaf or musically-challenged individual. Whenever someone tells me this, I encourage them to listen to Tom Waits. This guy's almost un-listenable vocal stylings have endured a thirty-year career, with brilliant songs that make him one of the most respected and covered artists of our time. All you need to become a musician is a unique sound, soulful delivery, and a steadfast practice regimen. You have been singing, banging on instruments, and dancing since you were two, so I know you are destined for some kind of a musical future.

The best advice I can give you on this subject is to search for music that really moves you, and try to develop your own style from those joyful emotions. Seek out interesting chord progressions, adjust them to your liking, and hum along as you play. Soon enough, those hums will become meaningful lyrics, and the songs your own, a piece of your heart for the world to share. I just hope that whatever your musical taste may be, you will always be in search of substance and meaning over image and style. Does the song inspire you? Is there truth, soul, and conviction? But, most importantly, does it give you the chills?

# CHAPTER 8: PETS

I saw a great bumper sticker the other day that said, "The more people I meet, the more I love my dog!" These are my sentiments exactly; I'm a huge believer in the power of animals. They can enrich your life in so many ways, giving you unconditional love, and constantly reminding you to live in the moment. Animals are so carefree and impulsive that you just can't help but have it rub off on you as well.

My love for animals has always been apparent, however, in the germ-free environment I grew up in, pets were strictly prohibited. After years of whining, I finally convinced my parents into buying me a hamster when I was ten, but because of our opposite sleep schedules, the relationship never took form. Besides, this wasn't the type of furry companionship I was yearning for. I wanted an animal that could supply undying devotion and lifelong friendship.

Once I moved into my own apartment after college, I impulsively adopted a cat from the local shelter. "Bro" was a very intelligent feline, but he was way too independent for me. He would hang out under the bed for weeks at a time, and could care less if I even looked at him. I tried every furry rodent possible and soon moved onto fish, reptiles of all sorts, and even dabbled in birds for a while; but to no avail, I still wasn't satisfied. Pets are an inordinate amount of work, and I felt that the love you get has to be worth the trouble. I always had a special place in my heart for dogs. Even as a kid at relatives' houses, all the cousins would be playing Manhunt and I'd be wrestling in the yard with the family canine. I don't know why I had such an affinity for dogs. I guess we just understood each other.

It would be twenty-seven years before I would finally be able to have a dog of my own, a yellow Labrador Retriever named Ezekiel Jerome, "Zeke" for short, with the Jerome being a reference to Jerry Garcia. I spent several weeks researching different breeds and tried to figure out which one would be the right match for me. There were so many I loved; the majestic Newfoundland (too much drooling), the adorable English Bulldog (respiratory problems), the protective German Shepherd (too high-strung), or the droopy-faced Basset Hound (too stubborn).

After much consideration, I decided a Labrador was the best choice. During my studies, I discovered that there were two different blood lines among labs: English and American. The American lines were primarily used as hunting dogs; they have long thin snouts, skinny bodies, long legs, wiry tails, and boundless energy. While the English lines are short in stature, have a shorter snout, boxy head, barrel shaped chest, and an otter tail. These dogs were used mainly as show dogs and possess a much calmer disposition. Many uninformed Labrador enthusiasts mistakenly purchase American pups, and wind up having their houses destroyed and lives torn apart. This exact scenario is hilariously depicted in the heartwarming book *Marley and Me* by John Grogan.

Lucky for me, Mommy was a dog expert, having had many as a child and even five at one time for a brief period. Her favorite dog of all was a black Lab named Gail. She still gets teary-eyed when her name comes up in conversation. Now that we had decided on a Lab, the next step was to locate a reputable breeder. In my ignorance, I believed you could just go down to your local pet store and pick a wonderful puppy from the cages without a problem. I soon found out that acquiring a dog through this method can become a lesson in torment. You see, almost all pet stores get their puppies from puppy mills. These are dreadful places where dogs are kept in cages twenty-four hours a day, and forced to breed and have multiple litters, often from incestual blood lines. These deprived animals never see the light of day, and live miserable lives for the sole purpose of pumping out money-making pups.

The dogs are nothing more than merchandise to the sickos who run these places, and worst of all the puppies they turn out are usually riddled with health problems, costing their new owner thousands in vet bills and endless heartache. One horrible story comes to mind: an elderly man was arrested in the town where I grew up for running a puppy mill. When his house was raided, the police found over fifty Cocker Spaniels in his dingy basement, living in tiny stacked cages, filled with urine and feces dripping downward. They were sickly and malnourished, and many of the puppies were dead from starvation.

### Life Rule #20: Never buy a dog from a pet store.

Anyway, back to Zeke; we were able to locate a reputable breeder and when the day finally came, we drove to a farm in New Jersey to pick him up. As we walked up the driveway, a pack of fuzzy little pudgeballs came charging out of the barn to greet us, and it was love at first sight. As the other pups wrestled around and sniffed each other's butts, Zeke jumped right into my arms and I immediately knew he was the one. Although raising him was quite the frustrating experience, as the months passed and he slowly matured, he became the most loving companion I could have ever asked for. Words cannot begin to express how I feel about this dog. I literally owe my life to him.

The summer of 2001, I was living on the south shore of Long Island in a beach bungalow. One night we were taking our usual sunset jog and I decided to take a plunge in the ocean afterward. Zeke always accompanied me on my swims, but being a water dog he knew better than to venture passed the breakers. This particular night, the surf was quite rough and except for us, the beach was completely deserted. Upon diving in, I could feel the riptide grab hold of me with incredible force, and pull me under to the rocky bottom. When I came to the surface, I was gasping for air, spitting up salt water, and further from the shore than I had ever been. I knew that rule #1 in this situation was don't panic, but I panicked, and panicked big time! I started paddling, kicking, and screaming feverishly for help. As the waves bombarded and the current relentlessly pulled me out to sea, I remember thinking, "So this is how I'm gonna die. I can't believe it. Please God help!"

Suddenly out of the rushing white water and haze of the setting sun, I saw the image of a white creature paddling toward me, like one of those adorable baby seals you see on nature shows. I was battered and barely keeping my head afloat when Zeke's snorting muzzle came face to face with mine. I mustered up all the strength I could and grabbed onto his tail and continued to pray. I could barely hold on through the raging surf, but Zeke's stubby legs never stopped churning and somehow I managed to maintain my grip.

Moments later I was in knee deep water being dragged toward the dry sand. I was dumbfounded and utterly exhausted. I couldn't believe the miracle that had just transpired. As if nothing had happened, Zeke shook off his coat and picked up a nearby stick to play fetch with. It was just a game to him, part of his everlasting attempt to gain my love and attention. It was one of those magical moments when you realize how great it is to be alive, and not a day goes by that I don't look at Zeke and feel overwhelmed with gratitude.

They say that dogs have this chemical in their saliva that speeds up the healing process, and that's the reason why they are always licking wounds. I believe this to be true, and not just for physical wounds, but psychological ones as well. There were days when my depression would reach an all-time low and I couldn't even get out of bed in the morning without crying. And just when I thought I could bear no more and that life was hopeless, Zeke would come barreling in the room, lap up every tear, and stare me in the eye as if to say, "It's a beautiful day! Take me outside bee-otch!" Time after time it was encounters like these that gave me the courage to pull myself together, grab the leash, and face the world again.

As we'd walk through the neighborhood, I'd watch Zeke strut his stuff down the street with his happy tail wagging and I'd say to myself, "Look at this guy; he embraces each day with such incredible enthusiasm. Why can't I be like that, instead of worrying myself sick all the time?" I spent hundreds of hours training this dog, when it is I who should be learning from him. Instead of me commanding him to "sit, stay, and heal," he should be commanding me to "embrace life, be happy, and love your family." We could learn so much from our pets if we just took the time to love them. No one knows for sure that humans are the superior species on this planet. I mean, dogs don't pick up our shit in little plastic bags, do they?

What I do know is this: the last eight years I have spent with Zeke have been wonderful, and I don't know where I'd be without him. Every time I get out of bed and step on his head, or come through the front door and he attacks me like he hasn't seen me in years, I thank God for him. When you first came home from the hospital at three days old, we put you on the floor in your car seat and Zeke gave you a big sniff followed by a wet lick on the forehead. He then laid down next to you and hasn't left your side since. Over the years, you've ridden him, poked his eyes, pulled his ears and tail, dressed him up in different outfits, and even taken naps nestled in his soft polar bear fur. In fact, one of your first words was "eek."

And even though he's ninety pounds of mushy love, he also has a very protective side when it comes to his family. I've witnessed a startling ferocity when suspicious people approach us on the street, and when I'm not home at night I am secure knowing that he is on guard to look after you.

Adolescence can be a time when our pets are often forgotten. I realize that between boys, school, and your friends, you can barely even hold another thought in your head. But if you just take a moment out of your day to notice your pets, it will help you refocus on what's important in life. If given the chance, animals can teach you how to be selfless and are also fantastic practice for parenthood. Before I had Zeke, I was the most selfish and irresponsible person on the planet. I couldn't imagine a living creature having to rely on me for food, water, walks, medical treatment, and affection. Yet, after only a few months, I was completely transformed and found myself including Zeke in my every plan. Deep down all everyone really wants is to be loved and not judged. Who could be better at this than our pets? While they may stink, get fleas, shed, ruin stuff, and be very expensive, I'd take all that and then some for a lifelong friend until death.

# Chapter 9:
# School

Between grade school, college, and my career as a teacher, I have been involved in the school system for about twenty-eight of my thirty-four years. So I guess you could call this topic my area of expertise. All of my educational stages were both academically and socially challenging, but high school was by far the most mentally exhaustive. While it can be the greatest time of your life, high school can also be four years of misery. For me it was both: freshman and sophomore year were a nightmare, while junior and senior year were a total blast. I've had a lot of time to look back, analyze my experiences, and figure out if it was all worth it. Did I really need to learn all that awful math, physics, chemistry, and economics? As much as I'd love to tell you that it was all worthless, I just can't bring myself to do it.

In recent years, I've come to believe in education wholeheartedly, and feel that it really does play a critical role in your future. I know learning the endless facts, dates, and all the rote memorization crap is horrendous, but reading, writing, and speaking are three skills that are incredibly vital in becoming a successful person. Many people I know (myself included) squeaked through high school without ever cracking a book, writing a paper, or giving a single speech, and it really had negative affects on later life. I always managed to find a short cut, dishonest scheme, or someone to help me with any major assignment, and it really plagued me in college. This was probably the main reason I failed out in my junior year, that along with all the beer.

After all my years of education and having been on both sides of the desk, I've learned that school is about teaching people one thing and one thing only: discipline. That's about it; are you disciplined enough to follow rules, reach deadlines, work diligently, and get along with others? If you are, then you'll be rewarded with a piece of paper that says you jumped through all the necessary hoops, and have shown true resilience under pressure. Some call this piece of paper a degree or diploma. I call it a ticket to an easier way of life. Those who cannot hack the rules and rigidity of school wind up dropping out and discover quickly that life without that piece of paper is no picnic.

Our society is broken down into two main work forces: white collar and blue collar. Basically, one gets their hands dirty and the other one doesn't. White-collar workers are your doctors, lawyers, writers, bankers, and career-minded people. While blue-collar work usually requires more manual labor and unpleasant working conditions. I'm not putting down blue-collar workers in the slightest. Some have awesome jobs and live great lives, but the bottom line is that it's much harder work. In this ultra-competitive job market, it's even becoming difficult for college graduates to find fulfilling careers. So you can imagine the struggle for a person with only a high school diploma or less. Hell, I have three college degrees and I pull in a whopping thirty-eight grand a year, barely enough to support my family.

Not too long ago, the future aspirations of many young women were merely to become housewives and mothers. This was even one of your mom's teenage desires. Not that this profession isn't a tremendous calling, but it definitely lacks in the salary department. Many would graduate high school, immediately get married, and become baby-making machines, relying on dear hubby for everything. Then one day dear hubby runs off with his secretary, leaving his wife a thirty-six-year-old single mother of three, with nothing going for her but a high school diploma and zero work experience. That's why some single moms have to become exotic dancers and prostitutes. They have kids to feed and no other options; a Burger King salary just wasn't cutting it.

Most girls don't get married at eighteen anymore. They've learned heartbreaking lessons watching their moms struggle through life without an education, working the night shift at the local convenience store. Girls of today realize the significance of having a degree, career, and financial stability to fall back on, should the worst happen.

School isn't for everyone though; for some, sitting behind a desk and listening to a monotone teacher drone on for hours can be pure torture. However, every person has the ability to learn in their own distinctive way. In college I was informed of a man named Howard Gardner, who was the founder of the Multiple Intelligence Theory.*^ He believed that all human beings acquired knowledge differently, and that every individual has the potential to be successful at something. Gardner's theory explained that everyone possesses a unique blend of seven intelligences, with some being more prominent than others.

1. **Linguistic/Verbal Intelligence: The Word Smith**

   These are people who are unusually adept at using and manipulating language. Not only can they speak and write with natural ease, but they also have the power to recognize even the slightest rhyme and cadence. These are your writers, poets, actors, comedians, and politicians with true leadership qualities.

2. **Logical/Mathematical Intelligence: The Analyzer**

   These are your number people who easily recognize patterns, relationships, and order. L/M intelligence comes at a huge advantage in the fields of scientists, mathematicians, philosophers, computer programmers, doctors, accountants, lawyers, and criminologists.

### 3. Musical Intelligence: The Groover

These people have the ability to enjoy, perform, or compose complex pieces of music. They can easily decipher pitch, timbre, rhythm, and melodic intricacies, as well as the emotional implications that music creates. They are constantly humming, tapping, singing, and noticing sounds others may not. These people are tomorrow's composers, producers, singers, conductors, instrumentalists, and recording engineers.

### 4. Spatial Intelligence: The Visualizer

Visualizers have the ability to perceive and manipulate forms or objects, and create a visual representation of words. Architects, artists, engineers, fashion designers, interior designers, photographers, and graphic artists all rely heavily on these talents.

### 5. Bodily/ Kinesthetic Intelligence: The Mover

These individuals have the ability to use fine motor skills to solve problems, create products, or convey ideas. If sitting still in a chair even for a moment feels like an eternity, then you may possess the aptitude to become an athlete, police officer, fire fighter, dancer, inventor, or performance artist.

### 6. Interpersonal Intelligence: The Social Butterfly

Butterflies were born with the gift to gab. They also have the knack to empathize with others, and help them with their problems. Teachers, social workers, psychologists, counselors, sales, nursing, management, and anthropologists all utilize these skills in their daily work.

### 7. Intrapersonal Intelligence: The Individual

These people have the distinct capacity to understand oneself. They can easily recognize feelings, dreams, ideas, goals, and emotions. If you can sit around thinking for most of the day and never run dry of interesting ideas, then writing, counseling, art, philosophy, or psychology may be in your future.

With the way the modern public school system is set up in America, people with linguistic and mathematical intelligences are the only individuals that will truly stand out, all others are set up for failure. Most educators care little that Jimmy can run, jump, sing, draw, sculpt, or empathize with others. They are merely concerned that he can memorize information, excel on standardized testing, and make them appear to be effective teachers.

There are many tests out there that can show you which of the seven intelligences you display, but I feel this is something you must discover on your own. It won't take much investigation, chances are you already know your strengths and have known since kindergarten. Nurture these strengths, and don't ever let anyone tell you that they are meaningless.

## Teachers

One of the biggest obstacles that you will face in your academic career—something that will frustrate, annoy, and torment your every waking moment—will be your teachers. In my opinion, about half of the teachers you will have in your life will be power hungry and abusive morons, and that's probably low balling the figure. I should know, I've worked side by side with these people everyday for the last ten years. I'd even go as far as saying that many of them don't even like kids. Teaching was their "plan b" in life, and now that their dream career hasn't panned out, the students will pay dearly for this failure.

Take my fifth grade teacher Mrs. Hoffer for example, who I still believe to be the anti-Christ. She was so vindictive and nasty, that I can still taste the agony of being in her class. Mrs. Hoffer was a tyrannical ruler; her cruel punishments and ability to bring the strongest willed student to tears was second to none. I remember waking up every morning with a stomachache and dreading having to hear her retched voice again. Many an afternoon, I copied the dictionary with aching hand, sat in her "baby chair," knelt in the coat closet, or even wore a bib and pacifier until I was "ready to act my age." All these years later, I still think of her immoral tactics and realize the negative impact she had on my life. It's people like her that give teachers a horrible name.

I hear them in the faculty room everyday, ripping kids to shreds. No topic is off limits, from personal family matters and messy divorces, to private medical issues; all the while laughing and cackling it up with the rest of the hens. These people only get hired in the first place because they are well-spoken and have the proper credentials, not because of any experience with children. This one guy I worked with had Einstein's I.Q. but negative social skills. He barely let the kids breathe, and was eventually fired for saying inappropriate sexual content to his sixth grade class.

You must understand: most of the crappy teachers in the world are merely jealous of your youth and carefree attitude. Maybe they were geeks in high school and now they want revenge on the cool kids. They'd give anything to switch lives with you, instead of being the middle aged slouches that they have become.

On a more positive note, dealing with unbearable teachers develops great character, and is also excellent training for the many ball-busting bosses of tomorrow.

I'd condemn the whole educational system in a heart beat, and become one of those eccentric home schooling advocates if it weren't for the remaining 50 percent of the teaching profession. These are the people who are caring, fair, patient, entertaining, and genuinely love kids. It's teachers like this that are the sole reason I am standing in front of a classroom today. Here are a few gems from my day:

**Mrs. Roy: Kindergarten**. Whenever a distant memory of this woman comes to mind, I can't help but smile. She was just the sweetest thing, all four foot, eleven inches of her. Yet she had the heart of a giant, and made everyone of us feel like her favorite. I can still remember fighting with the other kids to be line leader, so that I could hold her hand in the halls. She sang to us at nap time, and whenever we cried her hugs were an instant remedy.

**Mr. Santos: Eighth Grade Music Appreciation.** This guy was the hippest teacher I have ever known. He was a singer/guitarist in a rock band and a local hero to many. He performed concerts for the school, and used works of the Beatles and Jimi Hendrix to enhance his inspiring lessons. His passion for music was contagious, and I still picture his mullet covered head flailing about whenever I hear a Seventies guitar anthem.

**Mr. Fitzsimmons: Tenth Grade History.** "Fitz" was a world traveler with an electric personality. He was hysterically funny, took us on cool trips, spoke to us like adults, and told the most outrageous historical stories, including the tale of Catherine the Great, the empress of Russia. Legend has it that this woman's insatiable sexual appetite led to her untimely death, after she was crushed by a male horse. This may have been the only time in the history of education, that an entire class of tenth graders was completely riveted with attentiveness.

**Mrs. Boone: High School Speech Therapist.** This woman had such a profound affect on my life. She was the first person to treat me like an intelligent human being and not a mental midget. She listened to me, helped me find my voice, and eventually hooked me up with hundreds of other people who shared my affliction.

**Mrs. Calderone: Eleventh Grade Biology.** Mrs. "C" was much like a loving mom. She got to know everyone on a personal level, shared stories from her life, chaperoned trips, ran clubs, and had awesome parties. She was my all-time favorite teacher. When she died a few years ago, her funeral felt like my ten-year high school reunion.

**Professor Gilden: College Multi-Cultural Education.** This gentleman was a seventy-five-year-old ex-jazz drummer, cancer survivor, father of seven, and 1960s civil rights activist. The stories of him being shot at in the Deep South marching for equality, or even arrested many times standing up for his beliefs, were a true inspiration and a testament to his convictions.

**Professor DiMartino: College Creative Writing.** After receiving a dreaded "C- Me" on my first writing assignment, I was fully prepared for yet another condescending browbeating by an intolerant teacher. Surprisingly, this guy sat me down in his office and not only told me that he admired my voice in the story, but also offered these encouraging words, "You just might be onto something here, Pete." Over the next few months, he took me under his wing and taught me the essentials of writing from the heart and how to connect with a reader. Like most freshman at Suffolk Community College, I was merely a meaningless face in a sea of unsettled eighteen-year-olds. But to Professor DiMartino, I was a promising young man who may be stumbling onto a newly discovered talent.

As much as you want to hate and ignore every teacher you have, try your best to listen to the ones who are sincerely trying to help you. Give them a chance before you tune them out. I would always give a teacher a solid month before I made up my mind about them. Even the real winners, who sport the same pants every day, pick their ears with a pen, have dandruff-covered shoulders, or wear pit-stained shirts can teach you a great deal about the world. Learn from how they treat others and how they fully embrace life.

## Public vs. Private

Which provides a better education: public or private school? This question has been burdening concerned parents since the days of the one room school house. In my career, I've taught in both kinds of schools, so naturally I have strong opinions on this matter. Private schools are funded mainly from student tuition, charities, and donations. While public schools are funded from state monies and the parents' tax dollars. Since public schools are state funded they have much more money to spend on extra-curricular activities, sports, clubs, and whatever other luxuries they can afford. These things are very important in kids' lives, and can teach them to become well-rounded adults. That said, the biggest difference that I've noticed between the two school systems has to do with the population of kids, and not the education they receive.

One hitch about those brand new public schools is that they have to accept every kid within the district parameters, and unless they are a homicidal maniac they have to keep them, by law. To most parents, a million dollar football field and state of the art computer system is much more important than the few undesirables wandering the halls of the public schools. I happen to believe otherwise.

The overall atmosphere of a school is just as, if not more important than, extra-curricular activities. Children learn from their peers, this is fact; one bad kid can turn a whole school into a danger zone. These anti-social misfits can be any kind of kid from any background, even the ones you'd least expect.

On April 20, 1999, two teenage students walked into their suburban Colorado high school armed to the teeth with assault weapons and explosives. After a horrific killing spree, twelve students and one teacher were brutally murdered. Ironically, these helpless victims were far from the intended targets, but rather upstanding young adults in the wrong place at the wrong time.

The ensuing investigation uncovered that the killers were Dylan Klebold and Eric Harris, two quiet kids who had never caused trouble in the past. After thousands of interviews, grief counseling, and intensive analysis of the killer's deranged computer blogs, this horrible event was discovered to be an extreme case of school bullying gone awry. The killers were weaker kids, fed up with being abused and harassed on a daily basis. When the mistreatment became intolerable, they acted out violently in the worst possible way.

In the wake of this tragedy, copycat incidents started occurring all over the country in other public schools. And almost every time, some one-hundred-pound nerdy kid with a bad haircut would get pulled from his home in handcuffs, to a stunned nation full of people demanding to know why. I feel the answer is obvious: you consistently push a person to the brink of insanity and sooner or later they'll snap. Bullying is a much bigger problem than people think it is, something a forty-five-minute teacher seminar cannot cure.

I was bullied most of my life with endless wedgies, pink bellies, purple nurples, and lunch money muggings; it's hell for kids. One time I was attacked by two older boys in a middle school bathroom and had my face shoved in a filthy urinal filled with piss and pubes, while being repeatedly flushed. For weeks afterward, all I could think about was swift vengeance on those scumbags. It's totally natural for humans to experience emotions such as these. But try explaining that to the devastated parents of the slain children of Columbine High School.

The solution is quite clear: some kids just don't belong in school. There are always going to be kids who walk the halls with one purpose—to terrorize, intimidate, and humiliate. Derrick Anderson mocked my stuttering everyday with such viciousness, that I could not believe he had a soul. He would not relent until he saw tears, and then he would continue until he saw blood. This putz was the originator of "P-P-P-Peter," who once locked me in a cage that held basketballs in my underwear, and then pushed it out the side door during dismissal. Every time we passed in the halls he'd scream, "Th-Th-Th-Th-That's all folks!" after Porky Pig, the famous stammering cartoon.

The worst part of this issue is that there's not a single thing public schools can do to put an end to this problem. I've attended endless workshops and seminars and it's all crap. I don't know which is a bigger joke: "Bully Free School Zones" or "Drug Free School Zones." It is simply too much to monitor and impossible to control. The bullies are incredibly savvy and they strike when the time is right; hallways, bathrooms, wherever, and threatening with severe bodily harm if reported. And even if they are reported to administration, the punishment is barely a slap on the wrist, or at best a two-day vacation in which to sleep late and watch TV. You more or less have to commit a felony these days to get permanently expelled from the public school system. I've witnessed middle schoolers threatened with death and extortion, and still no disciplinary action was enforced.

Having taught fourth through eighth graders in both inner city and rural areas of New York and Florida, you could say I've seen the best and the worst. The last public school I worked at was forced to hire an armed police officer to roam the halls as security. When a student showed up in my class with a box cutter in his pencil case for "protection," I knew it was time to reassess my career.

Jodee Blanco wrote an awesome book on this topic called *Please Stop Laughing at Me*. It's a true story about being bullied from a female's point of view, and the sheer havoc it wreaks on one's self-image. Jodee's heart-wrenching tales brought back vivd memories from my childhood, and would eventually become one of the many inspirations for this book to you.

## Bully Deterrence

1. **Silence is your best initial defense.** Bullies live for the reaction they get from you. If you simply don't react, they will most likely move on to more vulnerable prey.

2. **Befriend one of the bully's nicer companions.** This is a great way to get a bully to lay off, also a tactic I used with much success. If you've been given clearance by someone they trust, they just may leave you alone.

3. **Tell an adult you trust.** You can even remain anonymous if you want.

4. **Attempt kindness.** Sometimes a bully is just an insecure kid who doesn't want to expose their true self. When they sense you are interested in their friendship, they may change their tune.

5. **Have a tough friend or two.** They don't have to be your best friends, but being associated with intimidating people can be a huge deterrent to a bully. A guy from my wrestling team named Danny Webber was a humongous meathead, but after we became friends in eleventh grade, Derrick Anderson never looked my way again.

6. **If you feel physically threatened and see no other way out.** Hit first and hit hard, then run! I'll always back you up with the administration if your actions were justified.

7. **Cyber-bullying.** According to *Time for Kids* magazine, one in three teenagers are harassed and/or threatened online via e-mail, instant messages, and chat rooms on a daily basis. Although this is still a relatively new problem, the experts at *Time* encourage teens to ignore it at first, but print a written record of every incident. And if it continues tell a trusted adult. Though, if I have my way you won't have any unsupervised internet time until you go away to college.

All of these tactics should be utilized with extreme caution. If you try the wrong one with the wrong person, it can have disastrous consequences.

## Private Schools

At the other end of the educational spectrum are your private schools. There are private schools where the students get the best of everything: sports, technology, extra-curricular activities, and clubs. However, these schools can cost more in one semester than most make in a year. Aside from the high-priced prep schools and Ivy League academies, I am talking about more affordable private institutions such as parochial schools.

My first teaching job was in a Catholic school. Not because I was looking to spread the word of God or anything, basically because they were much easier to find. Public school teaching jobs on Long Island were virtually unavailable. My friend's mother worked at a school and I practically landed the job on her kind recommendation alone. Having gone to public school my whole life, I was completely out of my element and baffled by the whole situation: the uniforms, incessant praying, rundown facilities, ancient curriculum, and Sister Rosalie, my seventy-four-year-old tough-as-nails principal.

As the year progressed and I adjusted to the parochial way of life, I began to like what I saw. Sure, I was working with a twelve-year-old history book, and my ceiling leaked buckets on rainy days, but the majority of the kids were respectful with me and each other. And this was in an impoverished crime-riddled area of Queens, yet these kids all followed the rules and obeyed the adults. The reason being, from day one the students were taught that if they broke any of the rules, they were gone. Sister Rosalie would kick them to the curb with just three infractions, without a dime of tuition reimbursement. The parents knew it was a tight ship, and fought hard to keep their kids in line to avoid the nightmare that was the public school just down the boulevard.

We had our share of troublemakers just like every school in the world, but there was a thin line to walk. The students were given a chance to adjust and change their attitude, or they were history. This was the only thing that kept them in order. Now these kids had not one sports team, and they had to eat lunch in their classroom every day. But they learned the three most important lessons a kid could ever learn: discipline, respect, and moral values. And most importantly, they always felt safe. This is the only way that bullying can ever be stopped in education; case closed. In the four years I spent teaching at Saint Stephen's, I never saw a fraction of the deviant behavior I experienced in two years of public school.

Presently, I am teaching in a private school for children of South American immigrants. It is also a Catholic school and it's been the most rewarding thing I've ever been a part of. The population is 99 percent Hispanic, with four white kids whose parents send them there for the nurturing environment. It's all about family values and hope at this school, and this is why private schools are superior in my opinion. And also the reason why I'll dance on street corners for nickels if I have to, to send you to one. The lessons you learn are unparalleled, and your interpersonal skills will flourish.

Education is key; whether you like school or not, the sooner you realize its importance the better. Unless you want to be saying, "Would you like fries with that?" for a career, then you better hit the books, missy. You don't have to tell me how hard it is and how much you hate it. School's supposed to be hard, or else all the knuckleheads in the world would become doctors and lawyers. If you can just work your butt off for these few years, you can have it all in life: a fulfilling career, beautiful house, nice cars, and wonderful vacations. All of my friends used to harass my buddy Steve when we were out partying and he was at home studying for law school. Currently, four of us combined don't add up to his salary or exciting lifestyle. I'd now like to share some tips to help you succeed during your academic career, whatever that may be.

1.  **Take notes**. This was the worst part of school for me; I loathed taking notes. But it's a scientific fact that writing something helps you remember it more than just hearing it. And nothing works better during a cram session than writing them over again before a test.

2.  **Effort counts big time.** As a teacher, nothing impresses me more than a kid who tries his ass off. I've had some students who could barely write their own names. But they never stopped fighting, coming for extra help, and putting in the initiative with extra-credit projects. This speaks bounds about you, and will make most teachers cross rivers for you.

3.  **Never cheat**. Another shameful topic for me. I cheated like crazy in high school. I thought I was so slick: cheat sheets, wandering eyes, getting tests before hand, and even plagiarizing papers. And would you believe it, the first time I got caught was senior year during a final exam with a teacher I adored named Jane Stallworth. She confronted me after class and I had to fight back tears to deny it. I could have easily been denied my diploma, but thanks to Jane's compassion I was given the benefit of the doubt. Thank God I found my integrity in college and used my mind to succeed, rather than a scam. When you are dishonest with your education, you are only cheating your future.

4.  **Read and write for fun.** I did whatever I could to get out of reading in high school, going so far as making up entire book reports and research papers. Comprehensive reading is a learned skill. Don't get frustrated by early difficulties. Like all great talents it must be mastered slowly over many years. Developing a passion for reading will not only make school a cinch, it can also make your greatest dreams come

true. I hope that the countless bedtime readings of *The Runaway Bunny* weren't all for nothing.

The main reason why kids hate writing so much is because they are afraid of being ripped apart for their spelling and grammar mistakes. I've witnessed firsthand, that as soon as you allow students to write for fun without any fear of criticism, their ideas begin to flow and writing becomes an enjoyment. The famous book *On the Road*, by Jack Kerouac, was first written without any punctuation or the slightest regard for grammar. It was just three hundred pages of free-form thought, and it is still one of the best-selling pieces of literature of our time. Don't worry about all the run-ons, fragments, noun–verb agreements, and spelling errors. That will come eventually through trial and error. What's most important here is being able to transfer your stream of consciousness to paper. This one skill can turn you into an outstanding scholar, and set you apart from all others.

5. **Don't cut class.** Nothing pisses a teacher off more than a student who haphazardly skips class. I know it's so difficult to resist when all your friends are blowing off school to hit the beach or to party at someone's empty house, but it's just not worth it. With today's computerized attendance records, it is inevitable that you will get busted. This is a sure way to make enemies with your school administration and bring your grades way down as well. One of my buddies was actually prohibited from graduating with our senior class for skipping gym on numerous occasions. He was forced to go to summer school and graduate in August with the rest of the flunkies. I bet he wishes he would have just sucked it up and played dodge ball after that fiasco.

# College

In a few years you'll be going off to college, and that thought alone gives me much concern. Although I hate to admit it, I do believe everyone should go away to college, maybe not freshman year but definitely sometime. College is sort of like real life with training wheels on. You get to taste living on your own, responsibilities, and ultimate freedom, yet you are still under the care of the college and your parents' financial assistance. When I first went away to college I became a self-destructive madman within weeks, drinking every night, doing every drug I could get my hands on, and hooking up with any girl with a pulse. Lucky for my freakish memory, or I would have failed out the first semester. I actually made it through two years before eventually getting the boot. In the end, all the partying and missed classes finally caught up to me.

College taught me a lot, though. Mostly it taught me what <u>not</u> to do in life. Look back upon this section in a few years when you are ready to take this crucial step.

## Ten Tips for a Successful College Experience:

**1. No Greek life**. Before I left for school a few of my older friends warned me not to pledge anything, no matter what. However, three weeks in and I was attending the social mixers of all the major fraternities on campus. Never in a million years could I have pictured myself as a frat boy, but once I experienced it firsthand, it was irresistible. These guys all had four-story Victorian houses with thirty brothers living in each, the craziest parties, and the most beautiful girls lined the halls every night. It was like Hollywood in upstate New York, and these guys were the celebrities. Each frat had its own image; the football players, lacrosse team, rugby guys, rich kids, etc.—and wherever they went they were treated like royalty.

Then I saw them, Sigma Delta Gamma: the hardcore partiers. These guys were let ahead in line at every bar, drank for free, and had all the hottest girls in their back pockets. I had to see what these dudes were all about. At the first mixer I attended, they had strippers, ice-block shots, a six-foot gravity bong, and "beer slip and slide" in the main floor hallway. Nobody messed with them, and it was rumored that they had file cabinets full of exams and research papers for every professor on campus.

After much convincing, my reluctant roommate and I both decided to pledge. I had heard all the stories of the horrible things that happen during fraternity pledging, but I didn't believe it. Besides, it was only two weeks long, how bad could it be?

The first night my sixteen pledge brothers and I were led into the basement of their house, locked arm in arm, in the pitch black. When the lights came on we were bum-rushed by all fifty brothers to the deafening sounds of "Ace of Spades" by Motorhead, and beaten into oblivion. They all had stockings over their heads or demonic masks on, and they proceeded to rip our T-shirts, jeans, and underwear off, and pounded our naked bodies against the cold concrete floor. After a twenty minute onslaught, they finally relented and threw us against a wall nude and battered. Buckets of ice cold water were then thrown upon us, this in subzero January temperatures. They then made us eat disgusting things like chewing tobacco, hot chili-peppers, and human phlegm, and if we puked we had to get on our knees and lick it up.

We got home that first night and literally cried for our mommies. But it was known that if anyone quit they might as well leave school, for their social life would be over. My pledge brothers and I made a promise to tough it out to the end. And wouldn't you know it; one guy packed his stuff and took a bus home the very next morning. Because of this wuss, we got it even worse the following night. I won't gross you out with the rest of the gory details, but all twelve nights were just as bad as the first; including barefoot scavenger hunts in the snow, unauthorized head shavings, and the infamous "soup night," where we were forced to jump head first into a bathtub full of hot sauce, vinegar, and oatmeal.

When I finally became a brother, I must admit it was everything I dreamed it would be. We had the best parties, and now girls that wouldn't even look at me before were actually competing to hook up with me. Many times in the throes of intimacy I'd think to myself, "How the hell can this amazing girl be kissing—me?" With those three Greek symbols on my chest, I felt invincible. Yet, after one semester of living in the house, I realized that these guys weren't my real friends at all. They stole from each other, hooked up with each other's girlfriends, fought and hazed one another constantly. It retrieved all my nasty insecurities from childhood. I had taken great strides with my self-esteem issues, and these "brothers" of mine brought me right back to the agony of seventh grade. You'd think I would have learned my lesson in high school about superficial friendships, but I'm as thickheaded as they come.

Mommy also got swept up into the hype and pledged herself. According to her, it sounded almost as brutal as my experiences, just less physical. Some of the sororities stripped their pledges down to bra and panties, and circled their fat spots with Sharpie markers. They publicly humiliated them in the bars, assigned them degrading nicknames, and brought attention to their every insecurity. Looking back, we both wish that we never got involved in the whole Greek experience. When it's your turn to go to college, make your friends the old fashioned way—don't buy them.

**2. No classes before 10 AM.** Every college freshman says the same thing: "I'll make all my classes early and then I'll have the rest of the day for myself." Yeah right, anything before ten and you will never go; even ten is too early. One semester I enrolled in all night classes, and received my highest GPA ever. In college no one does anything during the day; sleep as long as you can. Just go to class!

**3. There is no such thing as going out for one drink.** Every night is Saturday night when you're away at school. It's either one-dollar pitchers, twenty-five cent beers, or ladies night, but every night is a party, and if you try to go out light, you're only kidding yourself.

**4. Stay far away from frat boys.** Fraternity boys are a whole new level of sleaze. Peep-holes in bathrooms, date rape drugs, and public sex shows are all regular weekend practices. My fraternity would dedicate part of our Sunday meeting for brothers to share who they hooked up with and every sordid detail—it was called "The skank report." Remember these words when the great-looking president of Lamda Lamda Lamda develops a thing for you.

**5. Befriend your professors.** I know this sounds like ass-kissing, but it really works. Go to their office hours for extra help and advice, get to know them on a personal level, and when it comes to grades they'll hook you up big time.

**6. Don't fall in love.** College is a guy's only chance to be a total slut. He needs this time to get it out of his system, and maybe become normal someday. If you go falling in love with the local dorm stud, he will break your heart in no time. Most college boys are physically incapable of monogamy, because until they can stop obsessing over getting laid and wasted every second; they will never be happy. Guys who don't sow their oats in college, are most likely the same ones who will later encounter a midlife crisis over their wasted adolescence.

**7. Make friends with someone with a car.** Odds are you won't have a car freshman year; I'm not paying your insurance. So, it's huge to know someone with wheels.

**8. Beware of the "freshman 15."** I've seen many people go from thin, athletic freshman, to pudgy, out-of-shape juniors in only a few years. Most of them never lost it either, and it soon became the "freshman 40." The average college diet consists mainly of beer, pizza, French fries, and chicken wings, without even a thought of exercise. Have a salad every once in a while.

**9. Never mix beer and liquor**. Have you ever heard that old saying, "Liquor before beer, in the clear"? Well, it's bullshit. On my twenty-first birthday, I had liquor before beer, and got so violently ill that I had to be rushed to the hospital for alcohol poisoning. And let me tell you, getting your stomach pumped is no pleasure cruise!

**10. It's all about the roommate**. This will make or break your first year. If they're cool, you'll love college; if they suck, you'll want to come home immediately. Mommy went to college with a good friend, which was a great move. I totally lucked out with my easy-going bunkmate Sean Lennihan. Yet, many of my friends suffered through freshman year with psychopathic roommates, including one guy who collected his pee in Mountain Dew bottles in the closet.

\* Gardner, H. 1983. *Frames of Mind: The Multiple Intelligence Theory.*
^ Cook Primary School. 2008. www.cookps.act.edu.au, Canberra, Australia.

# CHAPTER 10: WORK

There have been many times in my life when I've been so fed up with working; the daily grind, the pressure, the deadlines, the irritating co-workers, and all the shitty bosses. Sometimes I feel like just giving up and living in a trailer somewhere, working a low stress job, and enjoying myself for a change. But in reality, that would mean giving up many of life's pleasures, such as owning a home, retirement, vacations, living in a safe neighborhood, and economic stability. One way or another everyone has to work, spending almost every waking moment either preparing for, or unwinding from your chosen career. After a while you can even start to lose sight of who you are and what you believe in.

Suddenly you become your job. All your passion is consumed and you begin to resemble your own parents working their lives away. The alarm clock rings and you quiver in your pajamas at the thought of another day in your loathsome occupation. That's why life goes by so fast when you're grown. Because, when you're a kid you savor every waking moment, but when you're an adult you only savor weekends and vacations. So you wind up spending most of your life numb, letting time pass you by.

This is just something that we all have to accept. There are no shortcuts, believe me I've spent years searching for them. The truth is, if you ever want to have a nice life, then working is a must. The key here is to find a job you enjoy.

I've been working since I was fifteen years old. My measly five-dollar-a-week allowance wasn't cutting it anymore, so I decided it was time to become part of the labor force. Over the years I have had some crappy jobs, some decent ones, and a couple I absolutely loved. Yet, each one taught me so much about human nature, and this crazy thing called money.

If you think about the concept of money and what it represents for a second, it can drive you insane. We base our whole existence on this green-dyed paper, and some people would kill their own mother for even a bit of it. In the olden days, people traded for goods and everything was just peachy. "Howdy, neighbor, I'll trade you some eggs for some of that fine lookin' corn ya got?" Too bad it still can't be that way. But bartering goes against the basis of our capitalist government, whose main agenda is to make as much money as you possibly can until you die.

Now, it's true that money can't buy happiness, but it is a necessity if you wish to attain a comfortable life. What a "comfortable life" means is completely up to you. Is it three houses, fancy cars, and exotic vacations? Or, is it a modest lifestyle with middle class amenities? I have personally witnessed money destroy people, friendships, and families, including my own. My mother has been estranged from her siblings over money issues for many years. It truly is the root of all evil.

The million dollar question is: how can you make enough money to be comfortable, yet avoid ruining your life and becoming a miserable person? Well, it all boils down to life experience. You have to get out there and get your hands dirty to realize what you are all about, and what makes you happy. I knew from day one of my first job that backbreaking manual labor would never be for me. During the summer of ninth grade, a friend of my mother's offered me a job at his farm stand, where he sold fruits and vegetables. On my first day I was instructed to unload a truck full of gigantic watermelons, and sixty-pound sacks of potatoes; mind you, I weighed ninety pounds at the time. I'd come home from work every night covered in grime and aching like a seventy-year-old man, all for three dollars an hour. When Halloween came around and the pumpkin truck arrived, I knew this was more than I could stand; so I quit. And from that moment, I knew that my future career would have to be something intellectual.

My next place of employment was at a sixteen-screen movie theatre, which for me was the ultimate jackpot. While ripping tickets, sweeping sticky floors, and replacing urinal cakes sucked big time, this job had major fringe benefits. Being a movie buff, I was in heaven. I saw every movie that came out between 1989 and 1991 for free, plus all the popcorn, candy, and soda I could ingest. My fledgling popularity really began to take flight when I began letting everyone I knew in the back doors without a ticket. Even more importantly, this place was wall-to-wall babes at all times. Between all the employees, their friends, and the teenage movie goers—let's just say I seduced many a young lady in those darkened theatres. Life couldn't have been better, until a new manager came aboard and fired me for making out with a co-worker during a *Thelma and Louise* matinee. But I was eighteen now and yearning for more money, so I moved on unscathed.

I set my sights on an even bigger prize: the adolescent gold mine known as waiting tables. What a nutty occupation this turned out to be. I made awesome money for a kid, but I never worked so hard and kissed so much ass for every single penny. If you want to make cash at this job, you have to run around like a maniac, sweating bullets, carrying huge trays of food, fighting for elbow room in the kitchen, getting disgraced by customers, and all with a giant phony smile on your face.

In the restaurant business you have to accept that the customer is always right. These people get shit on all week at their jobs. On Friday night, they want to be treated like royalty and do the shitting for a change. I've had customers scream in my face, mimic my speech, and even throw food at me; but I took it, made my money, and swallowed my pride. Now, I'm not saying I didn't spit in a few soups or rub an occasional fork in my butt crack, but that's what you get when you piss off your waiter.

## *Life Rule #21: Never mistreat your food server and always tip 20 percent.*

People who work for tips make about two dollars an hour on the books, and most of them are struggling moms and college kids. They work their asses off and deserve a decent tip, unless they absolutely sucked or were rude to you. Anyway, waiting tables taught me to be humble, the true value of a dollar, and how to treat people. It also taught me another thing: restaurant employees party like rock stars. These people work hard all night, go out afterwards until sun-up, sleep until dark, and then start the cycle all over again. It was fun living the vampire life for a while; but after realizing I hadn't seen daylight in over a month, I decided I needed a job that would contribute more to a somewhat normal lifestyle.

This was about the time I realized I wanted to become a teacher. I'd been floating through community college without direction for two years, so I made a major life decision. I wanted to work with kids and maybe make a difference in their lives, like Mrs. Boone the speech therapist who first believed in me. To gain experience in the field, I took a job working with developmentally disabled children. I knew a girl who worked in a school/group home for autistic children. She told me they were looking for counselors, and even though it sounded tough, I felt up for the challenge. Autism is a strange disorder that affects social behavior, and forces those who suffer from it to live in their own private reality. I read up on it and went through a grueling six-week training class, yet nothing could prepare me for what I was about to experience.

What I didn't know was that most mildly autistic kids can live somewhat normal lives with limited family assistance. The kids I was about to work with were profoundly autistic, which is about as autistic as you can get. Their parents had no other choice but to send them away to this school as a last resort. They were severely abusive to both themselves and others; we're talking spitters, biters, food stealers, and self-mutilators.

Ironically, many autistic individuals possess some of the most amazing skills or talents. Harold, a twelve-year-old in my dorm, could whistle every Neil Diamond song ever written in perfect pitch. James could recite every Disney movie verbatim. Sometimes as a goof we'd mute the movies and bug out to his remarkable gift. This job really played on my heartstrings though. These poor kids were hardly ever visited by their families for birthdays, weekends, or holidays. Thinking about the many children who had to spend Christmas morning in the deserted dormitory still saddens me to this day. After two years at Maryhaven, Center of Hope, I was ready to pursue my dream of someday becoming a teacher.

There is still one more job I must mention—talk about a humbling experience. The summer in between my freshman and sophomore years of college, I worked with my friend who started his own clean-up business. However, this wasn't an ordinary clean-up business, he cleaned up dog poop. Picture me in the ninety-degree August heat, scooping fly-covered mounds of crap into a bucket, and dumping it into a truck. It was so humiliating; but how many people do you know who can literally say they have shoveled shit for a living?

## Take this Job and Shove It!

I know that being a quitter isn't something to be proud of, but that has more to do with things of significance, such as careers, dreams, meaningful relationships, and the like. When it comes to these mindless teenage jobs, if they piss you off, just walk the hell out! There are plenty of crappy jobs out there. Life is too short to work for some jackass and get treated like dirt for pennies. My dad instilled such a crazy work ethic in me, that I would always stick it out way too long in some of the worst jobs. But I must tell you, some of the most empowering moments of my life have been when I walked off a job mid-shift, with both my middle fingers raised high in the air. Don't ever let work people walk all over you.

If you are determined enough to pursue a fulfilling career, then quitting will never have to be a problem. I often wonder why kids have such grand career ambitions, yet when they grow up they settle so easily for mediocrity. I hear it everyday with my students: I want to be a doctor, a veterinarian, a singer, a pro athlete, actor, dancer, or, when I was little, a stunt man. Sure, these career choices require tremendous work, but some people just give up too easily. Do you think for a person who stutters becoming a teacher was easy? Actually it was unbearable, but I persevered and stayed true to myself. I knew that I could make a difference in kids' lives, and nothing was going to hold me back. I didn't want to live a life where I dreaded getting out of bed every morning. I needed something where I mattered. This is what you should look for in a career path.

## Life Rule #22: Enjoy the process.

The moment I get a new book, instead of just enjoying the story, I immediately flip to the last page to see how long it is, wondering when I'll be finished. Too many people live their lives in constant pursuit of a happy tomorrow, forgetting about today. These individuals waste away working jobs they hate, and dreaming of a place they may never reach. In order to avoid slipping into this zombie-like mind-set, you must learn to enjoy doing whatever it is that you are doing in the present.

I noticed this one day while jogging and trying to get back into shape. I was running and as usual thinking about how much I hated running. I couldn't wait to be done, take a shower, and fall into the couch with a bag of chips and a Heineken. Then it hit me. That's exactly what got me to this slovenly state in the first place. If I ever wanted to be in shape again, I was going to have to take this exercise thing more seriously. I had to learn how to enjoy the pain, and put my pessimistic mind to some good use.

One day I set out on my course and tried my best to enjoy the moment. I soaked in the beautiful Florida sunset, thought about ways to improve my attitude, and listened to the wind off the water. I ended up running seven miles that day, more than I ever ran before. I decided I was going to try and relate this philosophy to my whole life, and stop incessantly thinking about when my next vacation will be. Whether it's eating, exercising, making love, relationships, reading, and, most of all my career, I'm going to have fun doing it.

Out of the approximately nine thousand hours in each year, about 2,500 are spent working. That's more than a quarter of your life. Sometimes I'll have a horrible day at school, but I'll try to focus on a goofy kid or a funny joke and turn it into a positive. If you find it impossible to enjoy any part of your day, then it just might be time for a career change.

It can take some people many years of numerous career changes before they finally realize where they belong. Mommy slaved away in the advertising industry for five years before she decided to give teaching a try, and now she's happier than ever. This guy Tony was in a few of my college courses; he had such an amazing story. He quit his job as a truck-driver at age forty-three to become a teacher and spend more time with his kids. I had much respect for this dude. He had a mortgage and a family to care for. Now that's what I call a supportive wife.

One of the main reasons that people get stuck in jobs they hate is because the money is good, and they can't afford the schooling a career change would require. If this is ever the case in your life, I make you this promise: you are always welcome to move back in with us whenever you need to. Mommy's parents had seven kids, and at one point or another they all needed to move back home in hard times, including our family. We lived with Grandma and Pop when you were born, and we would have never made it without their help. This is where I learned the meaning of unconditional love, and I vowed to do the same for my kids someday if they needed it. So go out and find your dream career, be your own person, and never settle for anything that doesn't make you smile.

# Benefits

When I was a teenager, my father would tell me the same two things every day. One was, "check your oil," which I never did; and the other was, "I don't care what you choose to do for a living, just make sure it has good benefits." At seventeen that meant about as much to me as preparing my will, as I'm sure it sounds that way to you right now. I would soon learn that my dad was 100 percent accurate. Benefits are services that your job offers you along with employment, such as health insurance, dental coverage, retirement plan, paid sick time/vacations, and investment opportunities. I learned the vast importance of benefits in the winter of 1996, during the worst blizzard Long Island had seen in decades.

I fell down a flight of icy stairs at an apartment I was renting, and wound up knocking myself unconscious and fracturing two vertebrae. I was in a body brace for eight weeks and out of work for four months. Besides losing my mind, the medical bills I tallied up were staggering. Between my hospital stay, the plethora of tests, medications, doctor visits, and subsequent physical therapy, it totaled over thirty thousand dollars; this for a guy making about two hundred bucks a week. Thank heaven I was working at Maryhaven at this time with incredible health coverage. I only paid about eighty bucks out of pocket in co-pays over the whole six-month ordeal. If I hadn't had the benefits, I would have been sunk and in life-ruining debt for the rest of my days. It's exact situations like this that destroy people's lives and even send whole families to the streets.

As I mentioned earlier, your grandpa worked three jobs when I was a kid. He was an electrician's assistant at night, gas station attendant on weekends, and a county highway worker (the guys you see paving the roads) as his nine-to-five. My dad was a brilliant guy but he had no college education, so he had to start at the bottom and work his way up. He knew a county job would eventually offer excellent stability and great benefits for his family.

In a matter of a few years, he worked his way up to supervisor and eventually a highway inspector. Although he struggled greatly in the beginning, he is now living it up in retirement.

Someday you will be approaching your twilight years, and without the correct career choice as a young adult you could be working until the day you die. I talk to people all the time who are in their sixties and still have to work every day to survive. Even though we were pretty poor when I was little, my dad pulled us through and I admire him greatly for it. Many of his buddies that made big bucks when they were younger are now scraping by without any retirement funds. Throw this into the decision process when you are weighing future career options.

## Life Rule #23: Credit cards are evil.

When I first learned about credit cards, I couldn't believe what an amazing country we lived in. "You mean I can buy whatever I want, even if I don't have the money for it?" It sounded too good to be true. During freshman year of college, the local bank set up a booth in the student union in hopes of signing up inexperienced kids, like yours truly. With little convincing, I signed up for a student Visa with a thousand-dollar limit, took home my free T-shirt, and pondered the endless possibilities.

Within a few weeks it was maxed out and I had no way to pay it off. The bills came and I just didn't pay them. This is when I found out what the terms "bad credit" and "interest" meant. This is how they get you and why they are a billion dollar industry. If I loaned you ten bucks on Monday, and told you to pay me back fifteen bucks by Friday, and every day you were late I added two bucks; pretty soon you'd owe me a lot more than you bargained for. That's exactly what happens when you miss your payments, the interest accrues and you owe more.

My credit was ruined by the time I was twenty-four, and this is something that stays with you for a long time. When your mom and I began living together, we started using her larger credit cards to live way above our means. We went on extravagant vacations, bought expensive furniture, ate out in fancy restaurants, and even charged our whole Caribbean honeymoon. This was the last straw. We were newlyweds, twenty grand in debt, and already on the verge of bankruptcy. At this rate we'd never own a home or be financially secure.

Again, thank God for Grandma and Pop taking us in or we would have been royally screwed. We lived like paupers for a while, both worked two jobs, and eventually we were able to get our heads above water again. People without that kind of support system can wind up ruining their lives and becoming slaves to the credit companies. Although plastic currency has become a necessity in life, it should be reserved for emergencies only.

When it comes to money, honey, be careful what you wish for. I know being rich someday is everyone's dream, but with that kind of lifestyle comes much emotional baggage. From what I've seen, you get rich- you get miserable. And then one day you wake up not having a single person you can trust. We have a rich relative, who has slowly been severing ties with the family because he feels everyone wants his money, and you know what, most of them do. His phone rings around the clock and his mind is constantly spinning. Drugs and alcohol have become his only remedy.

I'm very happy with the current financial status of our family. Although there are many things that Mommy and I desire, we have everything we need: jobs that we love, beautiful children, and a modest home in a nice neighborhood. What more could a man ask for?

# CHAPTER 11:
# TELEVISION,
# TECHNOLOGY, AND
# THE MEDIA

Before I sat down to write tonight, there were two back–to-back stories on the news that were so gruesome that it sickens me to repeat them. First, a deranged man purposely threw his two young children off a fifteen-story balcony, killing them both; and, second, a jealous ex-boyfriend threw gasoline in a woman's face and lit a match.

Although these stories are about as horrific as can be, the thing that scared me even more was my callous reaction to both incidents. I barely felt anything while I watched the newscasters explain every graphic detail, and engage in emotionless banter between them. Does this make me some kind of monster, unable to empathize with the cruelty of the world, or rather someone who has been unwillingly desensitized by the media with their relentless attempts to shock, exploit, and invoke public fear?

Good old TV, where would we be without it? What began in the 1950s as a novelty item with four local stations, has now evolved into thousands of channels of digitally-enhanced entertainment. This magical invention with its many circuits, tubes, and wires contains all of our deepest fantasies and aspirations of who we would like to be. The thought of living even one day without it, is like imagining twenty-four hours without food or water. It is now in my thirties that I am finally trying to end the obsession that television has had over me since I can even remember. Being my only escape from family dysfunction, I'd spend hours, entire days, and whole weekends glued to the TV set. I eased my sorrows by dreaming of the fictitious lives I watched, and imagined that I was part of their world.

Most of my favorite childhood memories involve a television in some way. I'd build tents in my living room out of kitchen chairs and blankets, and just bask in the warm glow of the boob-tube inside my darkened hideaway. I stayed up all hours sneaking R-rated cable movies filled with obscenities that a young boy wasn't supposed to see. I watched every cartoon ever made and knew every sitcom rerun by heart. This was my reality.

For years I could recite the prime time line up of all the major networks on any given night. I was a walking *TV Guide*. Even in the present, it's still a daily battle not to fall right back into my addiction. Whenever free time presents itself, it's a challenge not to click on the tube and drift off into Neverland. The programming has gotten much more aggressive, violent, and sexually-explicit. The networks have become so ruthlessly competitive for ratings that there are no limits to the depravity they will air, as millions of impressionable youths struggle to make sense of it all.

Although, it hasn't been a total waste, my thirty-year obsession has allowed me to discover many things. One night as I wandered aimlessly through hundreds of channels, I came upon a pretty heavy realization. As I viewed the shows and commercials, I began noticing that my mind was thinking every self-deprecating thought imaginable: "You're too short, getting fat, going gray, teeth are turning yellow, I hate my hair, I need a new car, I shouldn't have zits at thirty-four, my breath stinks, my clothes suck, I have no money, and I hate my boring town!" These thoughts occurred sporadically throughout the night. Feeling overwhelmed, I grabbed my notebook and tried to write them down.

TV was controlling my thoughts, and subconsciously forcing me to analyze my every imperfection, and wishing them away. I was convincing myself that if I only had money and physical perfection, I could finally achieve happiness. This is the main purpose of television in my mind. Not to entertain or alleviate your worries, but to get you so infatuated with their shows and advertisements, that you will want to completely transform yourself and, therefore, consume products.

They've even begun to incorporate advertising into actual shows, with product placement and floating ads at the bottom of the screen. Do I really need to see a Viagra banner behind home plate during the World Series? Can't I even enjoy a baseball game, without the haunting thought that someday I may not be able to perform? The disturbing thing is that you hardly even notice these messages as they are passed into your subconscious, turning you into a mindless creature with one objective: "I want, I want, I want."

It's almost impossible to feel secure about who you are after a normal night of watching television. Visions of the flawless Hollywood types without an ounce of fat, perfect skin, amazing wardrobes, and awesome lifestyles stay with you as you retire to bed. How in the world can the average person look at all that and say, "Hey, my menial job, frumpy body, coffee-stained teeth, stringy hair, dated clothing, and tiny house suit me just fine."

There will be no "TV revolution." No defining moment where the people of the world throw their sets out the window and swear resistance from its mind control. As the world becomes more populated, and the ability for the average family to live a comfortable life becomes more unattainable, it is inevitable that this problem will only worsen. The days of households with one working parent are long gone. Now with both parents in the work force, the children are left at home with the television as their legal guardian.

What's a parent to do—not own a TV? That's unheard of in this day and age, and would most likely cause mutiny in the ranks of any home. The only fair and feasible plan Mommy and I could come up with was to try to limit television to a bare minimum, and be very strict as to what is viewed. Even though you'll probably hate our guts when your friends are constantly talking about MTV and other shows that you have to pretend you also watch. You'll just have to trust me on this one. I know all the reading and piano lessons suck right now, but in ten years you will be so grateful when you are a talented, intelligent, and secure young adult who inspires others.

Most of my students tell me that they watch TV and play video games between six and seven hours a day, including weekends where it can become an all day affair. Just last week, I was over a friend's house for dinner and his eight- and ten-year-old sons were ensconced in their video games. I sat down to watch. The object of the game they were playing was to steal cars, shoot at police, and destroy everything in their path. They were screaming things like, "Die sucka!" as fires erupted and heads exploded. It was such a long way from my 1982 Atari 2600 video game, with the two sticks and the ball bouncing back and forth. The teacher in me was thinking: how could these kids possibly enjoy story time on the rug, or a math lesson about fractions where sliced oranges are used as representation? Oh how fun!

This is why kids can't read or focus in school anymore. Because they are so over-stimulated at home, that when it comes to a book, they can't bear to look at it. My classes are practically jumping out of their skin listening to me teach, and I'm a pretty entertaining teacher. I juggle, tell jokes, do magic, break dance, play guitar, and talk in "gangsta" slang just to keep their attention, and it barely even works. I do everything short of shooting fire out of my ass to keep these kids entertained. How the hell is fifty-three-year-old Mrs. Smith with the lifeless voice, frigid personality, and jiggly triceps supposed to keep these kids motivated? I'll tell you how, she doesn't; she merely labels them as learning disabled and tries to get them services. You wouldn't believe how many kids are prescribed psychotropic drugs because of this.

As time goes by we will all have attention deficit disorder, unless parents can take a stand against this epidemic known as over-stimulation. Although most are just relieved that their kids are being quiet and staying in their rooms, it's destroying their imagination and ability to think for themselves. I'm no prude by any means, but I just can't sit back in good conscience and let my kid's minds and personalities get molded by television and video games. I wouldn't be able to live with myself if this happened.

## The Day the Music "Really" Died

In the early seventies, Don McLean wrote a catchy little tune called "American Pie." The song symbolized the 1959 plane crash and tragic loss of three of rock and roll's early pioneers, Ritchie Valenz, Buddy Holly, and the Big Bopper. Also known as "The Day the Music Died," the passing of these musical icons was an enormous blow to rock and roll. However, with the multitudes of new talent on the horizon, it would continue to persevere for decades to come. Until another tragic day in music history when I feel the music "really" died. August 1, 1981, the first day of MTV, music television.

It feels like yesterday when it premiered. My sister and I watched in awe, seeing our favorite singers perform in the flesh for the first time. Until then, you could only see famous musicians in magazines or the occasional late show appearance. Now you could finally see them in all their glory around the clock. The first video ever played was "Video Killed the Radio Star," by the Buggles. The eerie foreshadowing of this song couldn't have been any more precise, because that's exactly what has happened twenty-five years later; video has killed the radio star.

Before MTV, music was an art form, a masterful ability that select geniuses possessed with techniques that left thousands mystified. Music was something you experienced with your ears and emotions, but music television has single-handedly changed this. Over the course of two decades, they have transformed music into a visual experience rather than an aural one. Since human beings are mainly visual creatures, it made perfect sense for this evolution to occur. Who knew it would spin so out of control?

MTV would soon become a monster of a network, and more or less corner the teenage viewer demographic of the entire nation. They would eventually launch VH1, MTV2, and expand programming into making movies, TV shows, and game shows. In fact, they are the true inventors of the ever popular reality TV. All of the sudden, MTV became the epitome of everything that was cool and it told kids what to wear, how to talk, how to feel, what's hot, what's not, and how to think; and they all lapped it up like thirsty puppies. Because of this, musical artists come and go with the breeze nowadays. "Johnny and the Pocket Rockets" is the next big thing on Monday, and completely washed up by Friday. As music became more about the style of the artist and less about the actual content, the artists became dispensable.

A few months ago an "artist" named Ashlee Simpson, who is your basic run of the mill prom queen, was caught lip-synching during a live TV performance. When her audio track skipped, she ran off the stage humiliated and practically in tears. Nothing could symbolize the sorry state of popular music as that revealing incident. It seems that the new formula for musical success is to take a beautiful person, throw them in the recording booth, and then use studio magicians to turn them into the hot artist of tomorrow.

In the 1960s, the best musical talent was on the radio. This was your mainstream top forty. Many of these groundbreaking artists are still cranking out brilliant tunes to this day, and being honored for lifetime achievements. What's going to happen in twenty years when these people aren't with us anymore? Who will we honor and be inspired by, the Stevie Wonders, Bob Dylans, Neil Youngs, Bruce Springsteens, Paul McCartneys, and Bonnie Raitts? I'm not saying there aren't any present day geniuses around, but now you have to search them out underground. And they most certainly aren't among the top twelve finalists on *American Idol*. I rue the day when the Rock and Roll Hall of Fame is forced to change its name to the Hall of Sexy Bodies and Electronically Enhanced Music.

# CHAPTER 12:
# MOVIES

Here's a real shocker for you: I actually have a few obsessions that aren't harmful or potentially life threatening, and movies is one of them. For every ten lousy movies you see, they'll be one magical film that touches your heart and creates a moment you'll never forget. I still get chills when I think of the climatic crane kick in the *Karate Kid,* or the nail-biting escape scene from *E.T.,* and they both came out over twenty years ago. Amazing movies can have everlasting effects on your personality. They allow you to leave your life for a few hours and enter a world of fantasy and adventure. People judge films by many different criteria. Like music, everyone's a freakin' critic and many have not one nice thing to say. I judge movies by one criterion only. Did it make me think, laugh, or feel? If it did, it was a good one.

I remember going to the video store with my dad when I was younger. He'd always point out his favorite old movies and I couldn't have cared less. However, I promise you that my taste in movies is superb. All of the titles I am about to name will leave you speechless if given the chance, and they will still be regarded as great movies a hundred years from now.

*A Beautiful Mind:* The true story of a schizophrenic genius who struggles to come to grips with his disorder.

*A Time to Kill:* A black man's eight-year-old daughter is brutally raped by white men; he murders them in return and goes to trial.

*A Walk on the Moon:* A young mother almost loses it all, trying to recapture her wasted adolescence.

*American Beauty:* Startling tale of the intense drama that exists within normal American homes.

*American History X:* A riveting story of racial hatred and white supremacy in suburban America.

*Amistad:* A historical reflection into the atrocities of the African slave trade.

*Back to the Future:* Might be the best time travel tale ever.

*Basketball Diaries:* #1 don't do drugs movie.

*Boogie Nights:* A young man's journey through the seedy world of pornography.

*Borat: Cultural Learnings of America for Make Benefit Glorious Nation of Kazakhstan:* If you want to take a hysterical look at the idiocy of society, rent this tonight.

*Born on the Fourth of July:* A paralyzed soldier struggles through post-Vietnam life.

*Bowling for Columbine:* A disturbing documentary about America's obsession with guns and violence.

*Boys Don't Cry:* The true story of a young girl with a sexual identity crisis, who meets her brutal demise in Middle America.

***Brokeback Mountain:*** Believe it or not, a gay cowboy movie that cuts like a knife.

***Castaway:*** Trapped on a deserted island for five years, what would you do?

***Crash:*** A story of prejudice and racial stereotypes, with all of the remarkable plot lines coming together in the end.

***Dances with Wolves:*** The heart-wrenching story of the exploitation and brutal end of the Native American way of life.

***Dead Poets Society:*** "Carpe diem." The movie that made the whole world want to seize the day.

***Dragonfly:*** A man is mysteriously drawn to the place of his wife's death, for a life changing discovery.

***E.T.:*** I don't care how old it is, this movie will make you believe.

***Fargo:*** A twisting abduction tale about how money and greed are the roots of all evil.

***Fast Times at Ridgemont High:*** An Eighties favorite and the best stoner movie ever made.

***Fear:*** A psycho boyfriend ruins a young girl's life. Every sixteen-year-old girl should be forced to watch this movie.

***Fight Club:*** A cult classic about unleashing your inner beast; also Brad Pitt at his finest.

***Forrest Gump:*** My all-time favorite movie. A simple-minded man leads an extraordinary life of personal discovery.

***Frequency:*** A man discovers a way to communicate with his dead father.

***Garden State:*** An emotional look at the trials and tribulations of twenty-somethings.

***Girl, Interrupted:*** The story of troubled young women who find solace in each other during a stay at a mental health facility.

***Good Will Hunting:*** An abused orphan who also happens to be a mathematical genius, struggles with his past, and through friendship finds his way.

***Goodfellas:*** A cinematic adventure into the depths of organized crime.

***Hardball:*** Kids from the slums get a chance at greatness, from the most unlikely of coaches.

***Higher Learning:*** A revealing look into the dangers of college campus life. Everything they don't tell you in the brochure.

***It's a Wonderful Life:*** A classic tale that answers the age old question, what would the world be like if you were never born?

***Karate Kid:*** The best bully movie ever made.

***Little Miss Sunshine:*** American family dysfunction at it's all-time best.

***Mask:*** Truthful account of a brave young man living with a devastating physical deformity.

***Mean Girls:*** The best representation of teenage-girl angst on film.

***Memento:*** Mind-blowing mystery filmed with the scenes in reverse.

***Million Dollar Baby:*** Who would have imagined a movie about a female boxer could be so amazing?

***Monster:*** Chilling true story about a Florida prostitute turned serial killer.

***Mr. Holland's Opus:*** A musical composer and school teacher discovers how much he influenced lives with his music.

***My Girl:*** A touching story about the wonders of childhood friendship.

***My Life:*** A man dying of cancer makes a video for his unborn child.

***Napoleon Dynamite:*** A low-budget cult comedy classic. This guy is the nerd that we all felt like in high school.

***Pay It Forward:*** A movie about the endless possibilities of spreading positive energy.

***Pee Wee's Big Adventure:*** I cannot believe I'm including this one, but I adored this goofy fantasy flick as a kid.

***Project X:*** A film about the evils of animal testing that will enlighten your spirit.

***Rainman:*** A wealthy businessman connects with the adult autistic brother he never knew he had.

***Requiem for a Dream:*** #2 don't do drugs movie.

***Revenge of the Nerds:*** The geeks fight back against the beautiful people, and win.

***Saving Private Ryan:*** Set in a World War II flashback, this gripping tale is about the endless nightmares a soldier must live with.

***Schindler's List:*** The end-all Holocaust movie.

***Se7en:*** The most suspenseful serial killer movie ever made.

***Seven Years in Tibet:*** The tragic fall of the peaceful nation of Tibet.

***Shawshank Redemption:*** A man goes to prison for a crime he didn't commit, but never loses his hope.

***Shine:*** A musical prodigy with an overbearing father suffers a nervous breakdown and becomes a reclusive schizophrenic.

***Sling Blade:*** A film about mental illness and domestic abuse with an unlikely hero.

***Spun:*** #3 don't do drugs movie.

***Stand by Me:*** This is my coming of age movie.

***Super Size Me:*** A documentary about the poisoning effects of fast food.

***The Accused:*** A vicious film that depicts the evils of men.

***The Machinist:*** You can run, but you can never hide from your own guilty conscience.

***The Matrix:*** A post-apocalyptic Earth movie that will confuse the hell out of you, in a good way.

***The Outsiders:*** Cultures collide in this 1960s gang tale.

***The Passion of the Christ:*** A movie about the greatest story ever told; it is so realistic you will never look at a crucifix the same way again.

***The School of Rock:*** If you ever wanted to know what daddy is like in class, see this movie.

***The Silence of the Lambs:*** Hannibal Lector is the best on-screen villain ever.

***The Sixth Sense:*** This movie has the best surprise ending ever written.

***The Truman Show:*** A man's whole life has been a reality TV show, and he doesn't even know it.

***Thirteen:*** A good girl turns thirteen and gets involved with the wrong crowd; every parent's nightmare.

***This Boy's Life:*** A young boy struggles through a meaningless existence at the hands of his abusive stepfather.

***Titanic:*** The ultimate chick flick, this is the historically incorrect tale of the sinking of an unsinkable cruise liner.

***Traffic:*** Brilliant depiction of the American government's futile war on drugs.

***Unfaithful:*** A movie that proves infidelity always ends in tragedy (alright, so I have a thing for Diane Lane; big deal).

# Chapter 13: Breaking the Rules

In October of 1989, Vinny Torino and I skipped eighth period to go smoke weed and hit up the Wendy's drive-thru. Vinny was the kind of kid who caused trouble wherever he went, but he sure was a blast to hang out with. This guy had no fear whatsoever. He lived on impulse like a true sociopath; fighting, vandalizing, shoplifting, you name it, he did it. For instance, we once went to the movies together, and the first thing he did was buy the biggest box of Milk Duds he could find, to beam at people's heads from the back row. I knew that associating with him was going to be my eventual downfall. It was just too exciting to resist.

This day in particular we were out cruising around in his ten-passenger Chevy Suburban that he had aptly named, "the Party Barge." He'd take crowds of us out on the hills of Farmingville at break-neck speeds, spreading mayhem to otherwise peaceful neighborhoods.

Today it was just him and me, and lucky for us it happened to be leaf day. In a few select neighborhoods, people would rake all their leaves into piles by the edge of the lawn, and the town would come by with giant vacuum machines and suck them into a truck. One of our favorite activities was to drive through these leaf piles at top speed and turn them into smithereens. After destroying a few mediocre-size piles with great delight, we were ready to head back to school, when into our view came the mother of all leaf piles. Our mouths watered as we gazed upon this dumpster-sized pile in front of a luxurious estate. Vinny locked it into his sights, floored the gas, and we both screamed in harmonious excitement.

"Pour Some Sugar on Me" by Def Leppard blared from the speakers as the Party Barge's engine roared, and we pounded our fists in unison. Vin squinted his beady eyes and put his nose to the steering wheel, while I buried my fingers into the dash and held on for dear life. Seconds away from impact, I noticed the leaf pile ruffle in an unusual way, and purely by instinct I reached over and frantically pulled the steering wheel to the right. Vinny slammed on the brakes and we whipped into a 180 degree spin, screeching to a halt on the lawn directly across the street from our target. As the Party Barge laid motionless and Vinny was about to grab my throat in rage, we watched in astonishment as two preschool age boys popped out of the pile carrying plastic guns and ran toward their house in fear.

We couldn't move, speak, or even breathe for what felt like an eternity. Irate neighbors began coming outside to assess the situation, and Vin tore out of there with a fury. He dropped me off at school without one word spoken. I sat in my car for over an hour shivering, as the image of those two boys repeatedly flashed before my eyes. What if I hadn't grabbed the wheel? We would have crushed those kids to death. And because of all the pot that we had on us, in us, and our intentional reckless behavior, we would have no doubt been charged with vehicular homicide, and gone from carefree teenagers to murderers in an instant. Instead of being a teacher, husband, and loving father, I'd be inmate #253-047 living in a cage like an animal, and on constant suicide watch. One more second and my whole life could've ended along with those two little boys. Vinny and I never hung out again. I don't think either of us will ever forget that day.

That's how quickly a good time can turn into a life altering tragedy. I have so many stories like this of narrowly avoiding disaster. I chose to run with a fast crowd, so trouble was always near. One more deserves mention. A bunch of us were attending a raging woods party one night, getting wasted, blasting music, and dancing around a campfire. After a drunken keg tossing competition, the empty barrel was jokingly rolled into the fire by a guy named Eddie McCarran. As the hours passed and the party was winding down to just the die-hards, Amber Donahue and I had moved on to a more intimate setting.

The next morning I received a distraught phone call from my friend Chris, who informed me that the empty keg had later exploded in the fire and killed someone. Joe Weis was a super-cool surfer dude with the warmest personality ever. I didn't know him that well, but he didn't have an enemy in the world. The twisted metal had gone through his chest and practically decapitated him. His funeral was closed-casket.

Eddie McCarran was arrested, brought up on charges, and eventually prosecuted; another example of a silly mistake becoming a point of no return.

### Life Rule #24: Every action has its consequence.

When you're young, everything is all about fun. You never want to be the killjoy who says, "Hey, guys, maybe we shouldn't be doing this." Everyone might think you're a loser, and you also might miss out on an incredible memory. Sometimes you just have to trust your gut. If your stomach is twisting and turning, then you know that what you're about to do is a very bad idea.

Usually for girls, the real danger comes from the guys you associate with. You know the type, the ones who are constantly fighting, speeding, drinking, and having drugs on them. I know these guys can be irresistible to hang out with, but they are also the ones who will bring you the most misfortune. You can get in just as much trouble being with a sociopath as being one yourself. Furthermore, ignorance of the law does not protect you from breaking it. In other words, just because you didn't know a law existed, you're still screwed if you disregard it.

Here are some things we did when I was a teenager. I'm sure they've now morphed into actions of more severity, but I'd imagine some of them are still quite popular.

1. **Shoplifting**. I'd bet that this is still one of the most prevalent crimes amongst teenage girls. Even your saint-like Mom had a few run-ins with "five finger discounts" during her adolescence. The reason being is when you're sixteen and trying so hard to maintain an unaffordable wardrobe, the temptation is too great. The clothes are too easy to shove into your shopping bag. Just remember, when you think it is so easy and you cannot possibly get caught, you are most likely being watched. Nowadays, even dollar stores have surveillance cameras hidden where you cannot notice them. They are recording your every move, and later this can become proof of guilt in a court of law.

   One time in Steinbeck's department store, I shoved a fleece jacket I really wanted into my shopping bag and walked out. Within seconds, the seven-foot security guard was in my face and dragging me to a secret room upstairs. As he called the police, he showed me a video tape of my rather indiscreet caper. Luckily, I only got a slap on the wrist; a phone call home, and lifetime banishment from the store.

   Shoplifting can actually turn into an obsession. A few years ago a famous actress named Winona Ryder was arrested for shoplifting things from a store. Even though she had millions of dollars, she still could not resist the rush that walking out with unpaid merchandise can provide; just like drugs. Please try to use your best judgment and refrain from stealing. I know we aren't the richest family in town, and you probably wish you could have more. But nothing feels better than saving for something special and earning it on your own. Mommy and I will always try to help you get the things you really want. Just don't break the law, and more importantly, don't listen to your airhead friends.

2. **Using a fake ID**. In the old days, we'd just change our birthday with a colored pencil, or use an older friend's license to get into a bar or buy alcohol. Presently, with all the latest technology, it's harder to get away with it, and now the punishment is much more severe. I'm sure kids will always figure out new and improved ways to acquire phony IDs. It's quite frustrating when you're only a few months away from twenty-one and still can't buy beer. This is actually a very serious crime, and you can get in major trouble for possessing a fake ID. You have your whole life to go to bars. Don't rush it; plus they're way overrated.

3. **DWI**. Besides the risks of killing yourself and innocent others, drinking and driving can have many other serious consequences attached to it. The police are really cracking down on this crime. The legal blood alcohol content (BAC) continues to lower each year. Realistically, you can't even have one beer and drive or you'll blow over the legal limit, especially if you're a slender female. Even if you have food and four cups of coffee after drinking, only time (a lot of time) will sober a person up and nothing else.

Sometimes that doesn't even work. A guy I taught with once slept eight hours after a drunken New Years Eve, and when he was pulled over the next morning, he was given a breathalyzer and failed. Not only was he driving with a suspended license, but this was his second DWI in ten years. He was sentenced to two months in jail, lost his teaching license, and now has a permanent felonious record. He was an awesome teacher, too. When I think of him delivering furniture for a living now, it nearly breaks my heart. Drinking and driving is never the answer, just look at the losses I have suffered and please learn from them. With the simple turn of a key, countless lives can be forever shattered.

4. **Illegal things in your car.** You never know what the people in your car are carrying in their pockets, especially if you choose to hang out with a rowdy crowd. I don't care if they are your best friends since birth, when you get pulled over, whatever anyone is carrying gets shoved directly under the seat without a moment's thought. When the police find it (and they will), if nobody fesses up, possession falls on the owner of the car, and that's who gets arrested. I once gave a spaced-out kid a ride home from a Phish concert, and during the ride he informed me that he was holding hundreds of hits of LSD. I should have stopped the car right there, but like an idiot, I didn't. If I would have been pulled over my life would have been finished. Acid is one of the most serious drugs to get caught with. Do you think that kid would have spoken up for me?

Teenage boys love having their girlfriend's chauffer them all over town so they can get drunk, stoned, and unruly without care. And the more of his friends that join the party, the more chances are that you will get pulled over and searched. Even one empty beer can, pot seed, or bottle cap is grounds for complete search of the vehicle, and loss of everything you have worked so hard for. So, do yourself a tremendous favor and don't get in cars with these reckless maniacs, and never ever offer to drive. Just meet them there.

When you do get pulled over, if you do the right thing you may get away with a stern warning. Always keep in mind that the cop has all the power in the situation, and if he wants to he can use his pen to ruin your life. It is never a good idea to give attitude to a cop. Here's what you do: pull over slowly and immediately. Turn on your interior light, put both hands on top of the steering wheel, and be as courteous and apologetic as humanly possible. And never under any circumstances open the car door or try to get out. This method will get you out of many more jams than bitching and complaining ever would. One more thing, don't ever lie to them. These people get lied to for a living, they can smell it from a mile away and it really pisses them off.

5. **Injury/Death at your house party**. At the time of my legendary bonfire party, I had no idea that if anyone had gotten injured on my property or while driving home drunk, my parents would have been held legally responsible. They could have been sued, lost their house, and had criminal charges pressed against them, even though they were thousands of miles away. Thank God nothing like that did happen, but there have been many stories where it did, and the parents had to pay dearly with their house and life savings. I know I have it coming to me one of these days, but please don't have a big party at our house. When you're old enough, we can discuss it and figure out the right thing to do. In the time being, have mercy on us!

6. **Drinking/Drugs on school grounds**. There are always those rebels who simply cannot wait until Friday night to party; they want to bring it to school with them. Nevertheless, all high schools have security and you will likely get caught and maybe even expelled if you choose to participate. The school has the right to search any student at any time, lockers included. If you ever know anyone who is partying at school, stay far away.

At the tenth grade homecoming dance, my boys and I snuck a bottle of peach schnapps into the gym and got piss-wasted. Three of us were later nabbed by our pitbull-like assistant principal. Parents were called, suspensions imposed, and privileges were revoked, but we wore it like a badge of honor. Let me ask you this: how many reputable colleges do you think are going to accept a student who was expelled from their high school for drugs or alcohol?

7. **Fighting**. Hopefully we raised you in a way that you know fighting is never the answer. It is always best to search out an alternative to violence. I'm not saying that you should allow someone to physically assault you and do nothing. Girls these days can be just as vicious as boys when it comes to physical intimidation. Most likely, it will be the boys in your inner circle that do most of the scuffling. Just remember that one solid punch to a sensitive spot like the throat or temple can cause instant death. Imagine watching a young person die after a pointless fight over inflated ego. What if it was your boyfriend? When confrontations arise, use your words and brain.

8. **Pulling fire alarms**. Kids used to do this in my high school all the time to avoid exams. What seemed like a harmless prank could have ended with deadly consequences. Emergency crews and fire departments will respond to school alarms with utmost urgency. Innocent rescue workers and pedestrians are frequently maimed or even killed in these traffic emergencies; simply because an irresponsible kid wanted to avoid a geometry quiz.

9. **Dine and Dash.** Friendly's in the Smith Haven Mall was continuously packed to the rafters. There was always a wait in the lobby and a lengthy line at the check-out counter. To the average shopper this may have been looked upon as an annoyance, but in the minds of rebellious teens, it was the perfect opportunity to "dine and dash!" At least once a month, my friends and I would treat ourselves to an extravagant feast from soup to nuts, topped off with a ginormous ice-cream sundae. Then, at the ideal moment we'd make our way to the register, sift through the crowd,

and discreetly saunter out the door. We always got a charge out of this activity, boasting about our bravery and how we were sticking it to the corporate fat-cats. But in reality, the only person we were sticking it to was the down-trodden waitress.

As I said earlier, food-servers make slave wages by the hour, and can only survive because of their tips. In one of the chain restaurants that I worked, the managers would hold the server personally responsible for walk-outs, and would distribute penalties like docking pay, taking away big-money shifts, or even letting people go. And not only is this a crime called "theft of services," but you are really screwing over an undeserving person for your own selfish enjoyment.

10. **Mailbox mischief.** There's a disturbing scene in the movie *The Butterfly Effect,* in which a group of hooligans place a lit M-80 inside a neighborhood mailbox. While hiding in nearby shrubbery, unexpected disaster strikes when the container explodes in the face of a young woman holding a baby. I think the reason this scene bothered me so much was because I used to do things like this to annoying neighbors quite often. What I didn't know at the time was that those low-priced mailboxes that people buy at Home Depot and install themselves are actually federal property, and tampering with them in any way is a felony offense. One harmless smoke bomb or a quick inning of "mailbox baseball" could have resulted in serious charges or even jail. So the next time you want to get a neighbor's panties in a bunch, just swing by their house after midnight and knock and run.

A colleague of mine was recently interviewing for a coveted teaching position in a high-paying district, and would you believe the interview board called his old high school? He didn't get the job because of an isolated incident of vandalism during his senior year. They told him to his face that they didn't want to hire someone with such feeble moral values. I bet he never thought that would come back to haunt him.

While some of the consequences of your actions will be minimal, others can scar you for life. Living with regret for a stupid mistake can become a nightmarish reality. Try and picture how that kid who threw the keg in the fire is doing right now. He didn't mean it. It was a drunken blunder, one that he has to live with forever.

I know that when you're a teenager nothing is lamer than endless lists of rules and restrictions. But rules were implemented for a reason: to keep people's loved ones alive and well. So the next time your gut is talking to you, listen up kid.

# CHAPTER 14:
# DEATH

Working in a Catholic school, the one question I get all the time from my students is, "Why does God let people die?" I always answer with an explanation of the Chinese philosophy of "yin and yang" and how the universe must constantly be in balance with both positive and negative forces. There can be no light without dark, love without hate, or life without death. Although this idea is something I truly believe in, it never really satisfies my students, and often leaves them looking more perplexed than before they asked the question. That's the best I can do; how could anyone possibly explain the concept of death?

Last week, I was watching a show on my favorite channel Animal Planet. A group of scientists were following around a herd of elephants, when one of the babies became ill and died. As the rest of the herd carried on unconcerned, the mother of the dead baby was in dire straits. She laid next to her offspring and desperately tried to make it move with her trunk, all the while exerting deep sorrowful bellows. Hours later and completely exhausted, she stayed with the lifeless carcass and continued her mourning throughout the night, as the hyenas waited in the darkness.

Death causes such deep emotional pain, that our minds cannot even fully grasp the concept. People die every second of every day, and with each death droves of people are destroyed, never to be the same. When my friends died in that car accident, I remember crying so much that it physically hurt. The fact that they were gone from my life forever was just too much for my delicate soul to handle. My childhood ended that day, and I didn't know if I'd ever recover or smile again. I wished that five years would pass by in a heartbeat, so I could be healed and stop feeling the pain. But the truth is, you never fully heal from the loss of loved ones. It's been over ten years since Jimmy and Greg passed away, and the wounds still feel as fresh as ever. While I'm not constantly sobbing or an emotional basket case anymore, it's a rare day that a sad thought about them doesn't enter my mind. I'm still waiting for the day when I come to accept their loss.

Sometimes even the death of complete strangers can be just as devastating as the passing of a cherished loved one. September 11, 2001, was a magnificent fall day in New York City. It was one of those picture perfect days that you get like five times a year if you're lucky: clear skies, bright sunshine, and not a hint of humidity. It even made the dingy little borough of Queens feel like paradise. If not for it being a Tuesday, I would have no doubt been on the beach with Zeke throwing sticks and loving life.

It was one of those days that made me truly appreciate my third floor classroom with breathtaking views of lower Manhattan from across the East River. Unbeknownst to us and the rest of America as we settled into our morning routine, the world would be forever changed within moments. As I wrote the daily agenda on the blackboard, the screeching voice of Shoneika Hudson pierced through the silence, "Oh my God! The Twin Towers are on fire!" My stomach retched, and in an instant my twenty-eight sixth graders and I were glued to the plate glass windows in awe.

As smoke billowed from the south tower turning the sky into an eerie black smog, the sounds of panic began to echo throughout the hallways and other classrooms. Dozens of petrified kids looked to me for answers, and I tried to assure them that it was probably just a small fire that would be taken care of momentarily. And then the unthinkable happened. A 747 jetliner full of passengers crashed directly into the second tower right before our eyes. Jaws hit the floor in disbelief and several students latched onto me for comfort. As both buildings burned on the horizon it became quite apparent that the city of New York was now under attack.

Gasps and screams turned into an unbearable sniffling silence. In a state of panic, I began checking the status of my shell-shocked platoon. The absolute terror on their faces chilled me to the core. As I came to Justin Banister, he was hyperventilating and drenched in tears as he uttered these sobering words, "Mr. G, my mom works in the Twin Towers." It cut through me like glass, and for a moment I was without speech. The best I could muster up was an arm around his shoulder and an unconvincing, "Don't worry, she'll be fine."

Hysterical parents soon began picking up their children in preparation for the apocalypse, including one man covered in blood and debris. We would soon find out that a group of religious extremists with deep hatred for America were responsible for this outlandish offense. They had highjacked four planes filled with passengers, with the intent of crashing them into the Twin Towers, the Pentagon, and the White House in Washington D.C. All but one plane was successful in its suicide mission.

The entire world was in turmoil. Every person in every country sat glued to their televisions watching the carnage unfold and the death count increase with each passing moment. "How could this happen?" "Who are these people and why do they hate us so much?" These questions and many more would be the focus of every American for years to come. Both towers eventually collapsed as firemen, policemen, rescue workers, people's sons, daughters, husbands, wives, moms, and dads met their untimely fates. Close to three thousand people died horrific deaths on this day.

In the days that followed, heartbreaking stories began emerging from the survivors and people who lost loved ones. Justin Banister's mom was killed in the attacks, becoming part of the lurid statistics of this catastrophic event. He returned to school two weeks later like a walking zombie. Always the class clown, he was now carved hollow and in his grandmother's care. The school pulled together to comfort him and the others who suffered losses, but Justin would soon become undone as the weeks passed. I couldn't even imagine the pain that this eleven-year-old boy was going through; nothing I could do or say would ever make it better.

The rescue attempts soon turned into rubbish and body removal, as the weeks turned into months, and the smoldering flames continued to burn. 9-11-01 will forever be one of the worst tragedies in human history.

Dealing with loss can be the most difficult battle a person can face. Saying that death is a part of life, or that time will heal all, just doesn't give anyone the comfort they desperately need. Between you and your brother, we had another child that almost became part of our family. Like so many young women, Mommy had a miscarriage in her first trimester of pregnancy. We were both pretty busted up. While the baby was no bigger than a strawberry, we had names picked out and were already starting to love that little scuttle bug. Your mother was much more devastated than I. She walked around in a state of mourning for months. Not until she became pregnant again with Jesse, did I see her smiling face again.

## Learning to Cope

When death barges into your world, you are left so beaten and raw that you can feel like a helpless infant struggling to survive amidst the harsh elements. You forget how it feels to be happy, and constant sadness becomes your norm. While you may never fully heal, eventually you will learn ways to cope. A few weeks after my friend's deaths, I grabbed a spiral notebook and headed to the beach, pondering my grief and thoughts of my own mortality. I started to scribble away with no direction. At first it came out as the inane drivel of a mad man. However, as the hours passed and my writing continued at a feverish pace, I realized I was writing a letter to my lost brothers. Everything I wanted to say to them but couldn't was flowing out of me almost supernaturally.

I felt the emotional burden slightly lessening as tears and words covered the blank pages, much like the way a cup of coffee slowly brings you out of the dreadful morning grog and into reality. I wrote until my hand ached and the pages became barely legible, but this letter didn't need to be read. It was now out of my head and no longer consuming my every thought. I ripped out my eleven-page letter, rolled it up, and shoved it into an empty soda bottle with some sand for added weight. I launched it into the crashing surf with all my might, hoping it would eventually fall off the horizon and wind up in heaven for Jimmy and Greg to read. I had discovered a way to feel better and deal with my emotions. I began journaling every night religiously. As a matter of fact, this book was born out of those very sessions.

Whatever the format, putting pen to paper can be a life-changing experience. Poetry is another great method of dealing with grief. After 9/11 my school was in a perpetual state of sorrow. Nobody smiled for months. One day I jotted down a poem and hung it up in the faculty room in an attempt to comfort people. I was quite taken back when the whole school fell in love with this simple sonnet that I wrote in five minutes. Other teachers photocopied it and hung it in their classrooms, and even gave some to students. It sort of became our school's battle cry. In a way, this poem was one of the things that helped our school heal, and I'm damn proud of what it represents.

## "That Day"

It was the 11th of September, forever etched in history
There was smoke over the city- far as the eye could see

It started out- like any other day
Why oh why- did it have to go this way

I could not comprehend- just what was going down
There were pieces of building- falling to the ground

Our freedom was attacked my friends
Those words rang out so true
Thousands lost their lives this day
I wondered who I knew

Why is there such hatred
How can this be real
So many dreams were shattered
Now only time will heal

But Mr. Terrorist- I've got some news for you
You can knock down our buildings
But we're gonna make it through
To kill the soul of America- is impossible to do!


Keep Strong,

Mr. G

The key to recovering from a loss is to purge the pain out of you in any way possible; through tears, writing, primal screams, prayer, or even heartfelt conversations. Without an outlet in which to vent, you will most definitely become an active volcano ready to explode. Besides time and literal expression, the only other thing that I've found to ease this kind of pain is the comfort of others who share your grief.

Whether it's a best friend or a room full of twenty strangers at a support group, it's amazing what a sincere hug from a caring soul can do. If any positive can come out of all of this heartbreak, it's to learn to appreciate life. Even though we may never be prepared for something as horrible as death, there can be happiness in its wake.

# Chapter 15:
# Live and Let Live

Throughout your life, you are going to come across tons of people who are quite different from you and what you are used to. You may be startled at first by their unfamiliarity, but this is all just part of growing up. Learning to accept people for who they are, and not prejudging, is what truly defines the concept of maturity. Whether it's a different race, religion, sexual orientation, style, accent, beliefs, customs, or culture, this is simply who they are.

This is something I've been forever trying to change about myself. During graduate school I was paired with a girl from India to do a research project. She was very traditional and dressed in native garb, with multi-colored dresses and a scarf over her head. At first I felt very uncomfortable and negative towards her. Yet, Marzia turned out to be the kindest soul, and was my driving force through a few grueling courses.

Fifty years ago there was an organization of people called the Ku Klux Klan. The KKK was a group of white supremacists that despised anything other than white people, and would act on this hatred through random acts of violence. They were especially brutal in their attacks on African Americans. They burned crosses on people's lawns, gang beat people, and even hung children from trees in broad daylight, a term gruesomely referred to as lynching. Although their numbers have significantly dropped in the last quarter century, you'd be shocked at how many people of this nature still exist in hiding.

Being born and raised in New York, I wasn't exposed to many "isms" until we moved to the South, when all that would change. One night I was conversing with this guy in a sleazy Florida bar. After hearing my accent he said, "The only Yankees we like are the ones who marry Niggers and move back up north!" I felt like I had stepped back in time as his group of toothless friends high-fived him and laughed in agreement.

The harsh reality is that even though discrimination is on its decline, it will always be a part of our society. As long as people hate, they will teach their children to hate and therefore continue the existence of this evil attribute. Because of 9/11, I even find myself talking hateful things about Arabic people, and the actual killers were only a handful of extremists, not a race of millions. Just in the last ten years, appalling acts of hatred have occurred in this country that offer proof that we are still far away from racial equality and social harmony.

**1998, Laramie, Wyoming**. Two college boys lured a student named Matthew Sheppard, who was supposedly gay, out of a bar to an open field. They then proceeded to savagely beat and pistol whip the boy into a coma, and left him tied to a fence to die, which he did. This incident actually happened when I was in Professor Gilden's class. He was the guy I mentioned earlier who marched for civil rights in the 1960s. He was outraged by this occurrence and was organizing a candlelight vigil in our town square that very night. Being inspired by his convictions, I attended and held a candle and a "Homophobia is a disease!" sign. I can't tell you how many groups of drunken guys screamed hateful slurs and even threw things at us. For that brief instance, I caught a glimpse of what it felt like to be discriminated against.

One of my managers at Applebee's was openly gay. At this time I was extremely homophobic, and had the ridiculous idea that every gay guy within proximity wanted to jump my bones. A bunch of us were having beers one night after a shift, and in my stupidity I said something about homosexuality being a choice.

He turned to me with a look of disgust on his face and said these unforgettable words: "Do you really think that I would choose to be ostracized, discriminated upon, beat up, fired from several jobs, and forced to live in secrecy, just to be gay? Do you choose to like girls? It's part of my being!" As my shroud of ignorance lifted, never before had something made such complete sense to me. And other than learning to keep my big mouth shut more often, I realized that being homosexual is not a choice, and everyone has the God given right to love.

**2001, Jasper, Texas.** Three good ol' boys picked up an African American hitchhiker named James Byrd Jr. on a desolate stretch of highway. They then beat him, stripped him down, chained his feet to the bumper of their truck, and sped away down a gravel road, dragging him to an unimaginable death. The Civil War ended slavery in America, but many families never changed their opinions of black people. Generations later and the hatred still exists.

I had four African American kids in my senior class of 1,200. I didn't have my first black friend until college. I then found out why many of them appear to be on the constant defensive. They have an inborn fear of being discriminated against, so they put up an intimidating wall to keep people out. Wouldn't you? I often wonder if the time will ever come when we are merely looked upon as Earthlings, and not differentiated by our skin tone.

**2002, Long Island, New York.** A pair of local contractors picked up two Mexican laborers expecting to work for a day's pay. When they arrived at the vacant construction site, they were led into the basement of an abandoned building, slashed with knives, and beaten with shovels within inches of their lives.

There's a growing fear among American laborers that these migrant workers are stealing their precious jobs. Most of these men lack a college education, yet they have acquired an invaluable skill in which they can make a comfortable living, such as landscaping, masonry, or construction work. Now along come the migrant laborers who work double the hours for half the money. They don't complain, don't show up late and hung over, and don't ask for a pay raise every day; hence the discontent.

I grew up a few miles from ground zero for this type of hatred: Farmingville, New York. What was once a charming middle class township has now become a chaotic meeting place for contractors and their illegal workforce. Every morning there are literally hundreds of day laborers hanging out in parking lots, gas stations, and 7-Elevens along Portion Road. As I write these words, the residents of Farmingville are in the middle of a heated legal battle to win back their beloved town. Honestly, I'd be upset too if my town turned into a lawless mob scene over night. But when it all boils down, these are just poverty-stricken people searching for a better life for their families. What dad wouldn't do the same for his kids if he had to?

These are the people whose children I teach everyday. They are from Guatemala, Mexico, and Columbia. They are so kind, grateful, and family-oriented. When we have parent–teacher meetings, every single parent attends, some directly from the orange groves covered in grime, just to thank me. They have taught me many invaluable lessons about family, struggle, and community; something I may have never known. After volunteering for a home-tutoring program, I couldn't believe the squalid conditions these people were living in. Some houses had not a stitch of furniture and whole families living in each bedroom. Still, they were so happy to be free and together. Do they not deserve a better life?

I realize that the above acts of violence sound like stories from medieval times, but that's just not the case. Although these are very extreme instances, I'm sure if you simply look in the halls of your own high school, there is evidence of the same. Respect people for who they are, even if they are different. Everyone has the right to be themselves and be happy. What a boring world it would be if everyone was the same color, dressed the same, talked the same, and looked the same.

America is the greatest country in the world. It is a land where people of all kinds can come for a better life. And it is this diversity alone that makes it so extraordinary. I for one am wholeheartedly optimistic that someday this noble country of ours can truly become one nation under God. The answer lies within each of us …

*Life Rule #25: Teach your children well.*

# CHAPTER 16:
# NO REGRETS

In the summer before eighth grade, Ray and I made a time capsule out of an old steel toolbox. We filled it with anything we thought represented us at that time in 1985: money, pictures of us, *Playboy* magazines, baseball cards, and a written pact that stated our burning desire to move out of our shitty households and get an apartment together after graduation. We buried it deep in the ground of my parent's backyard, made a map, and hid it in a box of old toys in my basement.

Recently I was going through those same boxes when I was packing for our move to Florida, and I just happened to stumble upon the map now twenty years old. Ray had long since moved away and started a family of his own, but I still wanted to dig it up to relive that distant memory. After hours of muscling a cavernous ditch, to my delight the capsule was still down there just where we left it. On top of all the decaying contents was our written pact in a zip-lock bag. As I read it, I became choked up with tears. I could actually feel myself writing it and all the emotions that were present, the anguish, the frustration.

It sucked that I was such a miserable kid. I wished that time capsule was filled with joyous memories of a carefree childhood, but instead it reeked of sorrow. I thought, "How long can I allow myself to be a prisoner to my past? How long can I blame and hold grudges against all those who have done me wrong?" It was time to move on. I put everything back into the steel box and dropped it into the hole, covered it with dirt, and finally put my childhood to rest. As each shovelful hit the capsule, I felt more confident that someday I could live a regret-free life.

## Now What?

You never have to mention or discuss anything on these pages with me. All that I ask is when you are finished, you come out of your room and give me the most tremendous hug. Like the ones when you were small and you'd bury your face in my neck, squeeze with all your might, and never let me go. This book has been enormously cathartic for me, and I hope that it touched your heart. For it has been an integral part of the healing process and my much needed closure. I thank you again for giving me the inspiration to write it with such passion.

Although there are many things in this book that I am ashamed of, how can I possibly prepare you for adulthood without sharing the whole truth? If I taught you that life was easy and that your parents had faultless pasts, then someday you'd go out into the world like a lamb being fed to the lions. I just pray that you will always choose to judge me by my present and not my past.

Dear Lilly,

Today I turned thirty-five. Every birthday I wake up and thank God that I am still alive and have a wonderful family to love me. And best of all, your mother has given me the greatest present possible. We will soon be a family of five: Emma for a girl and Zachary for a boy. I couldn't be happier, because at this stage of the game I need all the love I can get. When I come home from a long day at work, and you and Jesse charge at me with outstretched arms screaming "Da-Da Da-Da!" it's better than any drug in the world. I can only imagine the joy of having three adoring rug rats to greet me at the door. But mostly, I can't wait to watch you all grow and become my trusted confidants.

Professor DiMartino taught me that nothing ends a nonfiction piece better than an enlightening quote. My therapist gave me this poem during my final visit. I guess it was her idea of a diploma for life. What baffles my mind is how it's nearly one hundred years old and still totally relevant for today. It just goes to show that the essence of the human spirit will never change.

If you could manage to do even one line of this poem each day, then you would be doing a substantial amount for the good of humanity. It hangs in my bathroom, and every morning whilst on my throne, I gaze upon it and try to visualize myself living the many messages it conveys. Read it whenever you become disheartened, and try to remember that life is too short for sadness. From this moment forward, I would like you to live your days with a purpose, and never stop believing in yourself. Promise me that you will do this and I will finally have peace of mind. However, merely promising me would be pointless, for you must more importantly …

Peter Greyson

## "Promise Yourself"

Promise yourself to be so strong
that nothing can disturb your peace of mind

To talk health, happiness, and prosperity
to every person you meet

To make all your friends feel that
there is something special in them

To look at the sunny side of everything
and make your optimism come true

To think only of the best, to work only for the best,
and to expect only the best

To be just as enthusiastic about the success of others
as you are about your own

To forget the mistakes of the past and press on to
greater achievements of the future

To wear a cheerful countenance at all times
and give every living creature you meet a smile

To give so much time to the improvement of yourself
that you have no time to criticize others

To be too large for worry, too noble for anger,
too strong for fear, and too happy to permit the presence
of trouble

Christian D. Larson 1912

# FYIs

Here are some last minute tidbits that don't warrant explaining, but just may come in handy someday.

1. Never sit in the front row at a comedy club.
2. The hardest people to love are usually the ones who need it the most.
3. Guys like girls who can camp.
4. A drunken person's words are a sober person's thoughts.
5. Getting up front at a concert is more hassle than it's worth.
6. New York City pizza and bagels are the world's finest.
7. Floss daily and you'll be one of the few seventy-year-olds with all your own teeth.
8. Use deodorant only; antiperspirants inhibit a necessary body function.
9. Always check for feet in the stall before you talk in the bathroom.
10. Keep a calendar of loved ones' birthdays.
11. Don't be a sentence finisher.
12. Always resist the temptation to stare.
13. Never laugh at someone else's pain.
14. Greed will destroy you.
15. Dance like nobody is watching.
16. A nap a day keeps the crankies away.
17. Guys physically cannot control it when they stare at other girls.

18. Respect the elderly and listen when they have something to tell you.
19. Learn a second language.
20. Never make a promise you don't intend to keep.
21. No one knows you better than your parents.
22. Don't believe everything you read.
23. Headphones will eventually make you hard of hearing.
24. Don't wash your hair everyday; you'll get a flakey scalp.
25. Stay away from running microwaves.
26. Boys lie; just checking.
27. When screwing things, it's "righty tighty" and "lefty loosey."
28. Never take the subway after dark in any city.
29. When with guests, never take the last one of anything.
30. One person can make a difference in the world.
31. "Just kissing" always leads somewhere.
32. Keep stuff for sentimental reasons.
33. Cheaters and liars always get caught in the end.
34. Never take someone's opinion to heart, except mine of course.
35. Avoid mirrors in brightly lit rooms.
36. Guys have no respect for slutty dressers; leave something to the imagination.
37. Never look a strange dog in the eye.
38. Never stand behind a horse.
39. Never order seafood at a diner.
40. Guys hate too much makeup.
41. Unless it's a pulsating whitehead, leave your zits alone.
42. Holidays can be the loneliest time for some people.
43. Motorcycles are death traps.
44. Braces cannot lock during kissing.
45. Those who anger you, control you.
46. A large amount of chocolate can kill a dog.
47. Seatbelts are a must, even in the backseat.

48. People mock what they do not understand.
49. Take lots of pictures.
50. Always brush your tongue.
51. Compliment at least one person a day.
52. Sing like nobody is listening.
53. Tattoos are permanent; picture an old lady with "princess" on her lower back.
54. Have a clue what is going on in the world.
55. People will always judge you by how you spell.
56. Kicking a guy in the balls should be reserved for the most desperate of situations.
57. Trash mouth is a huge turn-off.
58. Rodents make lousy pets.
59. Always double check the bowl after you flush.
60. Time is an invention.

# REFERENCES

Blanco, Jodee. *Please Stop Laughing At Me*. Adams Media Corp., 2003.

Byrne, Rhonda. *The Secret*. Atria Books, 2006.

Dalai Lama, and Howard Cutler, MD. *The Art of Happiness*. Riverhead Books, 1998.

Diamond, Harvey, and Marilyn Diamond. *Fit For Life*. Warner Books, 1985.

Francis, Raymond. *Never Be Sick Again*. Health Communications, Inc. 2002.

Fulghum, Robert. *All I Really Need To Know I Learned In Kindergarten*. Ivy Books, 1986.

Gardner, Howard. *Frames of Mind*. Basic Books, 1983.

Grogan, John. *Marley & Me*. William Morrow Publishing, 2005.

Humphreys, Christmas. *Zen Buddhism*. Diamond Books, 1949.

James, Muriel, PhD, and Dorothy Jongeward, PhD. *Born To Win*. Signet Books, 1971.

Kerouac, Jack. *On The Road*. Penguin Books, 1955.

Kraybill, Donald B., Steven M. Nolt, and David L. Weaver-Zercher. *Amish Grace*. Jossey-Bass Publishing, 2007.

Lamb, Wally. *She's Come Undone*. Pocket Books, 1992.

Levine, Peter A. *Waking the Tiger: Healing Trauma*. North Atlantic Books, 1997.

Pelzer, David. *A Child Called "It": One Child's Courage to Survive*. HCI, 1995.

Redfield, James. *The Celestine Prophecy*. Bantam Books, 1996.

Rodale, J. I. *The Healthy Hunzas*. Rodale Press, 1949.

Ruiz, Don Miguel. *The Four Agreements*. Amber-Allen Publishing, 1997.

Schlosser, Eric. *Fast Food Nation*. Harper Perennial, 2005.

Wolfe, Tom. *The Electric Kool-Aid Acid Test*. Bantam Books, 1968.

Wiseman, Rosalind. *Queen Bees & Wannabes*. Three Rivers Press, 2002.

Wurtzel, Elizabeth. *Prozac Nation*. Riverhead Books, 1995.

Wurtzel, Elizabeth. *More, Now, Again*. Simon & Schuster, 2002.

Manufactured By:    RR Donnelley
Breinigsville, PA  USA
May, 2010